Saint Dominic and His Mission

Saint Dominic and His Mission

Augustin Laffay, OP, and Gianni Festa, OP
Translated by The Dominican Sisters of Saint Cecilia
Foreword by Father Gerard Francisco Timoner III, OP

The Catholic University of America Press
Washington, D.C.

Originally published as *Saint Dominique et sa Mission*
(Éditions du Cerf, 2021).

The paper used in this publication meets the minimum requirements of American National Standards for Information Science—Permanence of Paper for Printed Library Materials, ANSI Z39.48-1992.

∞

Cataloging-in-Publication Data is available from the Library of Congress

ISBN (paperback): 978-0-8132-3978-1
ISBN (ebook): 978-0-8132-3979-8

To all those who undertake to follow the path traced by Our Father Saint Dominic

Let us imitate the fatherly footsteps as far as we can, and give thanks to the Redeemer who, on this road on which we walk, has shown such a guide to his servants, begetting us again through him in the light of this way of life; and let us beseech the Father of mercies, that, directed by that Spirit which leads the sons of God, we too may obtain, on a straight path, passing through the bounds which our fathers laid down, that same term of perpetual bliss and eternal bliss and eternal happiness which he has attained and enjoys forevermore. Amen.

—Jordan of Saxony, *Libellus*, 109

Contents

Foreword

After 800 years, is there anything about St. Dominic that has not yet been discovered, something unexplored and yet to be written? Over the centuries, is there anything about the founder and first friar of the Order of Preachers that has not been reflected on or remained unsaid? In the absence of any new discovery of an ancient manuscript, it seems that a new book on St. Dominic is simply adding a long footnote to all that has already been written over the years. So why a new portrait of St. Dominic?

St. Dominic embarked on a ***timely*** mission, for he saw around him a world in urgent need of a *new evangelization*; yet this same mission is truly ***timeless***, for every generation needs a *new evangelization*, that is, of the preaching of the One who is *always old* but *always new.* This "old-new" paradox is reminiscent of the notion of the "classic" as expressed by Hans-Georg Gadamer. A "classic" is both timeless and timely. It is timeless not because it is beyond the vicissitudes of history but because it becomes an event of meaning at every moment in history. It is timely precisely because it is "a timeless present which is contemporary with all other presents." In this sense, St. Bernard states that the scriptures speak *hodie usque ad nos.*[1]

The "classic," writes Sandra Schneiders, is like a musical composition, which can only be rendered in true fidelity to the musical score, but which will be performed differently by each artist. There is only *one* piece of music, but it receives a *unique* interpretation at each performance because of the variety of talents or circumstances of the event. Each performance of a work by musicians, whether in a concert or in another context, is not just a "copy" of the copy as it appears in the mind of the composer but is a "creative event." In a similar way, we understand that there are ***many*** ways to respond authentically to Jesus's ***unique*** invitation: "Come, follow me" (Mt 16:24).

As a saint whose life was dedicated to the preaching of the incarnate word, St. Dominic has "something to say" in all times and places,

1. That is, today and to us.

not because his life, in *itself*, would have the capacity to transcend time and place but because the Gospel that formed and transformed his life is *classical*.

The present book is like a new interpretation of a classic melody: the *same* but *different*. This book is about the same person, the same saint we know from so many previous books, but it presents him in a slightly different way. This interpretation combines the virtues of reliable historiography with those of an inspiring hagiography. It seeks to inform and inspire. It is therefore highly recommended reading for those who are getting to know St. Dominic for the first time, for brothers and sisters of the Dominican family who are in initial formation, or for those who know him well but wish to take a fresh look at this medieval saint whose life and mission have the capacity to bring forth new meaning when appropriated to the present, especially as the original French edition was written at a particular moment of grace, the eighth centenary of his birth to eternal life.

Gerard Francisco Timoner III, OP
Master of the Order

Preface

THE RENEWAL OF THE STUDY of original sources that has taken place since the nineteenth century has made it possible to not only know the life of St. Dominic better but has also to understand with greater accuracy the originality of his religious life. The *History of St. Dominic* by Father Marie-Humbert Vicaire in 1957 was a major achievement, decisive for its knowledge of the saint. Since then, progress on a critical edition of the sources of the history of the origins of the Order of Preachers and numerous studies, especially those undertaken through the impetus of Father Simon Tugwell, have made it possible to clarify and sometimes correct the knowledge that we have about St. Dominic. The publication in 2019 by Nicole Bériou and Bernard Hodel of *Saint Dominique de l'ordre des frères prêcheurs* [*Saint Dominic of the Order of Preachers*], a vast collection of written testimonies from the end of the twelfth through the fourteenth centuries, has finally made available an unparalleled collection of documents. These documents are richly annotated and rigorously presented for researchers and for those who love Saint Dominic. Without the work of these authors, and of many other scholars, this book attempting to present *Saint Dominic and His Mission* would not have been possible. From the various perspectives contained in these documents that are our inheritance, we wish to present the sanctity of St. Dominic.

The first part, "In the Footsteps of Saint Dominic" (I), seeks to reveal the sanctity of the Castilian canon who became the founder of an order of universal scope by following the account of him in the sources. The aim here is not so much to construct a new critical biography, analyzing at length the context into which Dominic's life is inserted, as to understand how he was perceived by his contemporaries and by the first generations of Dominicans. This biographical essay follows the chronology of the saint's life as outlined by Simon Tugwell and makes abundant use of the texts that were systematically translated by Nicole Bériou and Bernard Hodel.[1] The second part of

1. The notes provide a double reference to the medieval sources of the history of the Order of Preachers: the critical edition is first indicated by the

the book offers a succinct presentation of "The Dominican Way" (II) as it seems to emerge from the sources, following its course through the centuries up to our own time. The third part, conceived and realized by two art historians, Coralie Machabert and Claire Rousseau, evokes "The Image of the Founder" (III) through the presentation of sixteen works of art, ranging from the Middle Ages to the present day. Gianni Festa and Eleonora Tioli conclude this part by examining the historical and artistic significance of an intriguing Bolognese work, the Mascarella table, one of the oldest representations of St. Dominic. Finally, "References and Sources for the History of Saint Dominic" (IV) provides the rigorous chronology established by Simon Tugwell and offers a means for further research.

A book is always a collective adventure. Claire Rousseau and Coralie Machabert agreed to be part of it; we thank them fraternally, as well as Father Simon Tugwell, who generously granted us the use of his "Chronological Outline of the Life of Saint Dominic." We are also grateful to the Dominican friars Vincent Tierny and Innocent Smith, who gave us the benefit of their knowledge of canon law and the history of the liturgy. Without the wise advice generously given by Nicole Bériou and Bernard Hodel during the first draft of this work, and without the publication of their masterpiece, this book would not have been possible. We would like to thank them warmly. For the English version, we thank primarily the Dominican Sisters of Saint Cecilia for their tireless work on the translation of the text, as well as the copyeditor David Lampo and the whole team at The Catholic University of America Press, especially Trevor Crowell, who brought the work to completion.

---

name of the author, followed by the abbreviated title of the work and the references of the text; this reference is followed by the translation given in *Saint Dominique de l'ordre des frères prêcheurs: Témoignages écrits fin XIIe-XIVe siècle*, translated texts annotated and presented by Nicole Bériou et Bernard Hodel with the collaboration of Gisèle Besson (Éd. du Cerf, 2019) [abbreviated as Bériou-Hodel, followed by the page number]. The texts in their original version are available in a PDF File on the website of les Éditions du Cerf, https://www.editionsducerf.fr/librairie/livre/18834/saint-dominique-de-l-ordre-des-freres-precheurs-temoignages-ecrits.

The authors are two historians who are also sons of St. Dominic, to whom they gave themselves on the day of their religious profession. They are part of a tradition that intends to link the search for historical truth with filial devotion. This work was completed on the Aventine Hill, in the ancient convent of Santa Sabina, a place of great significance for the authors and the Order. They are indebted to their predecessors for having passed on to them the love of the Castilian religious who himself pushed open the door of this paleo-Christian basilica that Pope Honorius III had just given him in order to undertake and continue his work *in medio Ecclesiae*. That was eight hundred years ago. This work is also an act of thanksgiving: its authors hope that it will allow our contemporaries to discover the life of St. Dominic, and that it will encourage in their vocation those who, attracted by the missionary zeal of the Father of the Preachers, hear the call to follow him in preaching the Gospel of salvation to the world.

Augustin Laffay, OP
Archivist General of the Order of Preachers

Gianni Festa, OP
Postulator General of the Order of Preachers

Santa Sabina, May 24, 2021

Abbreviations

For more information about these sources, please see the Sources and Bibliography in the back matter of this book.

Acta canonizationis, Bologna	*Acta canonizationis*, ed. Angelus Walz, 123–67, in *Monumenta historica Sancti Patris Nostri Dominici*, fasc. II, MOPH 16 (Institutum Historicum Fratrum Prædicatorum, 1935).
Acta canonizationis, Toulouse	*Acta canonizationis*, ed. Angelus Walz, 176–87, in MOPH 16.
AFP	*Archivum Fratrum Prædicatorum*
AGOP	*Archivum Generale Ordinis Prædicatorum* (Rome, Santa Sabina)
ASOP	*Analecta Sacri Ordinis Prædicatorum*
Bériou-Hodel	*Saint Dominique de l'ordre des frères prêcheurs: Témoignages écrits fin* XIIe–XIVe *siècle* [*Saint Dominic of the Order of Friar Preachers: Testimonies written at the end of the 12th–14th century*], textes traduits, annotés et présentés par Nicole Bériou et Bernard Hodel avec la collaboration de Gisèle Besson [texts translated, annotated, and presented by Nicole Bériou and Bernard Hodel with the collaboration of Gisèle Besson] (Éd. du Cerf, 2019).
Chronica	William of Puylaurens, *Chronique: Chronica magistri Guillelmi de Podio Laurentii* [*Chronicle: The Chronicle of Master William of Puylaurens*], texte édité, traduit et annoté par Jean Duvernoy [text

	edited, translated, and annotated by Jean Duvernoy] (Éd. du CNRS, 1976).
De quattuor in quibus	Stephen of Salagnac-Bernard Gui, *De quatuor in quibus Deus prædicatorum ordinem insignivit* [*Of the four in which God distinguished the order of preachers*], ed. Thomas Kaeppeli, MOPH 22 (Institutum Historicum Ordinis Fratrum Prædicatorum, 1949).
Histoire albigeoise	Pierre des Vaux-de-Cernay, *Histoire albigeoise* [*Albigensian history*], nouvelle traduction par Pascal Guébin et Henri Maisonneuve (J. Vrin, 1951).
Legenda	Constantine of Orvieto, *Legenda*, ed. Heribert Christian Scheeben, 286–352, in MOPH 16.
Legenda maior	Humbert of Romans, *Humberti de Romanis legendæ Sancti Dominici*, ed. Simon Tugwell, MOPH 30 (Institutum Historicum Ordinis Fratrum Prædicatorum, 2008).
Legenda sancti Dominici	*Petri Ferrandi legenda sancti Dominici*, ed. Simon Tugwell, MOPH 32 (Angelicum University Press, 2015).
Lehner	Francis C. Lehner, ed., *Saint Dominic: Biographical Documents* (The Thomist Press, 1964)
Libellus	Jordan of Saxony, *Libellus de principiis Ordinis Prædicatorum*, ed. Heribert Christian Scheeben, 1–88, in MOPH 16.
Miracula S. Dominici	Sister Cecilia, *Miracula S. Dominici a sorore Cecilia recitata et a sorore Angelica in scriptis redacta*, in Simon Tugwell, OP, "Scripta quædam minora de S.

	Dominico [Some minor writings on Saint Dominic]," AFP 83 (2013): 64–115.
MOPH	*Monumenta Ordinis Prædicatorum Historica*
Monumenta diplomatica	*Monumenta diplomatica Sancti Dominici*, ed. Vladimír J. Koudelka, *auxiliante* Raymundo J. Loenertz, MOPH 25 (Institutum Historicum Fratrum Prædicatorum, 1966).
Vita	Vito-Tomás Gómez Garcia, *Santo Domingo de Guzmán: Escritos de sus contemporáneos* [*Saint Dominic de Guzman: Writings of his contemporaries*], prólogo [prologue by] José A. Martinez Puche (Edibesa, 2011), 581–624 (translation into Castilian, after the translation of Carro and the *Annalium*).
Vitæ fratrum	Fratris Gerardi de Fracheto, OP, *Vitæ Fratrum Ordinis Prædicatorum necnon Cronica ordinis ab anno MCCIII usque ad MCCLIV* [*The Life of the Brethren of the Order of Preachers and the Chronicle of the Order from 1203 to 1254*], ed. Benedictus Maria Reichert, MOPH 1 (Typis E. Charpentier & J. Schoonjans, 1896).
Vita sancti Dominici	Dietrich of Apolda, *Livre sur la vie et la mort de saint Dominique* [*Book on the life and death of Saint Dominic*], traduit et annoté par Amédée Curé [translated and annotated by Amédée Curé] (Œuvre de Saint-Paul, 1887).

Part I

IN THE FOOTSTEPS OF SAINT DOMINIC

Chapter 1

A Life of Saint Dominic

It seems that it never occurred to Dominic to provide material for his biographers. The holy founder of the Order of Preachers remained, according to the beautiful expression of Guy-Thomas Bedouelle, "hidden in the light."[1] The Dominican historian was inspired by this phrase, taken from a remark by Henri-Dominique Lacordaire comparing Dominic's action with that of his friend Simon de Montfort. This nineteenth-century Dominican who refounded the order in France wanted to underline the complementary nature of the two men:

> The sun of history illumines the breastplate of the warrior, revealing brilliant lights and deep shadows; hardly a ray falls on the garb of Dominic, but that, so pure and so holy, that the absence of a greater brilliancy is in itself a striking homage. Dominic is in obscurity because he has withdrawn from tumult and from bloodshed, because, faithful to his mission, he has opened his lips but to bless, his heart but to pray, and his hands but for deeds of mercy, and because virtue, when hidden from man, is invisible to all, save God.[2]

We have no *Confessions* of Dominic as we have of St. Augustine, no founding text as we have in the *Rule* of St. Benedict, no spectacular conversion like St. Francis of Assisi, no mystical experience like that of St. Ignatius of Loyola. No one recorded the preaching of the "Father of Preachers." His written work consists of three poor and

1. Guy Bedouelle, *Saint Dominic: The Grace of the Word*, trans. Sister Mary Thomas Noble, OP (Ignatius Press, 1987), 59.

2. Henri-Dominique Lacordaire, *Life of Saint Dominic*, trans. Mrs. Edward Hazel (Burns and Oates, 1883), 95–96, accessed December 27, 2021, https://archive.org/details/lifesaintdomini00domigoog/page/n118/mode/2up?q=montfort%27s+armour.

brief missives handed down to us in much later copies. There is nothing of his feelings in them, and we have no direct insights into his person. We have, as it were, only the casting mold formed by the impressions of those who knew him, but not the sculpture of St. Dominic himself. We must form his likeness from the sources of the thirteenth century.[3] Chronicles contemporary with his life sometimes mention him in passing: the *Histoire albigeoise* by Pierre des Vaux-de-Cernay[4] or the *Chronica* by William of Puylaurens.[5] We can add some traces in the registers of an inquisitorial investigation carried out in Toulouse in 1245 and 1246, which provide a list of those persons who were reconciled by Dominic thirty years before the institution of the courts of the Inquisition. There are also diplomatic and juridical sources: chancery documents and bulls that provide a legal basis for the foundation of the Order. All of this remains quite external to the mystery of his human existence.

The Dominicans themselves produced sources, but they focused more on his work and his order rather than on Dominic. The *Little Book on the Beginning of the Order*, or *Libellus*, by Jordan of Saxony (c. 1185–1237), the primary source of information about Dominic's life, was written by his first successor, who knew him personally for only a few months.[6] The first *Constitutions* and the Acts of the General Chapters of 1220 and 1221, which have come down to us in much later copies, also say something about Dominic, but only by

3. In Spanish, reference may be made to the work edited by Vito Tomás Gómez Garcia, *Santo Domingo de Guzmán. Escritos de sus contemporáneos* (Edibesa, 2011). In French, a recent state of the sources, accompanied by an abundant bibliography, can be found in the masterpiece *Saint Dominique de l'ordre des frères prêcheurs: Témoignages écrits fin* XIIe-XIVe *siècle*, texts translated, annotated, and presented by Nicole Bériou and Bernard Hodel with the collaboration of Gisèle Besson (Éd. du Cerf, 2019).

4. Pierre des Vaux-de-Cernay, O. Cist., *Hystoire albigeoise*, trans. Pascal Guébin and Henri Maisonneuve (J. Vrin, 1951).

5. Guillaume de Puylaurens, *Chronique: Chronica magistri Guillelmi de Podio Laurentii*, ed., trans., and annot. Jean Duvernoy (Éd. du CNRS, 1976).

6. Heribert Christian Scheeben, *Libellus de principiis Ordinis Praedicatorum*, MOPH 16 (Institutum Historicum Ordinis Prædicatorum, 1935). See also Jordan of Saxony, *On the Beginnings of the Order of Preachers*, trans. Simon Tugwell, OP, Dominican Sources: New Editions in English (PARABLE, 1982).

linking the man and his project.[7] Even the documents of the canonization process of 1233 and the liturgical legends composed for the office of the saint are suspect of wanting to present a "St. Dominic" as the friars dreamed him rather than the real Dominic, seeking the road to the kingdom for himself and for men in the midst of the vicissitudes of his time. The *Miracles of St. Dominic* by Sister Cecilia offers the participation of the nuns in the memory of Dominic; *The Nine Ways of Prayer of St. Dominic* sheds light on his mystical life; and anecdotal or exemplary accounts give a glimpse of the human and spiritual traits of the saint. But in all these texts, the biographical elements are inserted into literary genres whose rules seem to distance Dominic from the questions that the modern reader asks. If they tell us something of his deeply religious soul, these documents do not meet the requirements of contemporary criticism for writing a biography. From the very beginning, Dominican historiography has been tempted to take its inspiration from a Franciscan model that was not its own: that of the unique and charismatic inspirer to whom all the intuitions and decisions of the foundation would belong. But St. Dominic is not St. Francis; Fanjeaux is not Assisi. Once he has left a place, Dominic does not return to it, except in passing. His place in the world is linked to an office entrusted by the church: that of preaching.

Because of these difficulties, St. Dominic received a critical biography only in the second half of the twentieth century: the work of Father Marie-Humbert Vicaire, first published in 1957.[8] In the last sixty years, this *Dominique et ses Prêcheurs* has been amended, corrected,

7. Antonin H. Thomas, *De oudste Constituties van de Dominicanen* (Leuven, 1965); *Acta capitulorum generalium ordinis Praedicatorum*, ed. Benedictus Maria Reichert, vol. 1, *Ab anno 1220 usque ad annum 1303* (Ex typographia polyglotta S. C. de Propaganda fide-Apud Josephum Roth, 1898).

8. Father Vicaire's work had been preceded by a series of studies and critical editions of the sources of Dominican history, due in particular to the first members of the Dominican Historical Institute (Angelus Walz, Antoine Dondaine, Marie-Hyacinthe Laurent, Vladimír Koudelka, and so on). Marie-Hyacinthe Laurent was a member of the Dominican Historical Institute and a member of the Dominican family. Marie-Humbert Vicaire claimed the Dominican Pierre Mandonnet as his master.

and enriched in several points by other experts.[9] The English Dominican Simon Tugwell occupies a special place among scholars for having offered fundamental contributions on the life of St. Dominic and for having prepared critical editions of several of the most important medieval sources.[10] His use of philology, criticism, and textual history have led him to engage in a fruitful discussion about some of Father Vicaire's assertions. The Italian historian Luigi Canetti has also produced some of the most important works concerning the birth and development of the hagiographic image of St. Dominic. He has studied the order's devotion to the "holy founder" in depth, paying particular attention to the first century of the order's existence.[11] Finally, the recent volume *Saint Dominique de l'ordre des frères prêcheurs*, edited by Nicole Bériou and Paul-Bernard Hodel, has provided sources on the history of Saint Dominic, enriched with introductions and numerous notes, as well as a biography that takes into account the most recent historiographical developments.[12] The work

9. Marie-Humbert Vicaire, *Dominique et ses Prêcheurs* (Éd. Universitaires - Éd. du Cerf, 1977). The collection of the *Cahiers de Fanjeaux* was born with the acts of a colloquium held at the birthplace of the order, in the Lauragais region, in 1965, on the initiative of Father Vicaire and Canon Delaruelle. The following year, *Saint Dominic in Languedoc* was published in *Cahiers de Fanjeaux* 1 (Privat, 1966). The characteristics of the collection were defined at the time of the publication of this first volume. The success of this meeting has not diminished in the fifty-five years of its existence.

10. Among Simon Tugwell's articles, particular note should be taken of "Notes on the Life of St. Dominic," AFP 65 (1995): 5–169; 66 (1996): 6–200; 67 (1997): 28–59; 68 (1998): 5–116; 73 (2003): 5–141. See also "For Whom Was Prouille Founded?" AFP 74 (2004): 5–125. The editions include texts by Peter Calo, Peter Ferrand, Jordan of Saxony, Humbert of Romans, Cecilia, etc.

11. Luigi Canetti, *L'invenzione della memoria: Il culto e l'immagine di Domenico nella storia dei primi frati Predicatori* (Centro italiano di Studi sull'alto Medioevo, 1996).

12. In addition to this work, we should mention *Domenico di Caleruega e la nascita dell'ordine dei frati predicatori: Atti del 41° Convegno storico internazionale (Todi, 10–12 ottobre 2004)*, "Atti Accademia Tudertina, NS 18" (Fondazione CISAM, 2005). Reference should also be made to the works of Elio Montanari and Marco Rainini, etc. On the Toulouse context, see *La bibliothèque des dominicains de Toulouse*, ed. Émilie Nadal and Magali Vène (Presses Universitaires du Midi, 2020).

of these historians and of all those who have contributed to the revival of critical studies on St. Dominic and the time of the foundation of his order are at the source of the biographical profile that we present here, in the year of the eighth centenary of the *dies natalis* of St. Dominic, the day of his birth into Heaven.

Dominic the Spaniard: After 1170–1203

Dominic was born in Castile, in Caleruega, a small village not far from the famous Benedictine abbey of Silos, founded by another St. Dominic to whom the future founder of the Order of Preachers certainly owes his name. His parents married in 1170.[13] "His father was called Felix, his mother Jane," the Spanish hagiographer Peter Ferrand soberly notes.[14] Rodrigo de Cerrato, who collected these family memories early on, adds, "His father was a respectable man and rich in his own property. His mother, for her part, was a woman of good character, reserved, prudent, very compassionate towards the unfortunate and the afflicted, and among all the women of that country, she shone with the privilege of a good reputation."[15] We do not know much more than what these thirteenth-century sources reveal. Later historians, however, claimed that Dominic's parents descended from two illustrious families of *ricos hombres*, the Aza and the Guzmán.[16] Contemporary critics have questioned and even revoked this illustrious lineage, but it has remained customary in the Hispanic world to refer to the patriarch of the Preachers as Dominic *de* Guzmán. On the other hand, his parents had a reputation for sanctity, and his mother was even beatified in 1828 by Pope Gregory XIII on the basis of the recognition of continuing devotion to her memory.[17] According to the sources at our disposal, at least three sons and probably a

13. Thierry d'Apolda, *Vie de saint Dominique*, 11; Bériou-Hodel, 996.

14. Peter Ferrand, *Legenda sancti Dominici*, 4; Bériou-Hodel, 801.

15. Rodrigo de Cerrato, *Vita*, 2; Bériou-Hodel, 1043.

16. Anthony Lappin, "On the Family and Early Years of St. Dominic of Caleruega," AFP 67 (1997): 5–26; according to the author, Felix, who is described as "vir venerabilis et dives in proprio suo" by Rodrigo de Cerrato, was probably a wealthy "bourgeois."

17. Innocenzo Venchi, *Catalogus hagiographicus Ordinis Praedicatorum*, editio altera (Postulatio generalis, Romae, 2001), 161.

daughter were born of this marriage.[18] Dominic's family seems to have formed a fervent environment: his brother Mannes became a Dominican; his other brother, also a priest, devoted himself in their village to the service of the poor; *nepotes*, nephews or cousins of Dominic, also entered the Order of Preachers.[19]

It is in the legend of Peter Ferrand that we first find a story that has a long history in Dominican hagiography and played a notable role in the iconography of the saint. Even before she had conceived Dominic, Jane had a dream: God showed her the son who was to be born of her in the form of a young dog holding in its mouth a flaming torch with which he was to go throughout the world.

> By this it was foreshadowed that a remarkable preacher would be born of her, who would carry the torch of a *fiery word*, by which he would kindle with great vehemence *the charity that was growing cold* in the hearts of *many*, and, by the barking of a zealous preaching, would turn away the wolves from the flocks and awaken to the vigilance of the virtues the souls asleep in sin. *This was* also *proved by subsequent events*, for he admirably rebuked the vices, fought against heresies, and exhorted the faithful with great care. Indeed, *his words burned like torches*, for he came *in the spirit and power of Elijah*.[20]

The episode has a precedent in Cistercian history: in the eleventh century, Aleth of Montbard, pregnant with Bernard of Fontaines, the future abbot of Clairvaux, had a similar dream of a small reddish-white dog barking incessantly. In the tenth century, the monk Robert de Tombelaine explains in his *Commentary on the Song of Songs*:

> The holy preachers are sometimes called dogs by resemblance: by assiduous preaching, which is like unwelcome barking, they endeavor to keep away the enemies, whoever they may be, from the flock of sheep. These dogs catch the foxes for Christ; as they

18. On the details of St. Dominic's family, see Bériou-Hodel, 1071n1.

19. *Vitae Fratrum*, pars 2a, 1. English citation at http://www.domcentral.org/trad/brethren/breth02.htm#0201.

20. Peter Ferrand, *Legenda sancti Dominici*, 3.

> faithfully love their leader, working for his sake, and by rounding up the heretics, they bring them from the prisons of darkness into the light of truth.

To guard the flock of the faithful in unity, to bring to the truth those who have lost their way, to protect, according to the image of the *Song*, the vineyards of the Lord from the voracious foxes: these are the missions to which Dominic dedicated himself.[21] These images explain the origin of the iconographic motif of the dog, which is so often attached to him, much better than an improbable pun on his name: the Latin words *Domini canis* taken literally mean the Lord's dog.[22]

Alfonso VIII ruled in Castile. In 1177, after recapturing Cuenca from the Muslims, he concluded a treaty with the King of Aragon to share future conquests in Andalusia. In 1195, however, the defeat of Alarcos forced the king to be less ambitious. The establishment of the Almohad Empire had given unity, strength, and tenacity to Spanish Islam. The Mozarabic Christians, mistreated by the Muslim princes, sought refuge in the north of the Iberian Peninsula. It was not until the victory achieved in 1212 at Las Navas de Tolosa by the Christian coalition formed by the kingdoms of Navarre, Aragon, Castile, and Portugal, supported by groups of horsemen from all over the West, that the *reconquista* against the Almohads took a decisive turn and opened the door to Andalusia for Castile.[23] Until then, it

21. Song of Songs 2:15: "Catch us the foxes, the little foxes that ravage the vines, for our vines are in flower" (*Jerusalem Bible* translation). The commentary of Robert of Tombelaine was edited by Migne under the name of Gregory the Great in the *Latin Patrology*, vol. 79, col. 500 C.

22. Pierre Mandonnet, "Note de symbolique médiévale: Domini canes," *Revue de Fribourg* 8 (1912): 561–77; article reprinted in *Mémoire dominicaine* 29 (2012): 17–29. The great medievalist forcefully reminds us that in Latin, *canus* is not *canis*: "*Dominicanus* is no more reminiscent of Dominic's dog, or the Lord's dog, than *Franciscanus*, which is of similar formation, is reminiscent of St. Francis's dog."

23. This battle of Las Navas de Tolosa marked the end of a period of "holy war" that had begun as early as the tenth century. A first expedition had taken place in 1064; when a coalition won the victory in 1212, the Iberian Peninsula was already largely in the hands of the Christians, and ecclesiastical

was necessary to remain vigilant: from the top of the fortified tower of the village of Caleruega, the *torreón*, one could watch the south as far as the eye could see. Defending the Christian faith and safeguarding the kingdom were one and the same. To confront the Muslim world and complete the reconquest, religious life in Castile gave rise to soldier-monks, the Knights of Calatrava, linked to the Order of Cistercians. During Dominic's childhood, therefore, the Spanish people anxiously awaited a definitive political and military solution, but there was no lack of pride: the kingdoms of Spain had their own laws, appointed their own bishops, and the Christian people shed their blood with courage to reconquer their land.

Jane and Felix consecrated their child to a priestly vocation; they therefore separated themselves from him so that he would be "imbued with this office."[24] As far as we can tell from the historical sources, Dominic never rebelled against this choice and instead entered willingly into this vocation, fully embracing the spirit of his state while living with an uncle who was a priest. This is what Jordan of Saxony reports: "From his earliest years," his parents, and especially his uncle, the archpriest, trained him "in the practices of the church, so that, as one whom God has foreseen as a 'vessel of election,' he would absorb in childhood, like the proverbial 'new-made pot,' an odor of sanctity which he would never thereafter lose."[25] He was then sent to Palencia to study the liberal arts following the trivium (grammar, logic, rhetoric) and then the quadrivium (arithmetic, geometry, astronomy, music).[26] After several years of this training, the young cleric finally devoted himself for four years to the science

---

reorganization was well advanced. See Jean-Marie Mayeur, ed., *Histoire du christianisme des origines à nos jours*, vol. 5, *Apogée de la papauté et expansion de la chrétienté (1054–1274)*, ed. André Vauchez (Desclée, 1993), 281–84.

24. Peter Ferrand, *Legenda sancti Dominici*, 4; Bériou-Hodel, 801.

25. Jordan of Saxony, *Libellus*, 5; Tugwell, 1.

26. Jordan of Saxony, *Libellus*, 6; Tugwell, 1: "Afterwards he was sent to Palencia to be formed in the liberal arts, because there was a thriving arts faculty there at this time. When he thought he had learned enough of the arts, he abandoned them and fled to the study of theology, as if he was afraid to waste his limited time on less fruitful study. He began to develop a passionate appetite for God's works, finding them 'sweeter than honey to his mouth.'"

of the Holy Scriptures by confronting the biblical text through reading, meditation, and memorization. As Jordan always assures us:

> His eagerness to imbibe the streams of Holy Scripture was so intense and so unremitting that he spent whole nights almost without sleep, so untiring was his desire to study; and the truth which his ears received he stored away in the deepest recesses of his mind and guarded in his retentive memory. . . . The verdict of Truth himself pronounces him blessed: as his said in the Gospel, 'Blessed are those who hear the word of God and keep it.'"[27]

Later, it was said that he knew the Gospel of Matthew and the epistles of St. Paul by heart, the testimony given of Dominic by Friar John of Spain during the canonization process.[28] The schools of Palencia, founded on the initiative of Alfonso VIII, constituted such an excellent center of ecclesiastical science in Castile that the first Spanish university was founded there. In this way, St. Dominic was able to benefit from the translations of Aristotle made in Toledo. These were texts from the Arab world, enriched with the commentaries of Averroes. Palencia was also open to the rest of Europe. "Dominic certainly met clerics from France and Italy," notes the historian Patrick Henriet, "and the theology he learned was perhaps already marked by Parisian innovations."[29] The young Dominic thus received a rigorous and advanced training that made him an intellectual in the manner of the Middle Ages.[30]

It was in Palencia that a well-documented incident occurred that reveals the spirit that animated the theology student. It has been told and illustrated in the Dominican world since the thirteenth century and become emblematic of Dominic's charity. Jordan of Saxony reports that there was a severe famine in Spain:

27. Jordan of Saxony, *Libellus*, 7; Tugwell, 1.

28. *Acta canonizationis*, Bologna, 29; Bériou-Hodel, 725.

29. Patrick Henriet, "Dominique avant saint Dominique ou le contexte castillan," *Mémoire dominicaine* 21 (2007): 20–21.

30. Henriet, "Dominique avant saint Dominique," 20–23. The training he received in Palencia "in a center that was very open to the outside world" and his subsequent integration into the chapter of Osma, "a prestigious ecclesiastical institution," heralded a brilliant ecclesiastical career.

> [Dominic] was deeply moved by the plight of the poor, and resolved, in the warmth of his compassion, to do something which would both accord with the Lord's counsels and do as much as possible to remedy the needs of the poor who were dying. So he sold the books which he possessed, although he needed them very much, and established an almonry where the poor could be fed. . . . He exemplary kindness so moved some of the other theologians and masters that they too began to give more lavish alms.[31]

According to the testimony of Brother Stephen of Lombardy during the canonization process of 1233, Dominic even declared, "I will not study on dead skins when men are dying of hunger."[32] The significance of such a gesture should not be underestimated: for a student, to sell his books and parchments in order to found an almshouse was to renounce himself and his career in order to save the life of his neighbor. The legend of Peter Ferrand also claims that during the same period, Dominic offered himself as a slave to buy back the freedom of a man who had fallen into the hands of the Saracens:

> A woman had come to him to lament the fact that her brother was being held prisoner by the Saracens. But he, who was filled with the spirit of piety, wounded by a feeling of compassion in his heart, offered to sell himself for the redemption of the captive. But the Lord did not allow this, as He reserved him for more abundant fruits of justice and for the conversion of a great number of souls.[33]

Dominic's behavior and his spiritual attitude attracted the attention of Martin de Bazán, the bishop of Osma. This episcopal see had been refounded after the *reconquista* by a Benedictine prelate of French or Languedoc origin, Peter of Bourges († 1109). Peter's action was part of the great movement of the Gregorian reform.

31. Jordan of Saxony, *Libellus*, 10; Tugwell, 2.

32. *Acta canonizazionis*, Bologna, 35. Testimony of Brother Stephen of Lombardy: '*Nolo studere super pelles mortuas, et homines moriantur fame*'; Lehner, 123.

33. Peter Ferrand, *Legenda sancti Dominici*, 18; Bériou-Hodel, 817.

He made every effort not only to define the borders of his diocese in the face of competing and neighboring bishops but also to endow his see with strong ecclesiastical institutions. This action continued the policy of Gregorian reform that had been underway in the church for a century. It was necessary to safeguard Spanish Christianity at a time when the Muslims were very close and threatening. Peter undertook the construction of the cathedral, and his successors continued the work and, on the foundations of the Romanesque church, developed the structure in the Gothic style. The establishment of a chapter of canons subject to the rule of Saint Augustine was part of this same spirit of renewal. These clerics, who were obliged to lead a common life, were to celebrate the Divine Office in the cathedral church, offer their advice to the bishop, and take part in the affairs of the diocese. Dominic joined the chapter of Canons Regular of Osma when Diego was prior, that is, superior of the community. He quickly found his place there and was exemplary in his practice of the religious life proper to canons. It was there that he developed the habit, which he kept until his death, of devoting a large part of the night to personal prayer. According to Jordan, he asked God in particular to "grant him true charity, which would be effective in caring for and winning the salvation of men; he thought he would only really be a member of Christ's Body when he could spend himself utterly with all his strength in the willing of souls, just as the Lord Jesus Christ, the Savior of us all, gave himself up entirely for our salvation."[34]

In hagiographic style, Jordan explains, decades after these events:

> Like the olive tree that flourishes and the cypress that grows taller, [Dominic] walked the floor of the church day and night, devoted himself unceasingly to contemplation, and hardly showed himself outside the monastery. God had granted him the singular grace of weeping for sinners, for the unfortunate, for the afflicted: bearing their misfortunes in the depths of the sanctuary of his compassion, he let the ardent emotion from which he was boiling inside escape out of his eyes.[35]

34. Jordan of Saxony, *Libellus*, 13; Tugwell, 3.
35. Jordan of Saxony, *Libellus*, 12; Bériou-Hodel, 612–13.

The author of the *Libellus* adds an important detail concerning the religious and spiritual formation of the young canon: as a reader of St. John Cassian, he drew on the patristic sources of the monastic life:

> He read and loved a book entitled *Conferences of the Fathers*, which deals with the vices and with the whole matter of spiritual perfection, and in this book he strove to explore the ways of salvation and to follow them with all the power of his mind. With the help of grace, this book brought him to the highest purity of conscience and to considerable enlightenment in contemplation and to a veritable peak of perfection.[36]

This movement toward God was based on a solid common life, lived without pretense. In accordance with the Rule, he depended on the community for all his needs and had no personal effects; he ate in the common refectory and shared the dormitory with the other canons. Dominic responded so well to his vocation that he became subprior of the chapter in 1201. In the same year, Bishop Martin died; Diego, then prior of the chapter, was appointed to succeed him in the episcopal see of Osma.[37]

On the Roads of Europe: 1203–1215

Before evoking the figure of the "venerable servant of Christ, Master Dominic," Jordan of Saxony directs his readers' attention to Bishop Diego of Osma. He notes zeal for the reform of the church and austerity of his personal life in his actions, describing in Bishop Diego all the attributes of a saint:

> There lived in Spain a venerable man named Diego, the bishop of Osma, who was renowned for his knowledge of the Bible and for the worldly respectability of his birth, but who was particularly distinguished for the remarkable integrity of his character and behavior. His love was so totally given to God that he renounced himself and sought only what belongs to Jesus Christ, turning his mind and will especially to finding some way

36. Jordan of Saxony, *Libellus*, 13, Tugwell, 3.
37. *Monumenta diplomatica*, n. 2.

> of winning many souls for Christ. He was determined that his Master should receive back his talent with generous interest. So he sought out, wherever he could, men who were commended by integrity of life and character and, by any means at his disposal, he tried to draw such man to himself and to give them benefices in the church which he ruled.
>
> If any of his subjects were sluggish in their desire for holiness, being more interested in worldly things, he urged them in words and inspired them by his example to adopt a more commendable pattern of behavior and a more serious form of religious life. As part of this program, he did his best, by means of frequent exhortations and unceasing encouragement, to persuade his canons to agree to follow the Rule of St. Augustine and to live as canons regular, and as a result of his efforts, he succeeded in winning their minds to his purpose, though some of them resisted him.[38]

The reputation of such a man was well established at the Castilian court, where he was also active. He was a friend of Dominic's and found in him a cleric who could assist him effectively, and the opportunity arose for closer collaboration. At the end of 1203, Alfonso VIII sent Diego to northern Europe to negotiate the marriage of his son Ferdinand to a young girl from the nobility of those countries.[39] Dominic took part in the embassy. At the age of thirty, he was probably leaving Castile for the first time. The journey promised to be long and full of adventure; crossing countries was unknown to the Castilian clerics. The group crossed the Pyrenees and came to Languedoc, a region that stretches from Toulouse to Saint-Gilles du Gard, on the right bank of the Rhône, not a homogeneous political entity. These lands were mainly under the control of the Count of Toulouse, the King of Aragon, and their vassals, among whom the Viscount of Albi, Béziers, and Carcassonne was particularly prominent. The powerful king of France, Philip Augustus, even at a distance, could not fail to covet these vast and rich lands.

38. Jordan of Saxony, *Libellus*, 4; Tugwell, 1.
39. Jordan of Saxony, *Libellus*, 14; Tugwell, 4.

The desire in the West for a life rooted in poverty and modeled on the Gospel was evidenced to a high degree at the end of the eleventh century. Some fervent Christians were claiming the possibility of leading a poor life as individuals *secundum formam sancti Evangelii*, following the evangelical counsels. They also expected such an attitude from the church and the clergy, who were considered too rich and powerful, thus manifesting a contradiction in their words and in their lives. This movement was coupled with new aspirations of educated laymen: the spreading of the word of God and a life shaped by the Gospel but lived outside traditional religious communities. The reform promoted by Gregory VII a century earlier had accentuated the difference in lifestyle between clerics and laity to encourage the former to lead a life more in keeping with their state. Some groups of lay people had become independent from the clergy, And like other regions of Europe around 1200, the Languedoc was thus dotted with religious groups on the fringes of Catholic orthodoxy. Today, the historian Jean-Louis Biget describes them as dissidents.[40] Their way of life can be described as essentially an internal deviation from the norm rather than a kind of religious heresy developed by stubborn theologians on the margins of the church. These dissidents, who sometimes led their followers into error, are difficult to grasp precisely. The texts of their opponents speak of them abundantly, but it is risky to reconstruct a heretical treatise exclusively from the somewhat combative writings that were written to oppose them! Two major movements nevertheless emerge from the nebula: the Waldensians and the "Good Men."

The Waldensian movement, founded by a pious merchant from Lyon, Waldo or Waldes, claimed radical poverty and itinerant preaching for lay people. According to polemical treatises setting out the Catholic viewpoint, the Waldensians were characterized by their insubordination to the clergy and maintained that it was better to obey God than men, not recognizing any hierarchy. They rejected the necessity of worship and denied the usefulness of churches because of the ubiquity of God. However, they admitted the dogmas of the

40. Jean-Louis Biget, *Hérésie et inquisition dans le Midi de la France* (Picard, 2007), 14–16.

incarnation and redemption, so that Pierre des Vaux-de-Cernay considered them less dangerous than the "Good Men."[41] This first movement was discreetly present in the Midi. In the eyes of their opponents, "Good Men" formed a kind of alternative church.[42] This name appears for the first time in 1165 in the Albi region; the term Albigensians was therefore used to refer to them in a derisive manner. Since the nineteenth century, the word "Cathar" has been used extensively, but incorrectly. Catharism refers to a heresy fought on the banks of the Rhine in the eleventh century, described as a dualism by its most fierce opponent, the Benedictine abbot of Schönau, Eckbert. But the word is absent from the southern sources of Dominic's time, so its use is to be discouraged.[43]

According to their Catholic opponents, for example, the chronicler Pierre des Vaux-de-Cernay, who wrote after 1212, the Good Men believed in two principles: the good God (*benignus Deus*), creator of the celestial world, and the evil God (*malignus Deus*), the Devil, creator of the visible, imperfect, and corrupt universe.[44] They argued that no communication was possible between the two creations. Men were actually apostate angels, cast into this world for their punishment. Christ did not become incarnate but took on a human appearance (this is the old Christian heresy of Docetism) to bring these spirits back to the celestial world through a series of purifying reincarnations. The Roman Church was under the authority of the Devil; its places of worship, images, and bells encouraged idolatry, and the

41. Biget, "Situation religieuse du Languedoc en 1206," *Mémoire dominicaine* 21 (2007): 46–47.

42. Biget, "Situation religieuse du Languedoc en 1206," 41–45.

43. Biget, "Situation religieuse du Languedoc en 1206," 42: "The terms 'Cathars' and 'Catharism,' used generically and exclusively since the publication of a work by Arno Borst [*Die Katharer*, Schriften der Monumenta Germaniae Historica 12 (Deutsches Institut für Erforschung des Mittelalters, 1953] to characterize the adherents and the religion of the Languedoc dissidents, seem to be irrelevant, as they imply a unity and universality contrary to the facts."

44. Henri Maisonneuve, "Pierre des Vaux-de-Cernay," *Catholicisme: Hier-Aujourd'hui-Demain*, vol. 11 (Letouzey et Ané, 1988), col. 398–99. His *Histoire* ended in 1218, during the siege of Toulouse in which Simon de Montfort perished. He was then lost.

sacraments were useless, especially marriage, which perpetuates sinful flesh. The lives of the good men were guided by the Gospel alone, to the exclusion of the Old Testament (this, too, is the old heresy Marcionism).[45] In the essential ritual developed by these Albigensians, the gospel book was placed on the head of the adult worshipper by a "good man" during the *consolamentum*, the baptism in the Spirit, which committed him immediately to a life of perfection. The *consolamentum* was granted at the end of a kind of "novitiate." As Jean Duvernoy points out:

> The infusion of the Holy Spirit by the laying on of hands, Paul's baptism, a baptism of "fire and Holy Spirit," as opposed to John the Baptist's water baptism, brings about the arrival of the "comforter," the Paraclete promised by Christ at Pentecost, hence its name *consolamentum*, *consolament*, i.e., paraclesis.[46]

The "consoled" or "perfected" were then bound to an ascetic life in which no fault was permitted. The prohibitions were many and rigorous: no lies or oaths; no meat or eggs; and absolute sexual continence, including for married people. These commitments resembled real vows. The modalities may vary according to the rituals that have come down to us, but they follow the same path of moral exigency and a concern for doctrinal purity.[47] In order to fulfill these precepts in an even more radical way, the "perfects" met in small spiritual communities. Some "Good Men" travelled throughout Languedoc to confer the *consolamentum* on those who requested it. The ceremony required the presence of an ordained minister, who laid hands on the new perfect and gave him the Lord's Prayer. In his explanation of "the religion of the Cathars," the historian Jean Duvernoy insists that the Catholic contemporaries who denounced the heresy of the "Good Men" "always placed the rejection of infant baptism by water

45. Biget, *Hérésie et inquisition dans le Midi de la France*, 42–45. The author gives a synthetic view of the religion of good men based on the polemical works of Alain de Lille, Bernard de Foncaude, Ermengaud, Raoul of Fontfroide, and the *Liber antiheresism*, edited by the Dominican Antoine Dondaine.

46. Jean Duvernoy, *Le catharisme: La religion des cathares* (Privat, 1976), 151.

47. Duvernoy, *Le catharisme*, 143–70.

in the forefront." This rejection, perceived as particularly scandalous by contemporaries, distinguished these dissidents from other religious groups that desired evangelical and apostolic life but were respectful of sacramental baptism, which is the foundation of Christian life.[48]

The success of the "Good Men" is understandable: the movement allowed the laity a great deal of independence, even if among them there may have been a kind of clergy; they combined word and example and apparently did not compromise with the Gospel. Jean-Louis Biget's research shows that this movement of dissent in Languedoc was mainly the work of the social elites: a small aristocracy of knights in the rural towns, merchants and bourgeois in the cities.[49] Indeed, the time had come for the end of a certain dominion held by the clerics. Other groups of the population were gaining the skills of reading and using Latin. They wished to gain the same autonomy in the religious sphere as they were striving to achieve in the political sphere, and in the process, they demanded a less ritualistic and more interiorized religion. The external elements, the customs to which a large part of the population was attached, were therefore rejected. These new elites disdained or placed less importance on the embellishment of the liturgical devotion to holy images and saints, sacramental life, etc. The movement of the "Good Men" was to remain quantitatively low; the common people remained mostly faithful to the church. For example, in the town of Béziers, which a chronicler wrote in 1209 was "all infected with the venom of heresy," the religion of the "Good Men" concerned at most only 10 percent of the population. Elsewhere in Languedoc, the percentage probably did not exceed 5 percent of the population.[50]

In a climate exacerbated by the quarrels between the pope and the emperor, in a period of change in feudal society, in an atmosphere that seemed to betoken the end of a world, clerics could be deeply concerned about the existence of these dissidents and certain groups being formed around heretical ideas. Pauline teaching could support their fears:

48. Duvernoy, *Le catharisme*, 151.

49. Biget, *Hérésie et inquisition dans le Midi de la France*, 96–100.

50. Biget, *Hérésie et inquisition dans le Midi de la France*, 130.

> Now the Spirit expressly says that in later times some will depart from the faith by giving heed to deceitful spirits and doctrines of demons, through the pretensions of liars whose consciences are branded, who forbid marriage and enjoin abstinence from foods (1 Tm 4:1–3).

As Nicole Bériou and Bernard Hodel note, the doctrines of the Calabrian abbot Joachim of Fiore, who died in 1202, fed the eschatological expectations of the thirteenth century and opened the way to new forms of preaching in the church. In his *Exposition on the Apocalypse*, Joachim sees in the angel sounding the sixth trumpet the figure of the "preachers of truth" who will confront the servants of the Antichrist in the sixth age of salvation history.[51] Clerics who were concerned about church unity were troubled by the spread of these words and concerned about the tensions created by certain dissident groups, which were acquiring a hierarchical structure and a more defined doctrinal system. Resolving questions of heresy, or dissent, as such, was a matter for the pope and the bishops.[52] But the latter were weak: they were close by blood, friendship, or interest to those who ventured into the paths of heterodoxy. Their hands were tied. In a decree of 1199, *Vergentis in senium*, Pope Innocent III had nevertheless presented heresy as a crime of divine treason "because it is much more serious to outrage the eternal majesty than to outrage the temporal majesty."[53] He asked that the temporal punishment correct what the spiritual discipline could not: that the property of heretics be confiscated until they return from their error. The penal solution, however, was not equal to the ecclesiastical crisis.

On crossing the Pyrenees, Dominic discovered the heresy of the Albigensians. In Toulouse, the prelate and his retinue were taken in by a heretic. Dominic, says Jordan of Saxony, "took action with force

51. Bériou-Hodel, 272.

52. Biget, *Hérésie et inquisition dans le Midi de la France*, 176. On this theme, see also the recent thesis by Pierre-Marie Berthe, *Les dissensions ecclésiales, un défi pour l'Église catholique: Histoire et actualité* (Éd. du Cerf, 2019), 250–61.

53. Innocent III, Bull *Vergentis in senium* (March 25, 1199), quoted in Marie Bassano, "Normativer l'anormal: L'esprit juridique des sommes anti-Vaudois de la fin du XIIe siècle," *Revue de l'histoire des religions* 228 (2011): 549.

and ardor, discussing and arguing at length with the host of the house, who was a heretic." The battle ended in victory. Dominic "brought him back to the faith, by the help of the Spirit of God, because the heretic was unable to withstand 'the wisdom and Spirit which was addressing him.'"[54] On this occasion, the canon used all the intellectual resources at his disposal: he argued and argued as they did in the schools of Palencia. No doubt he also understood that the faithful expected the clergy to be very holy and that disappointment was the reason why most of them welcomed heretical preachers. The population gave legitimacy to these preachers mainly due to their approval of the heretics' way of life.

Bishop Diego and his companion had a mission to accomplish and a long way to go. To bring a royal marriage of high political significance to a successful conclusion was no small matter. To which kingdom did Diego and Dominic go? It is difficult to say precisely. Jordan speaks of the Marches, a term that usually refers to a border region. Gerard de Frachet is the first to mention the Marche of Dacia, which some have interpreted as Denmark, but the mystery remains.[55] Nothing is known of their itinerary or their affairs except that they returned to Spain to Alfonso VIII with a promise of marriage according to medieval custom. To conclude the alliance definitively, they had to return to the family of the bride and bring her to Prince Ferdinand. In 1205, Diego set off for the north with Dominic. Unfortunately for the Castilian bridegroom, the girl had either died or become a nun. In either case, she was no longer marriageable! The mission was over, but this failed wedding, in which even the name of the bride is missing, is a hinge between Dominic's hidden life and his public life, the canonical life in the shadow of the cathedral of Osma and the missionary life on the roads of Europe, just as the episode of Cana operates as a hinge between the hidden life and the public life of Jesus in the Gospel of John.

Both journeys must have made a strong impression on the two Castilian churchmen. While travelling through Germany, Diego and

54. Jordan of Saxony, *Libellus*, 15; Tugwell, 4.

55. Bériou-Hodel, 614n1. We adopt the cautious attitude of these two authors.

his companion had heard about the destruction caused by the Cumans, the name given to the non-Muslim, Turkish-speaking peoples who had settled in eastern Europe since the end of the eleventh century. They had settled north of the Black Sea and further east in the steppes between the Caspian Sea and the Irtysh. Christianization of this population by the Georgians and the Russians had begun, but much remained to be done before these men would accept the Gospel.[56] Among them were pagan warriors who had been enlisted as mercenaries in a conflict between contenders for the German crown. They had then engaged, among other barbarities, in plunder and theft.

On their second journey, Diego and Dominic also met the Archbishop of Lund in Sweden, Andrew Sunesen (c. 1167–1228). This papal legate for the Nordic countries was a man of great political and cultural worth and possessed great apostolic energy. He was taking a keen interest in the young church in Livonia on the shores of the Baltic and was preparing a new undertaking in these lands in the form of a crusade to suppress paganism there.[57] This meeting, as well as the stories about the Cumans, convinced the two clerics not to return to their country directly but to go to Rome. Admitted to an audience with Innocent III, the Bishop of Osma offered to renounce the episcopate to devote himself entirely to the conversion of the pagan Cumans. The pope refused and sent the Castilians home.[58]

56. Jean Richard, *La Papauté et les Missions d'Orient au Moyen Âge (XIIe–XVe siècle)* (École française de Rome, 1977), 20–23. On the missionary commitment of St. Dominic, see Bériou-Hodel, 42–43.

57. According to the encyclopedist Michel Mourre, Livonia is a historical region of northern Europe, bordering the Baltic Sea. It remained unknown to Western Europe until 1158, when merchants from Lübeck established trading posts at the mouth of the Dvina. The Christianization of the inhabitants, the Lives, was undertaken at the end of the eleventh century by a canon from Holstein, who became the first bishop of these populations. In 1201, Bishop Albert transferred his see to Riga and one year later founded the Order of the Glaive-Bearing Brothers, which later merged with the Teutonic Knights. See Michel Mourre, *Dictionnaire de l'Histoire* (Bordas, 1990), 532.

58. Marie-Humbert Vicaire, *Histoire de saint Dominique*, vol. 1, *Un homme évangélique* (Éd. du Cerf, 1957), 134–35.

Disappointed, perhaps, but obedient, Diego and Dominic set off again to return to Spain. On this return journey, or perhaps on their first trip in 1204, they diverted their route to Cîteaux in Burgundy. The Cistercians represented the perfect example of traditional religious reform following the plan of Gregory VII. Diego is said to have successfully solicited a group of white monks from Cîteaux to run a monastery of women that he had established in his diocese.[59]

Arriving in Montpellier in the early months of 1206, the Castilians met the Cistercian legates commissioned by Pope Innocent III to convert the heretics of the Midi. These men, led by the abbot of Cîteaux, Arnaud Amalric, were discouraged. Military repression seemed to be the only way to fight against religious dissent because of the power struggles between the great feudal lords on the one hand and the anguish caused by the growing number of heretical speeches on the other. Breaking this attitude of defeatism, the bishop of Osma proposed that the Catholics adopt a mode of life in line with the desired goal: the return to full Catholic communion of the infidels. According to Jordan of Saxony, he told the legates:

> No, brethren, I do not think that you are setting about things in the right way. In my opinion, you will never be able to bring these people back to the faith just by talking to them because they are much more inclined to be swayed by example. . . . Use a nail to drive out a nail. Chase off their feigned holiness with true religious life. The imposing appearance of the false apostles can only be shown up for what it is by manifest humility.[60]

And he advised them "to act and teach after the example of the Divine Master and to go on foot, without gold or silver, imitating in everything the apostolic preaching." Diego embraced the idea of acting as an "evangelical man" to destroy popular anticlericalism. Basically, it was a question of following the recommendations given

59. The hypothesis is formulated by Simon Tugwell, "Notes on the Life of St. Dominic," AFP 58 (1998): 59–60.

60. Jordan of Saxony, *Libellus*, 20; Tugwell, 6.

by Jesus in the tenth chapter of the Gospel according to Saint Matthew: to set out without gold or money, without a bag for the journey or a change of clothes, to beg for food and shelter and to offer the peace and the word of the Gospel to anyone who wanted it. Setting an example, the prelate sent his baggage and companions back to Osma—with the exception of Dominic—and set out with two legates to preach and argue against the heresy. That same year, 1206, in an entirely different context in Umbria, Francis renounced his possessions and obtained from the Bishop of Assisi the status of a penitent within the church. But while Francis found in the teachings given by Christ to the disciples the answer to an urgent personal question, Dominic was merely obeying his bishop who intended to confront a missionary problem evangelically. In this sense, the adoption of a mendicant apostolic style on the part of the saint seems to have been dictated above all by circumstances, as a means to an end. Later, the order would be confronted with the question of the choice of mendicancy and whether to justify and deepen the reasons for which it was originally adopted. During Dominic's lifetime, some of his companions expressed their reluctance or even disagreement with the adoption of such a weighty poverty. Bishop Diego's proposal of apostolic and mendicant priests, however, was to leave such an impression on Dominic that he finally decided to link strictly evangelical preaching and radical poverty in the new order.

The experiment carried out by Diego and Dominic—though short-lived—was deemed conclusive. The two men left for Osma where Dominic resigned in the spring of 1206 as sub-prior of the chapter. He returned to Languedoc with Diego and some Spanish preachers, probably in July 1206, to support Bishop Fulk of Toulouse who wanted to encourage and spread the Castilian initiative in his diocese. A famous troubadour, then a Cistercian monk and abbot of Le Thoronet, Fulk had been appointed bishop of Toulouse in 1201 and took his mission very much to heart.[61] With his

61. After leading his wife and children into religious life, Fulk took the Cistercian habit at Le Thoronet in 1195 and became bishop of Toulouse ten years later. A faithful and firm supporter of Dominic, he died in Toulouse in 1231.

help, the business of preaching in Languedoc could gain momentum. At the General Chapter of Cîteaux in September 1206, the organization of a great campaign against heresy in the Midi was set in motion, following the strategy proposed by Diego. The preachers were to work in radical poverty according to the evangelical model of the poor and itinerant apostles, and the austerity of their lives was to be a guarantee of truth. Diego reported to the pope in November 1206. Far from being offended or even concerned by the initiatives taken by a bishop who he had sent back to his diocese a year earlier, Innocent III fully endorsed his views. Raoul, the Cistercian abbot of Fontfroide, was appointed papal legate and official head of the mission, but Diego, accompanied by Dominic, gave it spirit and impetus through the preachers he had brought from Spain. This was the victory of an absolutely new apostolic way of life.

At the end of 1206, a preaching mission, or *praedicatio*, was established at the foot of the village of Fanjeaux at a place called Prouille in dilapidated buildings adjoining a chapel dedicated to the Virgin that had been a place of pilgrimage. Prouille, which was then part of the diocese of Toulouse, was at the intersection of routes leading to Carcassonne, Castelnaudary and Toulouse, Mirepoix, and Foix. Despite its modest location, it was an important center for heresy. In the village and its immediate surroundings, about twenty aristocratic families shared the feudal rights, and all of them belonged to the "Good Men's" movement. In 1204, four ladies, all widows, received the *consolamentum*. Among them was Esclarmonde, the sister of the powerful Count of Foix. Five or six communities of "good ladies," functioning almost like monasteries, had been established in the *castrum*, a former Roman fort. Girls from good families were received there from childhood. Some of them were thus led to become "perfect" themselves. In 1206, at the request of the lord Dominic of Osma, Fulk, the archbishop of Toulouse, granted Diego:

Dante mentions him in the ninth canto of *Paradise* (IX, 93), in the *Divine Comedy*. See Stanislao Majarelli, "Folco (Folchetto) di Tolosa," *Enciclopedia cattolica*, vol. 5 (Città del Vaticano, 1950), col. 1468–79.

> The church of Blessed Mary of Prouille and the adjoining land on either side of this church, for thirty feet as it is found in canon law, to women converted by the preachers delegated to preach against heretics and to repel the pestilential heresy, present and future.[62]

It was a question of grouping together in this place "converted ladies living religiously," so that they could continue to lead, in the heart of the church to which they had returned, the life of monastic prayer and asceticism to which they had already dedicated themselves.[63] A late seventeenth-century account tells how Dominic, passing through Fanjeaux at night in prayer, turned his face toward the plain and saw a globe of fire crossing the sky, spinning around and then landing on the chapel of the Virgin in the hamlet of Prouille. He resolved to establish there the monastery intended to welcome the "perfect" women he had just brought back to the Catholic faith.[64] This edifying story has nourished Dominican iconography up to this day. Whatever its historical authenticity, it is certain that Dominic's preaching met with some success, and not only in this aspect of guiding women toward a monastic way of life.

Of the three preserved manuscript texts written by Dominic, two concern reconciliations of heretics. Registers drawn up during the Inquisition, more than thirty years after Dominic's passage through Languedoc, bear witness to his influence. For example,

62. *Monumenta diplomatica*, appendix II, 181–82 [translated from the French: Bériou-Hodel, 486]. For this question, see the article by Simon Tugwell, "For Whom Was Prouille Founded?" AFP 74 (2004): 5–125. The gift was made "before the end of the year" in the old style, that is, before March 25, 1207.

63. *Monumenta diplomatica*, 11, May 15, 1211 [translated from the French: Bériou-Hodel, 491]. The gift of this church in Bram was made by Fulk, bishop of Toulouse, to the "converted ladies."

64. *The Life of the Glorious Patriarch Saint Dominic, Founder and Teacher of the Order of the Brother Preachers and of His First Sixteen Companions: with the Foundation of all the Convents & Monasteries of the One & Other Sex in all the Provinces of the Kingdom of France, & in the Seventeen of the Low Country*, by the Reverend Father Jean de Rechac of St. Mary, a priest of the Convent of the Annunciation in Paris, a convent of Strict Observance of the Order of Friars Preachers and historian of that community (Sébastien Huré, 1647), 691.

Arnaude de Fremiac, an inhabitant of Fanjeaux, declared that she had confessed to and been reconciled by Brother Dominic. He had given her the penance of wearing two crosses on the front of her clothes until she found a husband; the Albigensians were indeed reluctant to marry.[65] The remedy, which is not without humor in our eyes, was effective: Arnaude married after a year! The same tactic was used for Pons Roger. If he was given times of fasting, to do penance, he was also enjoined to eat on the three main feasts of the year, in particular, to consume the foods absolutely refused by the heretics.[66] As Bériou and Hodel note about Pons Roger's reconciliation:

> Beyond the penitential prescriptions, Dominic in reality sought to make perceptible through the accomplishment of concrete gestures the demands of a process of conversion which implied a return to the ecclesial community.[67]

The method was commendable, but it was not infallible, and the reconciliations obtained by the Castilian canon did not remove the risk of relapse. Raimonde, the wife of Guilhem Gasc, was once reconciled by Dominic "after having believed, as they themselves said," the errors of the heretics: "on visible things," "on the consecrated host, that it was not the body of Christ," "on marriage that it had no value," and "on the resurrection of the body, that there will be none." In 1246, she confessed before the inquisitors that she had sometimes worshipped, that is, bowed down to "Good Men," despite this reconciliation.[68]

The work of Diego and Dominic was beginning to bear fruit. In response, the heretics mobilized their forces. In April 1207, Diego returned from Spain, where he had gone to administer his diocese.

65. *Monumenta diplomatica*, appendix I.

66. *Monumenta diplomatica*, 8. See also Elio Montanari, "Gli scritti di Domenico," in *Domenico di Caleruega e la nascita dell'ordine dei frati predicatori* (Centro italiano di Studi sull'alto Medioevo, 2005), 254–55.

67. Bériou-Hodel, 69.

68. *Monumenta diplomatica*, appendix I, 178 [translated from the French: Bériou-Hodel, 141].

He and Dominic took part in a dispute at Montreal, only a few kilometers from Fanjeaux and not far from Carcassonne. The "Good Men" had appointed as their spokesmen the best known and best trained of their men: Arnaud Oth, Guillabert of Castres, Benoît of Termes, and Pons Jourdan. Diego and Dominic defended the orthodox faith alongside the legates Peter of Castelnau and Raoul of Fontfroide. Four lay arbiters were to decide the case, two knights and two burghers leaning towards dissent. The Castilians were armed for the exercise thanks to their academic, rhetorical, biblical, and theological formation. The debate was about the church, its nature, its relationship with Christ, and its sacraments. Arguments were exchanged for several days in front of many listeners, and then the writings of both sides were handed over to those four lay arbiters to whom the two groups had given the authority to decide. But as these men did not wish to decide, the two sides separated, leaving the matter unfinished. According to William of Puylaurens, who claims to have investigated the matter years later, the Catholic side won because about 150 heretics were converted to the faith.[69] A miracle, reported in Pierre des Vaux-de-Cernay's *Histoire albigeoise*, also publicly demonstrated the victory of the Catholic party: the heretics, explains the Cistercian historian, tried to burn a written argument that Dominic had entrusted to them, but three times the parchment sprang out of the fire intact. They intended to hide the incident, but "a knight who was with them, and who had some adherence to our faith, did not wish to hide what he had seen, and told it to quite a number [of people]."[70]

At the time of this dispute, the twelve abbots of the Order of Cîteaux, who had been designated by their chapter of September 1206, arrived at last, each accompanied by a *socius*, that is, a travelling companion, "carrying only modest funds and without horses, in order

69. William of Puylaurens, *Chronica*, 9; Bériou-Hodel, 131–32. English version available in W. A. and M. D. Sibly, *The Chronicles of William Puylaurens* (Boydell Press, 2003), 25–26.

70. Pierre des Vaux-de-Cernay, *Histoire albigeoise*, 54 [translated from the French: Bériou-Hodel, 120–21]. Jordan of Saxony situates the miracle of the fire at Fanjeaux and describes it as an ordination intended to decide between those who had debated publicly. See Jordan of Saxony, *Libellus*, 24–25; Tugwell, 7.

to show themselves in everything as evangelical men."[71] They formed a group of about thirty people and dispersed themselves to engage in two preaching campaigns. Diego took advantage of these reinforcements to return to his diocese. In Pamiers, he took part in a dispute organized by Raimond-Roger, Count of Foix. A Waldensian leader, Durand de Huesca, was convinced by the Catholic arguments. He made his submission and obtained from the pope the right to continue practicing apostolic poverty and preaching with the consent of the local bishop.[72] This episode must have convinced the Bishop of Osma of the need to have a permanent staff capable of preaching competently while maintaining a lifestyle inspired by Christ's counsels to his apostles. He understood very well which way the wind was blowing: if the secular authorities continued to protect the heretics, sooner or later they would have to be brought back to the faith by force. The words addressed to the lords, who were supporters of the Albigensians, before he left for his diocese would prove to be truly prophetic. As Jordan tells us:

> Once, when he had plainly and publically exposed the errors and rebelliousness of the heretics in the presence of many of the nobility, and they mockingly defended the heretics who were

71. Roberti canonici S. Mariani Autissiodorensis [Robert of Auxerre], *Chronicon*, ed. O. Holder-Egger, *Monumenta Germaniae Historicae* 26 (Hannoverae, 1882), 271.

72. William of Puylaurens, *Chronica*, 8. Durand de Huesca, leader of the Aragonese Waldensians, worked in the last quarter of the eleventh century to demonstrate the Catholic faith of his master, Waldo (or Waldes). Just as Christ had chosen illiterate fishermen to proclaim the Gospel of salvation at the beginning of his public life, he again called upon humble believers, the Poor Catholics, to make up for the shortcomings of the clergy. Denouncing the corrupt Catholic clergy on the one hand, and anxious not to fall under the accusations that weighed on the Albigensians, on the other, Durand of Huesca wrote a Liber contra Manicheos between 1223 and 1230. He aroused the suspicion of certain prelates, despite the protection of Innocent III granted to the nascent order. The Poor Catholics disappeared during the first half of the thirteenth century. See "The Schools and the Waldensians: A New Work by Durand of Huesca," in *Christendom and its Discontents: Exclusion, Persecution and Rebellion, 1000–1500*, ed. S. L. Waugh and P. D. Diehl (Cambridge University Press, 1996), 86–111.

> ruining them, offering pleas in their favor which were quite sacrilegious, the bishop angrily lifted his hands to heaven and said, "Lord, stretch forth your hand and punish them"[73] (those who heard this realized afterwards that what he said was inspired by the Spirit when *persecution* gave them *understanding* of it).[74]

But Diego did not see his dream come true; he died in Castile in December 1207.[75]

Since the autumn of that year, Dominic had remained alone in Prouille with a few companions. In addition to the preaching, they had the responsibility to provide spiritual and material support for a group of women, former "perfects," living in community there. With the death of Diego, Dominic lost not only his bishop, but also his religious superior and the friend who had inspired him to lead a life of poor itinerant preaching. A misfortune was added to this grief. The Cistercian abbots, who had initially shown a willingness to take on the mission, gave up in the face of the difficulties encountered and the magnitude of their task. The compromises of the great local lords with the heretics and their tactic of using religious questions to settle political problems discouraged good will. The high society of southern France was composed of both supporters and dissenters within its ranks, with much ambiguity. The idea was beginning to take hold that only by an arduous path could Languedoc be delivered from all the heresy. Rather than wait for the storm that threatened to erupt, the abbots decided to return home. Abbot Guy des Vaux-de-Cernay remained alone as the official head of the preaching, but the future of the mission depended primarily on Dominic.

On January 14, 1208, the assassination of the papal representative in the Midi, the legate Peter of Castelnau, marked the start of the crusade against the Albigensians. The powerful Count of Toulouse, Raymond VI, was credibly suspected of having ordered the crime. He had been excommunicated by Peter of Castelnau because of his increasingly strong support for the heretics. Pope

73. Job 2:5.

74. Jordan of Saxony, *Libellus*, 33; adapted from Tugwell, 9. Regarding the last sentence, please see Isaiah 28:19.

75. Jordan of Saxony, *Libellus*, 30; Tugwell, 8.

Innocent III confirmed the sanction, and the count was forced to make amends.

King Philip Augustus of France declined the honor of leading the troops. He had to be on guard against England and the Holy Roman Empire. The crusade was therefore mainly a matter for the small lords of northern France. In July 1209, the crusader army was placed under the command of Simon de Montfort, hero of the fourth crusade to the East. From Béziers to Toulouse via Carcassonne, towns fell to the soldiers. In September 1213, Montfort defeated Raymond VI and his allies at the Battle of Muret. The *Legend of St. Dominic* by Constantine of Orvieto relates this military episode to the prediction that the saint made of the death of Peter II of Aragon a few months before it occurred. Questioned by a layman of the Cistercian Order who was distressed by the turn of events, Dominic is said to have affirmed:

> Certainly, it will have an end, the wickedness of these Toulousans; it will have an end, but the end is far off. In the meantime, the blood of many will be shed and a king will die, killed in battle in this war. . . . Do not fear for the King of France: there will be another king, and it will not be long before a setback in the present war will cut off his life.[76]

In 1214, the city of Toulouse capitulated and made its peace with the church. The battle of Muret marked not only the inexorable decline of the Albigensian movement and the definitive end of Aragonese expansionism in the west but also the first important step toward the future incorporation of the district of Toulouse, Languedoc, and other neighboring regions into the kingdom of France.[77] At

76. Constantine of Orvieto, *Legenda*, 55 [translated from the French: Bériou-Hodel, 913]. The text is taken up by Humbert of Romans, *Legenda maior*, 49.

77. "Histoire et légende: saint Dominique à Muret?" in *Le temps de la bataille de Muret: 12 septembre 1213*, Actes du 61e Congrès de la Fédération historique de Midi-Pyrénées (Muret, September 13–14, 2013), ed. Jean Le Pottier, Jacques Poumarède, Christophe Marquez, and René Souriac (Société des Études du Comminges, 2014), 521–32.

the time of the celebration of the Council of Lateran IV in November 1215, Simon de Montfort seemed to have the situation under control.[78]

So what did Dominic do in those bloody years? According to Simon Tugwell, he probably returned to Spain between 1208 and 1211, as he was deprived of a bishop and therefore a mandate. In any case, he returned to Prouille, accompanied by a handful of Castilian canons, before June 1211 with the consent of the new bishop of Osma and Bishop Fulk of Toulouse. According to Jordan of Saxony, "About ten years passed from the death of the bishop of Osma up to the Lateran Council, and all this time brother Dominic remained more or less alone."[79] He certainly resumed his itinerant preaching and went back to work to offer the sisters the opportunity to live authentic monastic life. Jordan recalls his zeal and tribulations when the troubles had not entirely ceased:

> The servant of God, Dominic, made such progress in virtue and in his reputation that the heretics became jealous. As he grew in goodness, they looked more and more askance at him. Their bleary eyes could not stand the brilliance of his light. So they made mock of him and followed him around, teasing him in various ways, bringing forth evil from the evil treasure in their hearts. But, while unbelievers mocked, the faithful were filled with holy joy because of him. All the Catholics felt such respect for him

78. The prophetic dimension of Dominic's life is highlighted by Constantine of Orvieto: "By what great favour of divine grace the man of God also shone with the spirit of prophecy, we like to make it briefly apparent" (Constantine of Orvieto, *Legenda*, 50 [translated from the French: Bériou-Hodel, 909]). Constantine's account of the prediction of Simon's death is particularly significant. Humbert of Romans's retelling of the story also emphasizes the friendship between the saint and the warlord: "[Nor should we pass over in silence the way in which the fall] of the excellent man Simon, count of Montfort, his intimate friend and familiar, who died in the region of Toulouse for the affairs of the faith which he was conducting there with energy, [did not escape the man of God, by the mystery of a vision revealed to him by divine power] before he dispersed the brothers from Toulouse" (Humbert de Romans, *Legenda maior*, 50 [translated from the French: Bériou-Hodel, 979]).

79. Jordan of Saxony, *Libellus*, 37; Tugwell, 10.

> that even the hearts of the nobility were touched by the charm of his holiness and the attractiveness of his character. And the archbishops and bishops and other prelates in the area considered him worthy of the highest honor.[80]

In fact, his way of life at the time combined austerity and fervor. An attentive housewife, Guillielma, with whom he stayed during his travels, affirmed that he had eaten more than 200 times in her house without her ever having seen him take more than a small piece of fish or two egg yolks, nor drink more than a cup of wine with three quarters water, nor eat more than a piece of bread. More than one witness said that he had never slept in a bed, even when he was ill.[81] Moral sufferings, humiliations, and asceticism accompanied these travels in Languedoc. By conviction, Dominic deliberately sought to beat the heretics at their own game. If it was austerity that they valued, he would outdo them, even to the point of preventing them from competing. Physical threats from his opponents probably alternated with jeers. The *Legend* of Peter Ferrand reports:

> The heretics ridiculed the holy man and mocked him in many ways, spitting on him, and throwing mud and other filth on him. Afterwards, one of them, led by repentance, came to confession and said that he himself had hit St. Dominic by throwing mud at him, and that in mockery he had tied strands of straw to his back.[82]

The same author states that when these men lying in wait who had threatened him with death came to their senses, they asked, "What would you have done if we had caught you?" Dominic is said to have replied:

> I would have asked you not to inflict a quick death on me by cutting it short as quickly as possible, but by mutilating each

80. Jordan of Saxony, *Libellus*, 36; Tugwell, 10.

81. *Acta canonizationis*, Toulouse, 15; Lehner, 142.

82. Peter Ferrand, *Legenda sancti Dominici*, 17 [translated from the French: Bériou-Hodel, 816].

> of my limbs little by little and one after the other; then, after having placed these limbs, cut pieces [of my body], before my eyes, after having finally gouged out my eyes, I would have asked you to abandon my half-dead and dilapidated body, and to let it bathe in its blood, or else to finish slaughtering it as you wished.[83]

However reliable the legend, physical threats and verbal abuse neither stopped nor diverted Dominic from his course of action. Fervent prayer sustained his apostolate for the conversion of souls. A witness at the Toulouse trial, the abbot of the monastery of St. Paul of Narbonne, testified under oath during the process of canonization that when Dominic was at prayer:

> When he prayed aloud, he could be heard on all sides saying: "O Lord, be merciful to Thy People. What will sinners do?" In this manner he spent sleepless nights weeping and bewailing the sins of others.[84]

Without participating in the activities of the crusade, Dominic did not disassociate himself from the crusaders or the clergy who accompanied them. He made his own contribution as a preacher by engaging in countless private dialogues with the inhabitants of the Midi. From January 1213 to May 1214, however, he remained in Carcassonne as curate to the new bishop Guy des Vaux-de-Cernay, who had gone to France to preach in support of the crusade. He became friends with the family of Simon de Montfort and blessed the marriage of his son Amaury. The leader of the crusade also helped Dominic to finance the *praedicatio,* the preaching mission, of Prouille. In 1214, Dominic received income from the town of Casseneuil, and then obtained the curial benefice of Fanjeaux. If Dominic's humble preaching activities attracted less attention from the chroniclers of the crusade than the dramas of the war, his action did not go unnoticed in his time. Three dioceses wanted him to become their bishop.

83. Peter Ferrand, *Legenda sancti Dominici*, 17 [translated from the French: Bériou-Hodel, 816].

84. *Acta canonizationis*, Toulouse, 18; Lehner, 144.

Each time he refused, even saying that he would take his staff and run away rather than accept an ecclesiastical honor. In 1233, during the process of canonization, Brother John of Spain, a member of the province of Provence and well acquainted with the events of Dominic's life in Languedoc, testified, "Two or three times he was selected for the episcopacy, but always refused; he preferred living with his brethren in poverty to being a bishop."[85]

Birth of the Order of Preachers: 1215–1221

In the early months of 1215, "At the time when the bishops were beginning to go to Rome for the Lateran Council, two upright and suitable men from Toulouse gave themselves to Christ's servant, Dominic."[86] They therefore made an oblation of themselves to the Castilian canon and thus became his companions and disciples. One of them, Brother Peter Seila, offered "some tall, noble houses which he possessed . . . near the Château Narbonnais,"[87] right up against the southern wall of the city of Toulouse. The deed of division of Peter Seila's inheritance, dated April 25, 1215, in fact, makes "Lord Dominic" and those who would live in these houses after him, the owners of Peter's share, and "it was in these houses that the brethren now first began to live in Toulouse, and from that time onwards all those who were with Brother Dominic began to humble themselves more and more profoundly and to adopt the manner of religious."[88]

With Fulk's support, Dominic gained the material resources necessary to found a sort of permanent institute of preachers in the main city of southern Languedoc. In the late spring or early summer of 1215, the bishop granted the status of diocesan preachers in perpetuity "to Brother Dominic and his companions, who proposed to walk in evangelical poverty and to preach the word of evangelical

85. *Acta canonizationis*, Bologna, 28; Lehner, 117. The bishoprics in question are Béziers and Couserans, also mentioned in the depositions taken in Toulouse. John of Spain mentions as well the bishopric of Comminges, the holder of which became archbishop of Auch around 1215.

86. Jordan of Saxony, *Libellus*, 38; Tugwell, 11.

87. Jordan of Saxony, *Libellus*, 38; Tugwell, 11.

88. Jordan of Saxony, *Libellus*, 38; Tugwell, 11.

truth."[89] Together with the prelate, the preachers agreed not to be attached to a particular church but only to receive help from what the diocese had reserved for the poor. The bishop also undertook to provide "all that will be necessary during their illnesses and when they sometimes wish to rest." Finally, the bishop stipulated that "if after one year there are any funds left, we want and rule that they be given to decorate these same parish churches or for the use of the poor, according to what the bishop deems expedient."[90] As Nicole Bériou and Bernard Hodel point out:

> This provision attests to the will not to hoard, unlike what happens in most ecclesiastical institutions, but to be satisfied with what is strictly necessary. It reflects Dominic's constant attitude since 1206 to bear witness to the Gospel in the face of the Albigensians by embracing poverty.[91]

Bishop Fulk also gave Dominic a hostel in June or July 1215 at the Porte Arnaud Bernard in Toulouse to receive converted women and the friars who cared for them.[92]

At the same time, hundreds of men were already following in the footsteps of Francis of Assisi on the roads of Italy. In the spring of 1215, Simon de Montfort asserted his power over Toulouse, and the church was revived in the city in which it had been forbidden. The presence of the preachers from the Lauragais region offered a strange spectacle. The first foundations of the Order of Preachers had been laid but within the limits of a diocesan institution. The conditions were, however, met to "adopt the manner of religious" and to receive vocations who would require training.[93] Dominic wanted six of his companions to attend the theology courses that a master was giving in the city, which did not yet have a university:

89. *Monumenta diplomatica*, 63 [translated from the French: Bériou-Hodel, 172]. Jordan of Saxony refers to this text: *Libellus*, 39; Tugwell, 11.

90. *Monumenta diplomatica*, 63 [translated from the French: Bériou-Hodel, 173].

91. Bériou-Hodel, 173n3.

92. *Monumenta diplomatica*, 64. Fulk does not mention a monastery. This likely is a reference to women converted from heresy.

93. Jordan of Saxony, *Libellus*, 38; Tugwell, 11.

> They informed this master that they were friars who were to preach the gospel of God against the infidels and to the faithful in the region of Toulouse, and explained that they had come to attend his school and that they desired and wished, with an eager heart, to listen to his lessons.[94]

This was only a beginning, however. Dominic remained a canon of Osma, as did some of his companions. The others had given themselves to Dominic and his *praedicatio*, but it was not a formally constituted religious community. Preaching had first presented itself to them as an office to be carried out on behalf of the church, and it was a demanding task. It was now appropriate that it should take the form of an institution, and the ecumenical council convened in the Roman Lateran Palace in November 1215 sanctioned the ambitious policy of Innocent III. Since the beginning of his pontificate, the pope had been committed not only to reforming the church but also to reforming Christendom, explaining to the princes that royal power received the splendor of its dignity from papal authority, just as the moon receives the light of the sun. Fulk and Dominic intended to take advantage of the opportunity to ask the pope for a more solid approval of the Toulouse community and its southern mission. Jordan of Saxony, who knows the rest of the story, notes soberly:

> Brother Dominic joined the bishop to go with him to the Lateran Council, to present with him a joint petition to Pope Innocent to confirm for Brother Dominic and his companions an Order which would be and would be called an order of Preachers.[95]

Perhaps it was on this journey that the Castilian founder met Francis of Assisi. The numerous iconographic representations of the fraternal embrace of Dominic and Francis testify in any case to the bond that the spiritual families of the two saints wanted to create between them. As conscious or unwitting founders of new orders,

94. Humbert of Romans, *Legenda maior*, 33; Bériou-Hodel, 978–79. On the "vision of the seven stars which appeared to a master of theology" in Toulouse shortly before Dominic presented himself to him with six companions.

95. Jordan of Saxony, *Libellus*, 40; Tugwell, 11.

Dominic and Francis saw their consecration to God and their Christian life from perspectives that were not those of the monastic or canonical orders of their time but of a new kind of order that could respond to the designs of the pope.[96]

In Rome, Innocent III heard Dominic's request. He took the community and property of Prouille under his protection, but instead of confirming the *praedicatio* of Toulouse immediately, he asked Dominic to return to his brethren and, "after full discussion with them, to choose, with their unanimous agreement, some approved Rule."[97] Then he would give the desired confirmation. The pontiff's prudence in this regard supported the preachers of Toulouse in their desire to become a true religious order, yet to avoid the proliferation of controversial initiatives, such as those that existed around Francis of Assisi or the former Waldensians, those who were called the "Poor Catholics," the pope encouraged traditional solutions. He did not want the combination of poverty and preaching to frighten and repel bishops but rather wanted preachers like those who had gathered around Dominic to be welcomed wherever they were needed. Writing around 1245 in a climate of fraternal rivalry between the Order of Friars Minor and the Order of Preachers, Constantine of Orvieto was the first hagiographer to mention in his *Legend* a dream of Inno-

96. Marie-Humbert Vicaire, in his biography of the saint, notes three encounters between Dominic and Francis mentioned in the hagiographical sources. With the exception of a brief passage in the *Book of Summaries on the Lives of the Saints* by the Dominican Bartholomew of Trent, all three are Franciscan (Bériou-Hodel, 1026). The first is said to have taken place at the time of the confirmation of the community of Toulouse by Innocent III; the second in 1218 on the occasion of the Franciscan chapter of the Porziuncola, called in part because of Franciscan tradition the "chapter of the mats" and mentioned by the anonymous author of the *Fioretti of St. Francis*; and, finally, a third meeting said to have taken place in 1221 in the presence of Cardinal Ugolino of Segni, the future Gregory IX. On these encounters and their historiography, see also Manuel-Antoine Cardoso-Canelas, "La rencontre entre saint Dominique et saint François: Perspectives iconologiques et variations mimétiques." In Augustin Laffay et Gabrielle de Lassus Saint-Geniès (dir.), *Études d'iconographie dominicaine. Europe occidentale (XVe–XXe siècle)*, Dissertationes historicae 25 (Institutum Historicum Ordinis Praedicatorum—Angelicum University Press, 2017), 25–45.

97. Jordan of Saxony, *Libellus*, 41; Tugwell, 11.

cent III that supernaturally confirmed the importance of Dominic's work for the whole church and was destined for a rich iconographic destiny. At first reluctant to accept the request for the confirmation of an "order that would be called and would be that of the Preachers," it was revealed to the pontiff one night:

> In a dream by a revelation that came to him from God, that the Lateran church was suddenly in great danger of ruin, as if its structure were disintegrating. As he watched this, both trembling and distressed, from across the way came the man of God Dominic, who put the whole crumbling edifice on his shoulders and supported it. Amazed, indeed, by the novelty of this vision and understanding [enlightened by] prudence its meaning, without suffering any delay, [the pope] praised the project of the man of God and cheerfully accepted his request, exhorting him to return to his brethren and to deliberate carefully with them.[98]

At the beginning of 1216, back in Toulouse after the Lateran Council, Dominic and his followers chose the Rule of St. Augustine, the same one they knew and practiced in the canonical tradition of Osma. The Rule of St. Augustine, which forms the basis of the legislation of the Friars Preachers, is not, however, exactly the one that the canonical movement of the late eleventh century had made

98. Constantine of Orvieto, *Legenda*, 21 [translated from the French: Beriou-Hodel, 885–86]. This vision became famous in its "Franciscan" version because of the fresco painted by Giotto in the Upper Basilica of Assisi: St. Francis is supporting the Lateran Church while the pope is dreaming. This vision would have been a divine sign in favor of Francis's rule. In fact, the Franciscan version of Innocent III's dream first appears in the *Legend of the Three Companions*, 51 (cf. *Francis of Assisi. Écrits, Vies, témoignages*, ed. Jacques Dalarun, vol. 1 [Éd. du Cerf-Éd. Franciscaines, 2010], 1139). The text is contemporaneous with that of Constantine of Orvieto, which is the first Dominican attestation of the episode. The iconography of St. Dominic quickly appropriated the scene to make it one of its recurring motifs: suffice it to say that it was engraved on the saint's sarcophagus in Bologna. The subject has been studied by André Vauchez, "Les songes d'Innocent III," in *Studi sulle società e le culture del Medioevo per Girolamo Arnaldi* (All'insegna del Giglio, 2002), 695–706, and taken up again in *Francesco d'Assisi e gli Ordini mendicanti* (Edizione Porziuncola, 2005), 81–96.

famous as the rule of "apostolic life." It consisted of two parts. The first part contained detailed prescriptions; the text of the Friars Preachers only preserved the first sentence, and only the second part was preserved in its entirety. It contained a set of spiritual and moral counsels. The text corresponds to St. Augustine's letter 211, with the difference that it is addressed to men. The rule was therefore not strictly normative. According to Jordan of Saxony, Dominic and his companions therefore adopted some stricter customs for food, sleep, clothing, and, "to ensure that no worldly responsibilities and worries would hinder their job of preaching, they decided and decreed that they would not own properties, but would only accept revenues with which to provide for the food they needed."[99] Poverty was embraced as a means of being conformed to Christ. These observances were essentially based on canonical traditions of strict observance (*arctiores consuetudines*), borrowed mainly from the Premonstratensians.

The house of Peter Seila had become too small to accommodate the apostolic preachers. In July 1216, the cathedral chapter of Toulouse gave Dominic and his companions the nearby church of St. Romain. Sixteen friars gathered there in a convent that they arranged in their own way by building a cloister and "cells suitable for studying and sleeping."[100] Preaching required not only a solid regular life but also intense intellectual activity. The death of Innocent III on July 16, 1216, and the election of Cardinal Savelli, who took the name of Honorius III, forced Dominic to return to Rome to ask the new pope for what had been promised by his predecessor. Honorius III was almost a stranger to him; he had to be told how the apostolic intuition of 1206 had been transformed into a new religious institution. The pope took his time, and Dominic's stay in Rome was extended. But Dominic was not a man to give up:

> In every reasonable purpose which his mind conceived, in accordance with God's will, he maintained such constancy that he hardly ever, if ever, consented to change any plan which he had formulated with due deliberation.[101]

99. Jordan of Saxony, *Libellus*, 42; Tugwell, 11.
100. Jordan of Saxony, *Libellus*, 42; Tugwell, 11.
101. Jordan of Saxony, *Libellus*, 103; Tugwell, 26.

Constantine of Orvieto placed a second episode of a miraculous vision in Rome, confirming the founder in his mission:

> As the man of God Dominic was in Rome and was praying in the Basilica of St. Peter under the eyes of God for the preservation and extension of the Order which his dexterity was propagating by making him its intermediary, *the hand of the Lord was upon him* and by a vision of the imagination he suddenly saw the glorious princes [of the apostles] Peter and Paul coming to him: the first, Peter, seemed to hand him a staff and Paul a book; and they added, "Go and preach, since you have been chosen by God for this ministry." Soon, in a moment, he seemed to see his sons scattered throughout the world, walking two by two and preaching the word of the Lord to the people.[102]

On December 22, 1216, Honorius III finally took under his protection the religious of St. Romain and their possessions, including Prouille, confirming them as religious of the Diocese of Toulouse.[103] In the curia, Cardinal Ugolino of Segni, the same cardinal who had supported Francis of Assisi and who, a few years later, as Pope Gregory IX, would canonize both Francis and Dominic, proved to be an effective supporter. New bulls granted by Honorius III widened the scope of action of the Preachers of Toulouse and confirmed the nature of their vocation: a bull of January 21, 1217, initially addressed to the prior and friars of St. Romanus "preaching" (*predicantes*) in the country of Toulouse, was corrected and sent to the "preachers" (*predicatores*).[104] This is not a mere detail! Dominic and his followers were no longer considered only as priests charged by a bishop to exercise temporarily the ministry of preaching but rather were treated as

102. Constantine of Orvieto, *Legenda*, 25 [translated from the French: Bériou-Hodel, 889]. Humbert takes up this episode almost to the letter: Humbert of Romans, *Legenda maior*, 27. The account of this apostolic apparition gave rise to an abundant iconography.

103. *Monumenta diplomatica*, 77; Bull *Religiosam vitam* (December 22, 1216).

104. *Monumenta diplomatica*, 79; Bull *Gratiarum omnium largitori* (January 21, 1217). The text was corrected before the friars received it. The abrasion and the change of name are still visible on the bull, which is preserved in the Archives départementales de l'Aude in Carcassonne, under the reference H 317, n° 1.

religious and totally dedicated to this office. This explanation is given as early as the thirteenth century by Thomas de Cantimpré, a committed defender of the mendicant orders and the famous author of *The Universal Good of Bees*. According to him, it was the notary of the pontifical curia who took the initiative to change the terms, thus justifying his act to the "apostolic lord":

> "Preaching" is a noun-adjective, even if it is permissible to make a participle a noun, and it is a common noun [that designates a person] acting; the noun "Preachers," on the other hand, is properly a noun, and it is a noun that refers both to a verb and to a person, in which the name of the office is expressed no more clearly.[105]

The name preachers has since then been used to designate what the Dominicans are and what they do; their task is to spread the Gospel with courage and perseverance without being distracted by other commitments. The mission could now expand to other shores. In fact, during the months of his stay in Rome, Dominic frequently visited Cardinal Ugolino and spoke of distant fields of activity.[106] In fact, he met a young cleric, William of Montferrat, in the cardinal's home, who he encouraged to study for two years in Paris and then join him in departing to "convert the pagans who live in Prussia and other northern regions."[107] William of Montferrat, who became a Dominican, bore witness to this Roman encounter with the future Gregory IX (who was at that time Bishop of Ostia). This meeting was indeed to change William's life. It also proves that Dominic's missionary desire had not waned.

On his return to Languedoc at the end of March 1217, Dominic assessed the political situation and was undoubtedly concerned. In his little treatise on the foundation of the Order, Stephen of Salagnac

105. Thomas de Cantimpré, *Le bien universel des abeilles*, 4 [translated from the French: Bériou-Hodel, 1141].

106. *Acta canonizationis*, Bologna, 12; Lehner, 107.

107. Vicaire, 227. The great family of Montferrat had been very involved in the crusade. The first name William is well attested in this family, but according to Nicole Bériou and Bernard Hodel, it cannot be stated with certainty that this religious belonged to this lineage; Bériou-Hodel, 708n1.

puts some harsh words in Dominic's mouth directed toward the inhabitants of Lauragais gathered in Prouille: "Where the blessing is of no avail, let the stick prevail!"[108] These words may have seemed prophetic. Simon de Montfort's conquest of Toulouse had been contested since September 1216. Count Raymond VI wished to take back his city, sure of the support of many of its inhabitants. Dominic's project of founding schools in Toulouse by bringing in Parisian teachers was therefore not without risk. The Friars Preachers might be considered among the spoils of war in the event of Raymond VI's triumphant return. According to Jordan of Saxony, Dominic had "knowledge by the Spirit" of new political dramas:

> He had seen a vision of a tall, beautiful tree, in whose branches a large number of birds were living. Then the tree was felled, and the birds which were sitting on it all took to flight. Filled with the Spirit of God, Brother Dominic realized that the great and exalted prince, the Count de Montfort, patron of many people, was soon to meet his death.[109]

Despite objections from all sides, Dominic decided to disperse the fifteen or so friars who had joined him. This act may have taken place in Prouille on the day of the Assumption of the Virgin Mary in the year 1217. As a legend of St. Dominic states, he knew that "seeds scattered bear fruit and when they are horded, they rot."[110] Some brothers left for Paris. Their leader, Brother Matthew of France, was given the title of abbot. Jordan of Saxony notes:

> He was the first and last in the Order to be called an "abbot," because afterwards, as a mark of humility, the brethren preferred to have their superior called "Master of the Order," not "abbot."[111]

108. Stephen of Salagnac-Bernard Gui, *De quatuor in quibus*, II, 3. On these words of Dominic, which are not attested anywhere else, see Bériou-Hodel, 1172–73.

109. Jordan of Saxony, *Libellus*, 46; Tugwell, 13.

110. Peter Ferrand, *Legenda sancti Dominici*, 27 [translated from the French: Bériou-Hodel, 827].

111. Jordan of Saxony, *Libellus*, 48; Tugwell, 13.

Later, it was also decided "that all the other inferior prelates would be designated by the term 'prior' or 'subprior,'" says Peter Ferrand.[112] Clearly, the foundation process was not yet complete, and there was some uncertainty regarding the organization of houses and the titles of superiors. The friars sent to Paris in two groups were to study with the masters of the university and establish a convent there.[113] From the end of 1217, the preachers attracted attention. Settled near the parish of Saint-Jacques, these preachers, a new kind of canon, received the nickname of "Jacobins" (from the Latin *Jacobus* for Jacques), which continued to describe the French Dominicans until the time of the revolution of 1789. Four other friars left Prouille for Spain. Two companions of the Iberian mission, Brother Peter of Madrid and Brother Sueiro Gomez, "made abundant progress in spreading the word of God." The former was superior of the province of Spain from 1221 to 1230. The other two, however, were not able to put down roots as they would have wished, and they later joined Rome and then Bologna.[114] In 1218, "some young and simple friars were sent to Orleans," Jordan tells us: "They were small seeds, as it were, but the much richer growth which came later all started with them."[115] Others were sent to Italy. They arrived in Bologna in 1218 and were probably welcomed in San Procolo before settling in *Santa Maria alla Mascarella*. "During their time in Bologna," according to Blessed Jordan, "they endured the most appalling poverty."[116] In mid-December 1217, Dominic himself set out for Rome to report the latest events to Pope Honorius III, informing him that Raymond VI entered the city of Toulouse and that Simon de Montfort had immediately laid siege to the city walls. The leader of the crusade was killed on June 25, 1218, during the military operations to reconquer the city.[117]

112. Peter Ferrand, *Legenda sancti Dominici*, 27 [translated from the French: Bériou-Hodel, 828].

113. Jordan of Saxony, *Libellus*, 51–52; Tugwell, 14.

114. Jordan of Saxony, *Libellus*, 49; Tugwell, 13.

115. Jordan of Saxony, *Libellus*, 54; Tugwell, 14.

116. Jordan of Saxony, *Libellus*, 55; Tugwell, 14.

117. Simon de Montfort, who had distinguished himself in Palestine during the Fourth Crusade, led the crusade against the Albigensians in 1208. Courageous and energetic, if not brutal, he took Béziers (1209), Carcassonne,

In Rome, Honorius III welcomed Dominic very favorably. On February 11, 1218, he issued the first of a series of bulls of recommendation ordering the ecclesiastical authorities throughout the world to assist and support "the friars of the Order of Preachers . . . whose useful ministry and religion we believe to be pleasing to God." For the first time, the pope recognized an order of preachers. He also confirmed the commitment of religious to poverty by specifying that those who bear the sign, "freely and faithfully proposing the word of God, attentive to the advancement of souls, following the Lord alone," must be surrounded by thoughtfulness in their laudable purpose and assisted in their need.[118] During his stay in Rome in 1218, Dominic also met a key figure in the early days of the order, a prominent clergyman who was accompanying his bishop to the tomb of St. Peter. Reginald, master-regent in canon law in Paris and later dean of Saint Aignan in Orleans, dreamed of a life dedicated to preaching and poverty. He was preparing to go on a pilgrimage to Jerusalem. When he fell seriously ill, he was visited by Dominic, who urged him to embrace "the poverty of Christ and to join the Order" in such a way that Reginald agreed "fully and freely to enter the Order, so much so that he bound himself to it by vow."[119] According to Blessed Jordan, following this vow, Reginald was miraculously healed by the Virgin Mary, who came to him and anointed "his eyes, ears, nose, mouth, navel, hands and feet with a healing balm," adding these words: "I anoint your feet with holy oil to make them ready to spread the gospel of peace." She then showed him the habit of the order.[120]

After he had completed his pilgrimage to the Holy Land, Reginald was sent by Dominic to Bologna as his vicar. Reginald's talent for oratory and his ability to recruit vocations were put to good use

---

and then won the battle of Muret (1213) against Peter II of Aragon. In doing so, he acquired vast domains at the expense of Raimond-Roger, viscount of Béziers and Carcassonne, and Raymond VI of Toulouse. He was recognized as the owner by Innocent III in 1215 and then by the king of France but had to face the revolt of the people.

118. *Monumenta diplomatica*, 86; Bull *Si personas religiosas* (February 11, 1218) [translated from the French: Bériou-Hodel, 191–92].

119. Jordan of Saxony, *Libellus*, 56; Tugwell, 15.

120. Jordan of Saxony, *Libellus*, 57; Tugwell, 15.

there, both with regards to the students and the teachers. "Hardly anyone was rock-like enough to be proof against its heat," writes Jordan, adding, "The whole of Bologna was in ferment."[121] Dominic's plan was therefore clear. The preachers were to recruit companions from the two greatest European university centers: Bologna and Paris.

Reassured by the pope's encouragement and anxious to keep together the groups of friars he had scattered, Dominic left in May of 1218 for Spain with Peter Seila and some companions. As he had done in the early days of the campaign in Languedoc, Dominic preached to all and engaged the unbelievers in debate. This time, he had to address not only the heretics but also the Jews and Muslims present in the Iberian Peninsula. During the canonization process, Brother John of Navarre, who witnessed these meetings, recounted that he was struck by the way Dominic treated everyone he met:

> Brother Dominic was friendly to all, rich and poor, Jews and pagans (who are very numerous in Spain). As [the witness] noted, he was also loved by all men, with the exception of heretics and enemies of the Church. He used to pursue these persons and refute them in debates and sermons. However, when he argued with them, he lovingly exhorted them to repent and return to the faith.[122]

In Madrid, he gave the habit to the sisters of a monastery that he established on the model of Prouille. A year later, he wrote them a letter, the only personal letter of the founder that has been preserved. He exhorted them to remain firmly attached to the monastic values of discipline and austerity and to fight the devil through prayer and fasting. While he confirmed the authority of his own brother, Mannes, over the community, he insisted that it was the responsibility of the nuns, not the brothers, to welcome new vocations. We will quote here the entirety of this letter because of its singularity. Although Dominic wrote a number of letters, only three of them have come down to us in the form of copies. In this text, the founder of the preachers speaks to his sisters in the first person:

121. Jordan of Saxony, *Libellus*, 57; Tugwell, 15.

122. *Acta canonizationis*, Bologna, 27; Lehner, 116.

Friar Dominic, Master of the Preachers, to the Beloved Prioress and the Entire Community of Nuns at Madrid: Health and Daily Progress.

Greatly do we rejoice and thank God because of your holy life and because He has freed you from the corruption of this world. Daughters, fight the ancient adversary insistently with fasting, for only he will be crowned who has striven according to the rules. If until the present you have not had a place in which to live your religious life, now you can no longer be excused, because by the grace of God you have buildings suitable enough for living the religious life. From now on I want silence to be kept in the forbidden places, the refectory, the dormitory, and the oratory, and your law to be observed in all other matters. Let none go out through the gate and no one enter except the bishop or some prelate for the sake of preaching or making a visitation. Be not sparing of discipline and vigils. Be obedient to your prioress. Avoid talking idly to one another. Let not your time be wasted in conversation.

Since we cannot help you in temporalities, we do not want to give any friar the authority to receive postulants, but only the prioress with the council of her community. Moreover, we command our dear brother, i.e., Friar Mannes, who has worked so hard and has joined you to this blessed state, that he arrange and dispose everything as shall seem good to him, so you might live a most religious and most holy life. Furthermore, we give him power to visit and correct and to remove the prioress (if it be necessary) with the consent of the majority of the nuns; and we give him permission that he may grant dispensations in some matters, if it seems fit to him.

Farewell in Christ.[123]

After this stay in Madrid and before Christmas, Dominic was in Segovia, where he founded the first Spanish convent of friars.[124] In 1219, the tireless mendicant went to Toulouse for the last time. From there he went to Paris, visiting the Marian shrine of Rocamadour on the way. The Parisian convent already had about thirty friars and was

123. *Monumenta diplomatici*, 125; Lehner, 91–92.

124. Jordan of Saxony, *Libellus*, 59; Tugwell, 15.

exerting its influence in the direction of Orleans, Reims, Poitiers, and Limoges. Vocations were pouring in. Dominic received William of Montferrat into the order at this time, and, as the latter recalled during the canonization process, Dominic discussed with him a mission to the Saracens and the Cumans.[125] His missionary dream never left him. As the *Legend* of Peter Ferrand attests, Dominic wore the missionaries' beard for a time after the dispersion of 1217, "while he was preparing to go to the land of the Saracens."[126] It was also in Paris that Jordan of Saxony met Dominic, and this encounter changed his life. Born in Westphalia and having graduated from the University of Paris, Jordan decided after careful consideration to join the order. He delayed doing so, however, in order to attract his fellow student and friend, Henry of Cologne, to the same ideal. They decided together to join at the beginning of Lent in 1220 and received the habit in the convent of Saint-Jacques.[127] In spite of these successes, a concern arose among the brethren during their stay in Paris. The friars were living as canons with an income for their house. Dominic "worked hard to convince them of the need for relinquishing and contemning all temporal goods—they should embrace poverty, live on alms, not carry money with them nor ride horses."[128] Their possessions were given to Cistercian nuns, but the friars seem to have had limited success in their efforts to live poverty more perfectly. Not everyone was prepared to live as they had in Toulouse at the beginning of the preaching. It was at this time, no doubt, that Dominic gave autonomy

125. *Acta canonizationis*, Bologna, 12; Lehner, 107.

126. Peter Ferrand, *Legenda sancti Dominici*, 27 [translated from the French: Bériou-Hodel, 827]. This fact is later taken up by Constantine of Orvieto and Humbert of Romans.

127. In May 1220, Jordan participated in the first General Chapter convened in Bologna. A year later, at the second General Chapter, he was appointed Prior Provincial of Lombardy. He arrived in Italy after Dominic's death. At the General Chapter in Paris in May 1222, he was elected to succeed Dominic in the government of the whole order and then devoted himself to the consolidation and expansion of the young religious family. He died in a shipwreck in 1237 while returning from a voyage to the Holy Land. He was beatified in 1826 by Leo XII. See Angelus Walz, "Giordano di Sassonia," *Biblioteca sanctorum*, vol. 6 (Città nuova editrice, 1965), col. 508–11.

128. *Acta canonizationis*, Bologna, 26; Lehner, 116.

of government to the friars of the Midi, under the leadership of Brother Bertrand of Garrigue. The first division of the order into provinces had begun.

From Paris, Dominic set out for Italy. At the end of August 1219, he arrived in Bologna and found a flourishing convent there. Things had changed after the arrival of Brother Reginald on December 21, 1218. The preachers, who were then few in number, lived in great poverty and benefitted from the hospitality of the Canons of Roncesvalles, who hosted them at their Spanish hospice near the church of *La Mascarella*. Reginald was a man after the founder's own heart. He aroused enthusiasm and a radical poverty. The community, which until then had languished, suddenly saw its numbers grow.[129] Under his leadership, the community was soon large and dynamic enough to found houses in Florence, Bergamo, and Milan. Soon it would spread to Verona, Piacenza, and Brescia, among other places.

Diana, daughter of the lord of Andalò, had aided the brothers with the establishment of their foundation in Bologna. Ardent as well as rich, this young woman had been a valuable ally. She convinced her grandfather, Peter of Lovello, to give the friars the church of St. Nicholas of the Vineyards. When the saintly founder arrived, she placed herself in Dominic's hands "before the altar of Blessed Nicholas in the presence of Master Reginald" and engaged the friars for the building of "a house of ladies which would be called and would be of the Order."[130] As in Prouille, Toulouse, and Madrid, women were closely linked to the preaching mission of the friars.

Dominic went to meet Pope Honorius III in Viterbo, perhaps accompanied by Brothers William of Montferrat, Buonviso of Piacenza, and Frugerio of Penna. He confided to the pontiff his desires to hold an inaugural general chapter and to undertake a mission to the pagans.[131] In his eyes, the era of establishing the Order of

129. Jordan of Saxony, *Libellus*, 58; Tugwell, 15.

130. ASOP 1 (1893):181–84, edition by Hyacinthe-Marie Cormier of the *Chronicle* of St. Agnes of Bologna, 3–4; Bériou-Hodel, 557. See also *Acta canonizationis*, Bologna, 46; Bériou-Hodel, 722n2.

131. *Acta canonizationis*, Bologna. For the depositions of Dominic's travelling companions in Italy, see *Acta canonizationis*: 12, 20, and 46–47; Lehner, 107–8, 111, and 132–34, respectively.

Preachers was coming to an end, and it seemed to him that he would soon be free to pursue his dream of preaching in the East. Once again, the pope shattered these missionary hopes. He wanted to remedy the chaotic situation of female monastic life in Rome and, to this end, asked Dominic to gather the Roman nuns in a new monastery near the basilica of San Sisto along the Via Appia. The ancient church of San Sisto, situated between Caelian and Aventine hills, had long been abandoned. Situated in a hollow, the land had fallen victim to negligence and had become a marsh. In addition, the church had suffered fire and looting in the wars and rivalries between opposing factions. The basilica had nevertheless attracted the attention of Innocent III, who wished to restructure the buildings to house within a single community the members of the seven monasteries in the city that were in decline or in ruins. Architects set to work demolishing the side aisles of the basilica and building the central nave. The result was a new church of more modest proportions that was better suited to accommodate a religious community of some sixty nuns. Honorius III took up the project of his predecessor, and when in December of 1219 the English canons of Sempringham, initially charged with the care of the new monastic institution, *de facto* refused to come to Rome, Honorius III entrusted the church, the work in progress, and the mission to Dominic.[132] His zeal for the nuns of Prouille was well known to the papal curia, and in 1218 at Dominic's request, Honorius III had renewed Innocent III's gesture by taking the Languedoc monastery under his protection.[133] Dominic took his task seriously, writing to the friars and nuns of Prouille, Fanjeaux, and Limoux to prepare themselves for a possible transfer to the Eternal City.[134] While waiting to be able to found the female community, he installed some brothers from Bologna within the walls of San Sisto. As a result, a convent of brothers was thus founded in Rome. In that same December of 1219, a priest from Friesach, in Carinthia, asked to be received into the

132. See Bériou-Hodel, 539–43: Benedetto da Montefiascone, *La fondation de Saint-Sixte de Rome* (Historical note serving as an introduction to the register of charters of the monastery).

133. *Monumenta diplomatica*, 90.

134. *Monumenta diplomatica*, 108, 113.

order and soon left for his country, thus spreading the order to the Germanic world.[135]

The opening of the first General Chapter of the Order of Preachers on May 20, 1220, testifies to the success of the young order. Jordan of Saxony, a witness and participant in the event, left an account of it in his *Libellus* that is as personal as it is succinct:

> In 1220 the first General Chapter of the Order was held in Bologna. I was present there myself. I and three others had been sent from Paris because Master Dominic had instructed us by letter to send four friars from the house in Paris to that in Bologna. I had not yet completed two months in the Order at this time.
>
> At the Chapter it was decreed, with the approval of all the brethren, that the General Chapter should be held one year in Bologna and one year in Paris, except that the following Chapter, in 1221, was to be held in Bologna. The same Chapter decreed that our brethren should thereafter no longer hold properties or revenues, and that they should give up those that they already held in the district round Toulouse. Several other constitutions were made there, which are observed to the day.[136]

This General Chapter brought together brothers from Bologna and Paris as well as from Toulouse and Segovia. These were the centers from which the order would go forth. As we can see from Jordan's account, the customs adopted in Toulouse in 1216 were no longer sufficient. Various problems had arisen, for instance, how to cope with the obligations of the great monastic fast on the roads; how to satisfy the canonical rules of lodging or prayer when travelling, or when the apostolate required a departure from the rules; and

135. Simon Tugwell, "Notes on the Life of St. Dominic," AFP 66 (1996): 163, edition of the text of a *Historia ordinis praedicatorum in Dania*; Bériou-Hodel, 385–86.

136. Jordan of Saxony, *Libellus*, 86–87; Tugwell, 22. See also *A Cathedral of Constitutional Law: Essays on the Earliest Constitutions of the Order of Preachers with an English Translation of Fr Antoninus H. Thomas's 1965 Study*, ed. Anton Milh and Mark Butaye, Bibliothèque de la Revue d'Histoire Ecclésiastique 112 (Turnhout, 2023).

what rules should be set for the woolen habit? In response to these difficulties, a principle of dispensation of unprecedented breadth was introduced. It allowed the superior to exempt a religious, a person who is a member of a religious order and has made vows, from anything that might hinder study, preaching, or the good of souls. Other provisions adopted at the chapter concerned the convent, which became the fundamental unit of the order. At the time of its foundation, a convent had to have at least twelve friars, be governed by an elected prior, and have a lector, that is, a master capable of teaching. Each Dominican convent was thus designed as a small school of theology, recruiting and training religious within its walls, therefore dispensing with the need to study doctrine elsewhere. At the Chapter of Bologna, Dominic appeared tired and worn out and even begged the friars to let him retire from office. According to the deposition of Brother Rodolfo of Faenza during the canonization process, Dominic said: "I am worthy only to be deposed, for I am useless and remiss." The witness adds: "Although the brethren would not remove him, they satisfied him by selecting certain deputies. While the chapter met, these would have power over him and the entire chapter to institute, define, and impose legislation."[137] Brother Dominic thus remained at the head of his brethren as Master of the Order—the title used to designate the superior general of the Preachers.

Having accepted the preference of his brothers, Dominic began to preach in Lombardy until he was exhausted. In his biography of St. Dominic, Marie-Humbert Vicaire dwells at length on this portion of Dominic's life, which seems to him to be crucial, even if, he says, "The documents which would provide accurate details of this mission are lacking."[138] Based on the testimony of Dominican witnesses during the canonization process, the historian expounds:

> In 1220, he would journey through the whole of Lombardy from the last days of May until the end of the year; between 1220 and 1221, he would traverse "almost in its entirety the Marches of Treviso" and "the territory of Venice." Lombardy,

137. *Acta canonizationis*, Bologna, 33; Lehner, 121.

138. M.-H. Vicaire OP, *Saint Dominic and His Times*, trans. Kathleen Pond (McGraw-Hill, 1964), 321.

> the Marches and Venice, in other words the whole of the north of Italy, he was going to comb through with his brethren, who were no longer young acolytes but men in full maturity, and perhaps one or other of the preachers sent to him by the Pope. The wandering sheep to whom he would be addressing himself were at last specified. They were all those who, in northern Italy, were systematically separating themselves from orthodox Christianity, and principally the Waldensians and the Catharists.[139]

For Father Vicaire, the campaign in Lombardy in 1220 was the fruit of the seed sown in the Lauragais region in 1203. Now the method had become clear.

Although the sources do not give us a description of Dominic preaching to the crowds, we do know that he revived the fervor of his brethren. According to the acts of the canonization process, he not only preached to the friars "almost every day" and gave a spiritual talk when he was in a house of his order but also preached and incited others to goodness when he was travelling and visiting religious houses "no matter of what order they happened to be."[140] We may not know the content of his sermons, but we do know that he both admonished yet consoled his listeners, visited those in need, and exhorted and heard confessions. In Italy, Master Dominic continued, as he had done since his years in Languedoc, to walk barefoot on the roads linking to towns or villages, carrying his shoes on his shoulder. On his way back to the villages, he put his shoes on again so he could be distinguished from the heretics. He did not need to be noticed for his penances, but the brothers who accompanied him were witnesses to it. Brother Buonviso, passing along a path where the stones were very sharp, heard the master complain: "What a wretch I am! Here I was once forced to put my shoes on."[141] It had rained, and the road had been impassable. The same companion of Dominic adds that the latter rejoiced when bad weather increased the difficulty of the road. He "praised and blessed God by singing the 'Ave Maris Stella' in a strong voice. When he finished that hymn, he began another, the

139. Vicaire OP, *Saint Dominic and His Times*, 321. See chapter 17.

140. *Acta canonizationis*, Bologna, 6; Lehner, 102.

141. *Acta canonizationis*, Bologna, 21; Lehner, 112.

'Veni Creator Spiritus.' He sang it all in a clear voice."[142] Dominic thus provided a singular approach of preaching to his followers.

In January 1221, after preaching in Lombardy to the limit of his strength, Dominic returned to Rome. The work on San Sisto was nearing completion, but the number of candidates for a more austere monastic life had dwindled. While waiting for a group of nuns from Prouille, the nuns came from the only two Roman communities: St. Bibiana on the Esquiline and St. Mary *in Tempuli* at the foot of the Caelian hill. A nun of St. Mary *in Tempuli*, Sister Cecilia, has left an important testimony of this reform of Roman monastic life and the role Dominic played in it. Her community, probably Benedictine, was located very close to San Sisto, and Dominic had established links with these nuns from his first extended stays in Rome. It was for them that he brought back small wooden spoons from Spain in 1219 as a gift of friendship. The young Sister Cecilia was so enthralled by the figure of the preacher that she later gave her sisters the only physical description of the saint that has come down to us:

> I would describe the appearance of Blessed Dominic in the following way. He was slender and of medium height. His face was handsome and somewhat ruddy. His hair and beard were reddish and his eyes beautiful. From his brow and eyes emanated a kind of radiance which drew everyone to revere and love him. He was always cheerful and gay, except when he was moved to compassion at the sight of someone's affliction. His hands were long and well-formed and his voice was of a pleasing resonance. He was never bald, although he wore the full corona, which was sprinkled with a few grey hairs.[143]

Sister Cecilia's enthusiasm for following in Dominic's footsteps was probably not shared by all her sisters. The abbess of St. Mary *in Tempuli*, after having made her first profession in Dominic's hands, set a condition for her acceptance of the endeavor: if the miraculous image of the Virgin Mary, which the nuns intended to bring with them were to leave San Sisto, they would be completely released from

142. *Acta canonizationis*, Bologna, 21; Lehner, 112.

143. Sister Cecilia, *Miracles of St. Dominic*, 15; Lehner, 183–84.

their profession. Dominic agreed to this. He told them that they should not leave the cloister to visit their relatives. The measure inflamed Roman passions. As Sister Cecilia later recounted:

> As a consequence, some of them repented of the profession they had made. Therefore, Blessed Dominic, knowing of this through the Spirit, went to them one morning and after Mass said to them, "My daughters, already you have changed your mind and wish to walk no longer on the Lord's highway. Now I want every one of you who still wishes to enter of her own will to repeat her profession into my hands."[144]

And so it was done. On February 28, 1221, the first Sunday of Lent, the nuns entered their monastery:

> Sister Cecilia, who was then seventeen years of age, was the first to receive the habit from Blessed Dominic as he stood at the front door. For the third time, she made profession into his hands. After her came the abbess and all the nuns of her convent, and finally a number of other religious and lay women, so that their number totaled forty-four.[145]

The following night, for fear of the Romans who did not want this transfer, Dominic, accompanied by two cardinals and a procession of barefoot faithful, brought the image of the Virgin Mary to the new monastery.[146] The Dominican operation was successful, and the Master of the Order took charge of the formation of the sisters of San Sisto. In the meantime, the friars who had occupied the place for the duration of the work, moved to the neighboring Aventine Hill. The pope's family, the Savellis, owned a fortress on this Roman hill and within whose walls stood the ancient Christian basilica of Santa Sabina. Honorius III donated it to the friars.

144. Sister Cecilia, *Miracles of St. Dominic*, 14; Lehner, 182.

145. Sister Cecilia, *Miracles of St. Dominic*, 14, Lehner, 183.

146. The icon followed the nuns who were transferred to the Monastery of Saints Dominic and Sisto in the sixteenth century and then to Monte Mario, also in Rome, in 1931.

The order was developing, and its place in the heart of the church was becoming clearer. Honorius III wanted to associate it with his projects. As Dominic had already stated on several occasions, the holy founder dreamed of concluding his course by leading a group of missionaries who would go to the pagans on the borders of Christendom. Friar Frugerio de Penna testified to this during the canonization process:

> He had a burning zeal for the salvation of souls, not only of Christians, but also of Saracens and other infidels, and exhorted the brethren to be like-minded. This love for souls was so great that he planned to go to the pagans and, if necessary, die for the faith, once his brethren were established.[147]

Brother Paul of Venice, a travelling companion of Dominic's at the end of his life, records Dominic's own words on the topic: "After we have organized and provided for our Order, let us go to the Cumans, preach the faith of Christ to them and win them for the Lord."[148] He also persuaded the pope to write to King Valdemar of Dacia to recommend the order to a ruler who was active in the Livonian missions. Whatever his wishes, Dominic was in Bologna on June 2, 1221, for the opening of the second General Chapter. There it was decided to send friars to Oxford because of the presence of the university, to Hungary, and to Poland. Other religious may have been sent to Greece. The territorial division of the order into provinces was also outlined:[149]

> After the General Chapter of 1221, Dominic travelled with Brother Paul to the region of Treviso before going to Venice where he met Cardinal Ugolino. In July he returned to Bologna. Exhausted, he lay ill. He had continued the habit of spending the night in church, praying and staying up as long as he could.

147. *Acta canonizationis*, Bologna, 47; Lehner, 133.

148. *Acta canonizationis*, Bologna, 43; Lehner, 130–31.

149. These first provinces are Lombardy, Provence, Spain, and the Roman Province. Bernard Gui also mentions Hungary, Teutonia, and England (Vicaire, *Saint Dominic and His Times*, 361).

During the day he often fell asleep at the table, overcome with fatigue. In the darkness, he would write by candlelight in the friars' dormitory, as he did in San Sisto before the nuns arrived. As he fell asleep, he would doze off fully clothed, wearing an iron chain around his body, having removed only his shoes. He would lie on the floor, on a chair, or sometimes on a simple wooden plank.[150] This regime exhausted his strength. In Bologna, a cell and a bed had to be found for him. When his condition worsened and it was decided to change his clothes, they realized that he had no change of clothes. Dressed in a coarse, patched, woolen tunic with a scapular that was too short and with his shoulders covered by a worn black cope, the former canon of Osma did not make much of an impression.[151] In the scorching heat of the Bolognese summer, they wanted to relieve the sick man by taking him to Santa Maria al Monte, to the small Benedictine priory established on the hill of Monte Mario overlooking the city. There Dominic again found the strength to speak before the friars. He gave them a very beautiful and moving sermon. Twelve of the most trusted friars from the convent of Bologna were then invited to attend him and they have given an astonishing testimony: Dominic admitted before them that although he had remained a virgin all his life, he found more charm in the conversation of young girls than in that of old women![152] After this episode, he insisted on being taken back to the city, telling his brethren, "God forbid that I should be buried except under the feet of my brethren. Carry me outside to die on the road so that you may bury me in our own church."[153]

When he returned to the convent, he assured the brothers that he would be more useful to them after his death. Brother Rodolfo of Faenza, who was wiping the sweat from his face with a cloth, for-

150. *Acta canonizationis*, Bologna, 31; Lehner, 119. The procurator of the convent gives a very credible testimony to Dominic's poverty and austerity. See also *Acta canonizationis*, Bologna, 47; Lehner, 133–34.

151. Stephen of Salagnac-Bernard Gui, *De quatuor in quibus*, III, 2, p. 33. The witness is Brother Moneta of Cremona.

152. Jordan of Saxony, *Libellus*, 92; Tugwell, 24.

153. *Acta canonizationis*, Bologna, 8; Lehner, 104.

mally attests during the canonization process to having heard Dominic say as much.[154] This promise is at the origin of the responsory *O spem miram*, which already appears in the liturgical office established in the thirteenth century.[155] As Jordan of Saxony notes:

> He certainly knew the One to whom he had entrusted the deposit of his labor and fruitful life, and he did not doubt the crown of justice that was now reserved for him: when he had received it, would he not be all the more powerful in presenting his petitions, since he would already have entered more surely into the powers of the Lord?

Dominic died in Bologna on August 6, 1221, while the prayers recommending his soul to God were being recited. "At last his soul was freed from the flesh to return to the Lord from whom it came, exchanging this dingy dwelling place for the everlasting comfort of a heavenly home," wrote Jordan of Saxony.[156] A miraculous vision, mentioned by the one who was to succeed Brother Dominic as head of the order, seems to confirm this judgment:

> That same day, at the very hour of his death, Brother Guala, the prior of Brescia and later bishop of the same city, had lain

154. *Acta canonizationis*, Bologna, 33; Lehner, 122. See also the deposition of Ventura of Verona. *Acta canonizationis*, Bologna, 8; Lehner, 104.

155. *Archivum Generale Ordinis Praedicatorum* (Roma) XIV L 1. This manuscript was produced between 1256 and 1259. The text of the responsory of the 9th lesson of the Office of Matins for the feast of St. Dominic is as follows: "O Spem miram quam dedisti mortis hora te flentibus, dum post mortem promisisti te profuturum fratribus: *Imple Pater quod dixisti, nos tuis juvans precibus.* Qui tot signis claruisti in aegrorum corporibus, nobis opem ferens Christi, aegris medére moribus"; Bériou-Hodel, 1484–85 (translation by the Dominican Nuns at Our Lady of the Rosary Monastery in Summit, New Jersey):

O wonderful hope which you gave to those who wept for you at the hour of your death,
promising that after your decease you would be helpful to your brethren.
Fulfill, Father what you have said, and help us by your prayers.
You shone on the bodies of the sick with so many miracles;
bring us the help of Christ, to heal our sick souls.
Fulfill, Father what you have said, and help us by your prayers.

156. Jordan of Saxony, *Libellus*, 94; Tugwell, 24.

> down and dozed off in the place where the brethren's bell-tower was in Brescia, and he saw a shining opening made in heaven, and through it a golden ladder came down. Jesus Christ was holding the top of it on one side and his glorious mother was holding the other side. At the bottom of the ladder he saw a friar, whose face he could not recognize, because it was covered with his hood, which is the normal way for our dead brethren to be buried. This friar was seated on a chair. Then Christ the Lord and his mother began to draw the ladder back up, until the person sitting at the bottom of it was brought up to their own level. He was then received into heaven, and the radiant opening in the sky was shut, and nothing more was seen. The brother who saw this vision went to Bologna, where he soon discovered that the servant of Christ, Dominic, had died on the very day and at the very time of the vision, as we learned from his own account."[157]

Dominic's Holiness

Dominic died with a reputation for holiness in a city that had enthusiastically welcomed his preaching. The virtues of the founder of the preachers could have immediately aroused devotion among a population eager for miraculous manifestations. After Dominic's death, explains Jordan, the devotion of the crowd and the veneration of the people was awakened:

> Many of them came along, who had been troubled by all kinds of diseases, and they stayed there for days and nights on end telling everyone that they had been entirely cured, and they brought mementos of their cures, fixing on to the tomb wax images of eyes, hands, feet and other parts of the body, depending on the nature of their infirmities and the kind of help they had received in their bodies or their affairs.[158]

Cardinal Ugolino was not far from Bologna. Friendship drew him to preside in person at Dominic's funeral, "knowing that he was a good

157. Jordan of Saxony, *Libellus*, 95; Tugwell, 24.
158. Jordan of Saxony, *Libellus*, 97; Tugwell, 25.

and holy man."[159] In a moral portrait written later and promising to be as famous as the physical description given by Sister Cecilia, Jordan notes the following characteristics of the founder of the Order of Preachers:

> Everybody was enfolded in the wide embrace of his charity, and since he loved everyone, everyone loved him. He made it his own business to rejoice with those who were rejoicing and to weep with those who wept. He was full of affection and gave himself utterly to caring for his neighbors and to showing sympathy for the unfortunate. Another thing which made him so attractive to everybody was his straightforwardness; there was never a hint of guile or duplicity in anything he said or did.[160]

The way seemed open for an official recognition of St. Dominic's holiness, but, as Jordan of Saxony notes, the friars discouraged the devotion that began to develop at his tomb after the first miracles.

> Many of [the brethren] were of the opinion that these miracles should not be broadcast, for fear that it would look as if they were trying to make money out of them, under the guise of piety. But in guarding their own reputation like this . . . they failed to consider how the church as a whole might have benefited, and they buried the glory of God.[161]

The discretion of the founder and the reticence of the friars allowed Dominic's figure to fall into relative oblivion even though the fruit of his labor was solid and lasting. The convents he had founded, especially that of Bologna, did not cease to grow. From 1228 onward, the memory of the founder had faded to such an extent that, due to the construction of the new church, Dominic's tomb was even exposed to the elements.[162]

159. Jordan of Saxony, *Libellus*, 96; Tugwell, 24.

160. Jordan of Saxony, *Libellus*, 107; Tugwell, 26.

161. Jordan of Saxony, *Libellus*, 98 [translated from the French: Bériou-Hodel, 662].

162. Jordan of Saxony, *Libellus*, 124; Lehner, 83.

Dominic had always been acutely aware of what charity demands of Christians. The preaching of the Gospel of salvation was, according to him, an urgent necessity for those who wanted to be authentic disciples of Christ. In 1233, expectation of the end of the world pervaded northern Italy. The region was shaken by the *Alleluia*, a preaching movement advocating the immediate reconciliation of all Christians and general conversion.[163] The Friars Preachers were involved alongside the Franciscans, in particular a Friar John of Vicenza who inspired a revival of devotion to Dominic.[164] Depositions of the miracles were collected and sent to the pope. The religious asked Gregory IX if Dominic's body could be transferred more solemnly to the conventual church. The pope, a firm supporter of the mendicant orders, warmly approved. He had just called upon the preachers as judges of the new inquisition tribunals and knew he could count on them. During the translation, celebrated on May 24, 1233, the smell of a wonderful perfume emanated from the tomb. It persisted eight days later when the relics were exposed for the veneration of those who could not be present at the opening of the tomb. The Friars Preachers then petitioned the pope for Dominic's canonization, and the official investigation began in the summer of 1233. The new canonization procedure was

163. André Vauchez, *Ordini mendicanti e società italiana, XIII-XV secoli* (Milan, 1990), 119–61; Vito Fumagalli, "In margine all'Alleluia del 1233," *Bisime* 80 (1968): 257–72; Augustine Thompson, *Revival Preachers and Politics in the Thirteenth Century Italy* (Clarendon Press, 1992).

164. According to André Duval, John of Vicenza, who was born around 1200, entered the order in Padua around 1220. But this is only conjecture: "He appeared in 1233 as the most popular of the preachers of Northern Italy who, pushing their action to the political level, controlled and reformed the communal statutes, and aroused a great movement of reconciliation and peace (the *Alleluia* of 1233). Venerated in Bologna as a saint and a miracle worker, John caused the solemn transfer of the remains of the founder of the Friars Preachers in May of that same year, a prelude to his canonization the following year." The height of his popularity was reached on August 28, 1233, near Verona, where he gathered a huge crowd. He then faded away and, although he is mentioned as an inquisitor in Lombardy in 1247, he subsequently escaped the notice of historians. See André Duval, "John of Vicenza," *Catholicisme: Hier-Aujourd'hui-Demain*, vol. 6 (Letouzey et Ané, 1967), col. 578.

initiated, and several dozen clerical, religious, lay, male and female witnesses were questioned. The commissioners appointed by the pope first questioned the friars of Bologna. Then some delegated commissioners, residing in Toulouse, were charged with collecting information on Dominic's activities and miracles in Languedoc. These depositions constitute a unique and valuable source of information about the apostolate and his message. At the end of the process, Dominic was declared a saint by Gregory IX in Rieti on July 3, 1234. His liturgical feast was first set for August 5, then moved to August 4, and finally to August 8. An impressive monument was erected over his tomb in Bologna, in the patriarchal basilica.

Chapter 2

The Sources of Saint Dominic's Life Between History and Hagiography

In the period between the death of St. Dominic in 1221 and the middle of the fourteenth century, especially during the general chapters that were held each year, the highest authorities in the Order of Preachers devoted much attention to the memory of the friars who had died in the odor of sanctity and to the promotion of the cult of those who had already been canonized. Although the *life* of St. Dominic, as the story of a man, has long been the subject of much research, as witnessed in particular by Father Marie-Humbert Vicaire's *Saint Dominic and His Times*,[1] the *evolution* of this hagiographic portrait, especially during the first decades of the order's development, has not aroused specific interest, at least not until the publication of Luigi Canetti's studies. These works have the merit of contextualizing the cult and the hagiographies of the founder during the formation of the Dominican identity embodied by the Friars Preachers of the first generations. In the following pages, we will try to present the hagiographic sources for St. Dominic and clarify the reasons that led the order to produce and diffuse these documents.

The Canonization of St. Dominic, the Process, and the *Libellus*

The Translation of 1233

Saint Dominic died on August 6, 1221, in Bologna, where he was first buried in the church of St. Nicholas of the Vineyards. Pope Gregory IX's bull, *Visibilium et invisibilium*, initiated the process of canonization on July 13, 1233, and on July 3 of the following year,

1. Marie-Humbert Vicaire, OP, *Saint Dominic and His Times* (Darton, Longman, and Todd Ltd., 1964).

Dominic was added to the list of saints as witnessed by the bull *Fons sapientiae*.[2]

One wonders why the canonization took place twelve years after Dominic's death, when in the preceding years the Order of Preachers had shown no sign of moving in this direction. As the anonymous author of an account of the translation of the saint's body recalls, miracles had indeed occurred at the tomb of the founder, but the friars had strenuously prevented the birth of a possible cult for fear that "their piety might appear self-serving."[3]

Contrary to the usual practice, the translation took place on May 24, 1233, that is, before the opening of the canonization process. This is probably due to pressure from Pope Gregory IX.[4] The night before the ceremony, the friars opened the tomb in the presence of the civil and ecclesiastical authorities (the chief magistrate of Bologna and the bishop of Ravenna, delegated by the pope), accompanied by the Master of the Order, Jordan of Saxony.

We know the details of this translation from an encyclical letter written, according to some historians, by Jordan himself.[5] Simon Tugwell believes that the author of the letter, one of the members of the Dominican convent in Bologna in the mid-thirteenth century, was an eyewitness to the translation.[6]

Between April and June of 1233, in tandem with preparations for the transfer of Dominic's body, the religious movement known as the "Alleluia," which had already spread in the regions of Emilia-

2. *Monumenta historica Sancti Patris Nostri Dominici*, MOPH 16 (Institutum historicum FF. Praedicatorum, 1935), 115–17, 190–94.

3. MOPH 16, 83n122.

4. Cf. Roberto Paciocco, "Il papato e i santi canonizzati degli ordini mendicanti. Significati, osservazioni e linee di ricerca (1198–1303)," in *Il Papato duecentesco e gli ordini mendicanti: Proceedings of the XXV International Conference (Assisi, February, 13–14, 1998)* (Centro italiano di Studi sull'alto medioevo, 1998), 263–341.

5. This is the opinion of Heribert Christian Scheeben, an eminent scholar on the life of St. Dominic. See Heribert Christian Scheeben, ed., *Iordani de Saxonia Libellus de principiis Ordinis Praedicatorum*, MOPH 16, pp. 1–25.

6. Simon Tugwell, *The So-called 'Encyclical' on the Translation of Saint Dominic Ascribed to Jordan of Saxony: A Study in Early Dominican Hagiography* (Oxford, 1987), especially 137–38.

Romagna and Veneto through Franciscan and Dominican preachers, spread in Bologna through the initiative of the Dominican, John of Vicenza.[7] The latter achieved important results, such as the reform of the statutes of the city of Bologna, adjusted according to the moral principles of the mendicant orders and the reconciliation between the civil power and the local bishop.[8] It is undoubtedly to John of Vicenza that we owe a sudden revival of interest in Dominic. One of the witnesses for the canonization process, Friar Stephen, then Provincial of Lombardy, tells us that John of Vicenza was the first to preach to the people about the holiness of St. Dominic. It seems, moreover, that it was John himself who took the initiative to encourage the city of Bologna to support the cause of Dominic's canonization.

The Little Book on the Beginning of the Order of Preachers, or Libellus

Blessed Jordan's *Libellus de principiis Ordinis Praedicatorum* was completed in the period between April and May of 1233.[9] This *Little Book*, or *Libellus*, is undoubtedly a primary source for the history of St. Dominic and the beginnings of the Order of Preachers.

The prologue does not mention the transfer of Dominic's body, and for this reason, it is likely to have been written before the ceremony. A *terminus post quem* is given by the mention of Fulk, Bishop of Toulouse, who died in 1231. Simon Tugwell believes that Jordan began writing his text well before the year 1233.[10]

7. On this movement, see André Vauchez, "Une campagne de pacification vers 1233: L'action politique des ordres mendiants d'après la réforme des statuts communaux et les accords de paix," *Mélanges de l'École française de Rome—Moyen Âge* 78 (1966): 503–49. Italian edition: *Ordini mendicanti e società italiana (XIII–XV secc.)* (Milan, 1990), 263–341.

8. On the activity of John of Vicenza in Bologna, see Augustine Thompson, *Revival Preachers and Politics in Thirteenth-Century Italy* (Wipf and Stock Publishers, 1992).

9. The discussion concerning the date of the *Libellus* is summarized in Bériou-Hodel, 602–3.

10. Jordan of Saxony, *Libellus*, 110–20; Bériou-Hodel, 667–72. The conclusion of the *Libellus*, that is, the story of a certain Brother Bernard possessed

The literary genre of this work is unclear; the author composes a mixture of history of the order and hagiography. Some elements clearly belong to the history of the foundation, such as the title of the text, which in many manuscripts is *Libellus de initio Ordinis*. Another example is the conclusion of the manuscript, in which Jordan, after praising Dominic's virtues, recounts in several pages the story of a certain friar, Bernard of Bologna, who was possessed by a demon. This episode is said to have led to the introduction in the Bologna convent of the custom of singing the antiphon, *Salve Regina,* in the evening. However, it is certain that this work cannot be considered simply as a history: the period following Dominic's death receives very little attention and is full of references to events of little importance. Moreover, the *Libellus* was used from the beginning for liturgical purposes as a source of information about Dominic's life. The paragraphs in which Jordan deals with the virtues of the saint are, in particular, purely hagiographic in character.

What, then, could have been the purpose of the *Libellus*? Simon Tugwell speculates that Jordan wanted to provide the Dominicans with an authentic portrait of the founder and to clarify the saint's relationship to the order at a critical time in its development in 1233, the year of the translation. In the prologue, Blessed Dominic is referred to as "the first who instituted this religion and was its master and brother." Jordan's aim was thus to present Dominic not only as the founder of the order but also as one of its brothers.[11] Another of Jordan's aims, again according to Tugwell, was to assert the primacy of Dominic's membership in the order and to prevent his image being used by members of John of Vicenza's movement, which was entangled with the affairs of the city of Bologna.[12] Jordan, in fact,

---

by the devil, seems to support this thesis: if Jordan had written his text in 1233, he would probably have remembered major events in the life of the order. See Simon Tugwell, "Notes on the Life of St Dominic," AFP 68 (1998): 21–33.

11. This image, moreover, faithfully reflects Dominic's attitude. Rodolfo of Faenza tells of his renunciation of his office at the first General Chapter in Bologna in 1220 and the proposal to elect Diffinitors with wide powers, even over the person of the Master General (cf. MOPH 16, p. 151).

12. Simon Tugwell, "Notes on the Life of St Dominic," AFP 68 (1998): 16.

had probably underestimated the activity of John of Vicenza and other friars who had acquired power and influence in the concerns of the laity. The decision of the General Chapter of 1234 to limit the interference of the friars in secular affairs seems to corroborate this hypothesis.[13]

However, it is very clear that the *Libellus* was completed with a view to opening a cause for canonization.[14] It was of particular interest to the Dominicans, who had fallen behind the Friars Minor in the number of canonized saints.[15] In composing his portrait of Dominic, Jordan wanted to avoid a circumstance in which the saint would play the role for the preachers that Francis had played for the Friars Minor. Indeed, the internal dissensions that the Franciscans experienced were caused by the authority that Francis's aura seemed to confer on his rule.

Luigi Canetti has emphasized Jordan's role as the first to promote the founder of the order as a model of sanctity, a position that was not to be challenged by later hagiography. Jordan's portrayal of Dominic, mixing biblical images with traditional hagiographic patterns, is faithful to the Dominican ideal established by the *Constitutions*. His Dominic is a model of regular observance and traditional monastic virtues. For the Dominicans of later centuries, respect for the *Constitutions* and the *Rule* would be more important than imitation of the founder's life. This distinguishes the Dominicans very clearly from the Friars Minor, who sought in the life of Francis the answer to the questions and demands of each age. As a result, the evolution of Franciscan hagiography was accompanied by violent and inevitable internal conflicts.[16]

13. *Acta Capitulorum Generalium Ordinis Praedicatorum, I. 1220–1303*, ed. B. M. Reichert, MOPH 3, p. 4.

14. Among the documents sent to the pope was the *Libellus*, the only "biography" of Dominic available in 1233 (cf. Simon Tugwell, *The So-Called 'Encyclical,'* 133ff). The addition of a biography to the dossier of the request for canonization was a common practice.

15. In 1233, the Franciscans already had two canonized saints: Francis of Assisi (canonized in 1228) and Anthony of Padua (canonized in 1232); the Dominicans had none.

16. See Giovanni Miccoli, *Francesco d'Assisi: Realtà e memoria di un'esperienza cristiana* (Einaudi, 1991), 190–93.

Dominic's Canonization Process

After the transfer of Dominic's relics, the bishop of Bologna and the municipal authorities petitioned the pope to initiate the canonization process. In response, on July 13, 1233, the pope entrusted three Bolognese clerics with the task of beginning the cause.[17] This was carried out in two phases, the first of which took place in Bologna and allowed for the collection of local testimonies.

The Dominicans of Bologna appointed a procurator in the person of Philip of Vercelli, who chose the witnesses and presented them to the papal delegates. Nine members of the order, whose names are known, were retained for this stage; the other testimonies, if any, have not been preserved.[18] Some of the records of the Bologna Acts have probably been lost.[19] It seems that Philip of Vercelli was responsible for the list of *articuli interrogatorii*, that is, the series of questions on the saint's virtues that allowed the investigators to proceed directly to the subject at hand, avoiding unnecessary digressions.[20]

A second stage of the trial took place in Toulouse, in the region of Languedoc, where Dominic had spent most of his life as an apostolic missionary. The witnesses who were called, both religious and lay, came from different parts of the Languedoc region. A majority of them were content to confirm the list of *articuli* already compiled;

17. *Monumenta historica Sancti Patris Nostri Dominici*, MOPH 16, p. 169.

18. *Monumenta historica Sancti Patris Nostri Dominici*, MOPH 16, pp. 123–67.

19. According to Simon Tugwell, the letter from the papal legates of August 19th, which opened the second phase of the trial in Languedoc, is proof of this. This letter states: "We have already heard many testimonies about his life, his conduct in Italy and some miracles." However, the hearing of only nine witnesses can hardly correspond to the Latin adjective *multos*; the collection of testimonies of miracles that occurred *post mortem* is also missing. The text of the bull of canonization also shows the existence of a large number of witnesses (cf. *Monumenta historica Sancti Patris Nostri Dominici*, MOPH 16, p. 193).

20. Father Vicaire believes that Dominic's trial was the first in which prepared questions, *articuli interrogatorii*, were used. Such a practice would become quite widespread. At the Bologna trial, only an abbreviated list of questions was used, supplemented when new testimony was added to the data already collected. See Marie-Humbert Vicaire, *Histoire de saint Dominique*, vol. 2 (Éd. du Cerf, 1957), 350.

a few, however, reported new biographical episodes. The Toulouse phase did not provide an investigation of miracles performed *post mortem*, which is not surprising given the distance between the city and Dominic's tomb. However, a few witnesses to the miracles performed during the saint's life were found.

A now-lost manuscript from the library of the Chapter of Osma, used by the Antwerp Jesuit William Cuypers for the dossier on St. Dominic in the Bollandist collection of the *Acta Sanctorum*, contained a list of twenty *post-mortem* miracles. According to Berthold Altaner, these must have been compiled at the time of the canonization process.[21] This list differs from other hagiographic writings, particularly in the use of a vernacular vocabulary, which confirms the text as a true record of the witnesses' testimony. In contrast, none of the miracles recounted occurred at Dominic's tomb, and no details are given of the acts of piety and gratitude performed by the beneficiaries of these miracles after their recovery.[22]

Luigi Canetti studied the acts of the canonization process with respect to the differences in emphasis in the two locales. His study shows that the virtue of Dominic most often mentioned by the Bolognese witnesses is that of *amor regularitatis*, that is, the rigorous observance of the rules of monastic life. The *zelus animarum*, or pastoral fervor, which according to André Vauchez is the typical character of the sanctity of the mendicant orders, is recalled more rarely. Zeal for preaching is mentioned even less frequently. The trial of Toulouse introduced a novelty: it added Dominic's supposed role of *persecutor hereticorum* to the list of standard questions, although it was only mentioned by a limited number of witnesses. As is well known, Dominic

21. Cf. *Acta Sanctorum Augusti Ex Latinis & Græcis, aliarumque gentium Monumentis, servata primigenia veterum Scriptorum phrasi, Collecta, Digesta, Commentariisque & Observationibus illustrata a Joanne Bapt. Sollerio, Joanne Pinio, Guillielmo Cupero, Petro Boschio, e Societate Jesu Presbyteris Theologis: Tomus I Quo dies primus, secundus, tertius & quartus continentur* (Antwerp, 1733), 558–59; Berthold Altaner, Der *heilige Dominikus: Untersuchungen und Texte* (Breslau, 1922), 9–10.

22. See Simon Tugwell's hypotheses on this point in the volume *Miracula sancti Dominici mandato magistri Berengarii collecta*, MOPH 26, pp. 21–109. The author of the first legend of St. Dominic, the Spaniard Peter Ferrand, knew and used this list; the accounts of the miracles were taken up by later hagiographers.

was not, and could not have been, an inquisitor; indeed, the papal mission in which he participated was not, technically speaking, an *inquisitio*. However, this role would later become associated with his image. This process went hand in hand with the integration of the duty of the inquisitor into the institutional consciousness of the order.[23]

The last canonization document in chronological order is the bull *Fons sapientiae* of Pope Gregory IX, in which Dominic and the Order of Preachers are placed in an ecclesiological and eschatological context that gives them an important role in salvation history. The pope makes use in his text of a biblical vision of the prophet Zechariah in which four chariots are described, drawn respectively by red, black, white, and piebald horses (6:1–7). This vision is applied to the history of the church: the red horses are the martyrs, followed by the black horses representing Saint Benedict and his monks; to give strength to the tired fighters, the white horses come next, that is, the Cistercians and the disciples of the Calabrian monk, Joachim of Fiore. Finally, at the eleventh hour, when the sun is about to set and charity is lacking, the mission of the piebald horses, Friars Minor and Friars Preachers, begins. This is an allusion to the description of the end times as given in the Gospel of Saint Matthew (24:12). The beggars are therefore the vigorous horses with their fawn and white coats that roam the world; they form the *militia promptior*, an army ready to fight. There is no lack of analogies in this text to the bull of canonization of Saint Francis, *Mira circa nos*. In the latter document, the eschatological allusion to the eleventh hour is also present. The members of the two great mendicant orders present themselves as the workers of the eleventh hour, who deserve the same wages as those who have worked in the vineyard since the morning. In the words of the parable in Matthew's Gospel, they are the last (*novissimi*) who will become the first (*primi*) (Mt 20:1–16).

Dominic's canonization is therefore presented as an important event, also from an ecclesiological point of view.[24] It consecrates,

23. Luigi Canetti, *L'invenzione della memoria: Il culto e l'immagine di Domenico nella storia dei primi frati Predicatori* (Centro italiano di Studi sull'alto medioevo, 1996), 223–24.

24. Paciocco, "Il papato e i santi canonizzati," 294–96.

before the whole church, not only the role of the Dominicans but also that of the mendicant orders, sanctioning their legitimacy and superiority over the older forms of religious life.

The "Lives" of Saint Dominic

Peter Ferrand

Since the *Libellus*, as has just been said, cannot be regarded as a true biography of St. Dominic, the first life or legend of Dominic is considered to be the one written by the Spanish Dominican Peter Ferrand.[25] The origins of this text are obscure. Heribert Christian Scheeben has speculated that Ferrand wrote the legend at Jordan's request immediately after the canonization; however, there is little evidence to support this hypothesis. According to Simon Tugwell, Ferrand did not work at another's request but rather on his own initiative. His legend would have been revised later, perhaps by a commission appointed for this purpose by the chapters of 1235 or 1236. The new version was then approved by the General Chapter of 1238 and used for liturgical purposes.

The main source for the legend of Peter Ferrand is Jordan's *Libellus*, which he follows almost to the letter except for the parts dealing with figures other than Dominic. The legend also lists the miracles mentioned earlier. It is the same list, probably expanded and stylistically improved, that must have been read to the pope at the time of the canonization.

The prologue presents an interesting and original element. It mentions the role of the preachers in the universal economy of salvation based on various biblical parables and the bull *Fons sapientiae*. According to Ferrand, the new order was sent by God in these last times, in keeping with the evangelical model of the servant who carries the invitation to go to the wedding banquet (Lk 14:17–18). Another New Testament image already present in the bull of canonization is that of the workers of the eleventh hour. The founder of the order, claims Ferrand, becomes the evening star, the *novum sidus*

25. Marie-Hyacinthe Laurent, *Petri Ferrandi Legenda S. Dominici*, in *Monumenta historica*, MOPH 16, pp. 209–60.

or *vesperus* that closes the day begun by John the Baptist, defined as *Lucifer*, the morning star.[26] The new religious order sent by God for the end times is, in fact, the first in terms of the importance of the mission it is called to fulfill.

It is obvious that there is a certain Joachimite influence in this discourse, which must be taken into account. Themes from the doctrine of the Calabrian abbot appear as early as the bull of canonization and are present as late as the *Liber vitas fratrum*.[27] Marjorie Reeves's research shows that the influence of the writings of Joachim of Fiore, whether authentic or apocryphal, was indeed significant.[28] It is thanks to her that Dominicans and Franciscans were able to be identified as the two orders of spiritual men that Joachim announced. The legend of Peter Ferrand was written before the 1240s, when Joachim's ideas were at their peak of popularity, especially in the Franciscan sphere. Therefore, it is likely that Peter Ferrand was influenced not only by Joachimite writings but also by an apocalyptic eschatology whose influence was noticeable beginning in the tenth century.[29]

Another particularly interesting element of the legend of Peter Ferrand is the spiritual testament pronounced by the saint on his deathbed, expanding the account in Jordan's *Libellus*. In the conclusion of the latter text, Dominic exhorts "twelve of the wisest brethren" who he has summoned around his bed to avoid the company of women:

26. See Marie-Humbert Vicaire, "Vesperus (L'Étoile du soir) ou l'image de saint Dominique pour ses frères au XIIIe siècle," in *Dominique et ses prêcheurs* (Éd. Universitaires—Éd. du Cerf, 1977), 280–304.

27. The *Liber* relates that the monks of Abbot Joachim greeted the Friars Preachers as those whose advent had been foretold by their master; cf. *Gerardi de Fracheto O.P. Vitae Fratrum Ordinis Praedicatorum*, ed. Benedictus Reichert (Charpentier & Schoonjans, 1896), 13; Bériou-Hodel, 314.

28. See Marjorie Reeves, *The Influence of Prophecy in the Later Middle Ages* (University of Notre Dame Press, 1993), 145ff and 161–74.

29. The emergence of apocalyptic eschatology is linked to the reform of the church under Gregory VII. It emphasized the reading of Revelation and its application to political and social realities, thus distinguishing itself from imperial apocalypticism, which was based on texts of extrabiblical origin.

> "Behold!" he says, "up to this hour divine mercy has preserved me in the incorruption of the flesh; nevertheless, I confess that I have not escaped this imperfection: the conversation of young girls charms my heart more than the talks exchanged with old women."[30]

Jordan was not present at the time of Dominic's death; the only two witnesses at the Bologna trial who gave evidence of the saint's death, Ventura of Verona and Rodolfo of Faenza, do not report this speech. For Simon Tugwell, such an exhortation to discourage seeking the company of young women makes no sense in the context in which it occurs: Dominic should have been addressing the younger brothers, not the "wiser ones." The original context could be an episode reported by Brother Ventura in which Dominic addresses the novices, or the episode—also recounted by Brother Ventura—of Dominic's general confession of his entire life before several religious. It is probable that Jordan conflated the two episodes.[31] The Bologna Chapter of 1242 decreed that the episode of Dominic's confession of imperfection should be removed from the legend of Peter Ferrand.[32] The legends of Constantine of Orvieto and Humbert of Romans published later did not include it.

This same episode has suggested another research question to historians. Luigi Canetti, for example, has supported the hypothesis of a link between the last word of advice given by Dominic on his deathbed and the problem posed by the *cura mulierum* and, more specifically, the care for the nuns in the order. Dominic's concerns were, in fact, reflected in Jordan's thinking. In Jordan's time, there was a "misogynistic" Dominican current determined to prevent any incorporation of

30. Jordan of Saxony, *Libellus*, 92; Bériou-Hodel, 659.

31. See Simon Tugwell, "Notes on the Life of St Dominic," AFP 66 (1996): 96–98.

32. This change was due, according to André Vauchez, to the need to respond to the model of sanctity that the Holy See valued at the time and which implied the permanent preservation of Christian perfection, the total absence of sin, which was more essential than the occasional practice of any virtue: *La sainteté en Occident aux derniers siècles du Moyen Âge d'après les procès de canonisation et les documents hagiographiques* (École Française de Rome, 1981), 602.

female monasteries. Jordan, who had shown himself to be a friend and protector of the nuns on several occasions, as his spiritual correspondence with Diana d'Andalò proves, may have sought a compromise with those who took a stricter stance.[33] In fact, the chapter of 1228 had already forbidden a friar to take on the direction of nuns or female penitents. At the time of the publication of the *Libellus*, the debates provoked by this decision must have still been lively.[34]

Another element of Dominic's spiritual testament is the curse associated with detractors of the vow of poverty. This event was described in all subsequent legends, with the sole exception of Bartholomew of Trent. "This illustrious father," notes Peter Ferrand, "forbade as rigorously as he could the introduction of temporal possessions into this Order, pronouncing in a terrible manner the curse of God and his own against anyone who would have the audacity to sweep away with the dust of earthly riches this Order, whose profession of poverty is its particular ornament."[35] Introduced by Ferrand into Dominican literature, this exhortation was universally regarded as an original part of Dominic's testament until its authenticity was questioned in the twentieth century.[36]

The acceptance of mendicant poverty in the Order of Preachers was not without obstacles. The Chapter of 1220 was the first to renounce property and fixed incomes, but this was only possible because of the personal influence of Dominic. It remains possible, therefore, that the words that Ferrand attributes to Dominic reflect the hagiographer's desire to remind his confreres of an ideal which was of the utmost importance to the saint.[37]

33. See Berthold Altaner, *Die Briefe Jordans von Sachsen, des zweiten Dominikanergenerals (1222–1237): Text und Untersuchungen* (Leipzig, 1925).

34. See Canetti, *L'invenzione della memoria*, 269–309.

35. Peter Ferrand, *Legenda sancti Dominici*, 43; Bériou-Hodel, 845.

36. An article by Raymond Creytens shows that the words of curse cannot be authentic; the rest of the speech about charity and humility being left as a legacy, the account of the curse is only a *topos* found in the lives of many other saints: "Le testament de saint Dominique dans la littérature ancienne et moderne," AFP 43 (1973): 29–72.

37. On the possible context of the curse, see Canetti, *L'invenzione della memoria*, 350–98.

Constantine of Orvieto

Although the legend of Peter Ferrand mentions several *post-mortem* miracles, it seems that this was not enough for the sensibilities of the time. There was a desire to spread the tidings of these newly discovered miracles. The General Chapter held in Cologne in 1245 therefore ordered that the accounts of the miracles missing from the legend of Peter Ferrand be collected and sent to the next chapter.[38]

There were also specific measures taken to promote the cult of Dominic. The Chapter of 1239 ordered the celebration of a weekly votive Mass in honor of St. Dominic in each convent.[39] A Confraternity of St. Dominic was founded in Bologna, and its statutes were approved in 1244 by the Master General John the Teutonic (John of Wildeshausen) to support these efforts.[40]

The German Master of the Order probably wanted a new legend of St. Dominic to be written from 1245 onward. In any case, it was he who sent Constantine of Orvieto the accounts of miracles collected after the Chapter of 1245. The prologue of the legend written by Constantine shows that the first task was to insert the new elements into the already existing legend; the idea of a complete renewal of the text came later.

Among the new miracles, the approximately twenty that occurred in the Hungarian monastery of Somlyo (today Érsomlyó in Serbia) are particularly interesting.[41] A relic of the saint was venerated there. Constantine records the accounts of these miraculous events before mentioning those that occurred at the time of the canonization. Dominic's relics were certainly brought to Hungary at an early stage and soon became the source of a cult. It is also interesting to note

38. *Acta Capitulorum, I*, MOPH 3, p. 33.

39. *Acta Capitulorum, I*, MOPH 3, p. 11.

40. Cf. Gilles Gérard Meersseman, *Ordo Fraternitatis: Confraternite e pietà dei laici nel Medioevo* [Confraternities and the piety of the laity in the Middle Ages] (Herder editrice e libreria, 1977), 578–79; Simon Tugwell, *Miracula sancti Dominici*, MOPH 26, p. 24.

41. *Sumlu* in the manuscripts. Somlyo is identified by György Györffy with Érsomlyó in Vojvodina (Serbia). On the location of this center, cf. Bériou-Hodel, 930n1.

how quickly the Dominican province of Hungary responded to the call of the Chapter of 1245.

It is notable that the development of the cult of St. Dominic within the Order of Preachers was parallel to that of the cult of St. Francis within the Order of Friars Minor.[42] A very clear example of this is a decision of the Dominican Chapter held in Cologne in 1245. A year earlier, in 1244, the Chapter of Minors in Genoa had ordered all the friars to make known to the Franciscan Curia all that they knew about the life, signs, and miracles of St. Francis so they could complete the *Vita prima* of Thomas of Celano. The material gathered was indeed used by Thomas to write the *Vita secunda*, which he completed in 1247. The similarity of the circumstances of the work entrusted to Constantine of Orvieto is striking. His legend was completed in the years 1246 and 1247 and presented to the General Chapter of 1247. It seems that both orders shared the conviction that the biographies of their founders did not do justice to their respective activities as wonder workers after their deaths.[43]

This coincidence is due in part to the similar needs of the two orders. The identities of both religious families were rooted in the examples of their founders that their members were called to imitate. Relations between the Friars Preachers and Minors at that time, however, were particularly difficult. This was especially due to the efforts of both communities to attract candidates to the religious life who were tempted by the competing order.[44] This historical context explains why the

42. Cf. Giulia Barone, "L'agiografia domenicana alla metà del XIII secolo," in *Aux origines de la liturgie dominicaine: Le manuscrit Santa Sabina XIV L1*, ed. Leonard E. Boyle and Pierre-Marie Gy (École Française de Rome, 2004), 368–77. On the manuscript tradition of the legend and Humbert's new liturgy, see, in the same collection, Simon Tugwell, "The Legenda of Saint Dominic in the Prototype and Other Manuscripts," 355–63.

43. Bériou-Hodel, 860–61.

44. To defend their cause, each community called upon the weapon of obtaining a papal bull. The Dominicans obtained from Pope Innocent IV the bull *Quo vos*, which forbade the Franciscans to attract novices who had already entered the Order of Preachers. In retaliation, the Franciscans reminded the pope of the bull *Non solum* of his predecessor, Gregory IX, which forbade the Dominicans to accept those who had not completed a full novitiate. On June 17, 1244, Innocent IV reissued the bull, specifying that the novitiate should last

Dominicans viewed the progress of the Franciscans with some anxiety. Fearing that they would be outdone, the preachers were careful that the Friars Minor did not surpass them in the promotion of their saints.

To return to Constantine of Orvieto, his task was to paint a Dominic who, in terms of his holiness, charisma, and powers as a miracle worker, could compete with Francis. Consequently, Dominic appears in Constantine's legend as the only founder of the order: it was he alone who went to Pope Innocent III to have the project of a new institute (*inchoandi ordinis*) approved. Constantine is the first to mention that the pope hesitated before giving his approval. On the one hand, he omits all details concerning the preaching mission that Dominic and Fulk had set up within the diocesan framework of Toulouse. On the other hand, Jordan of Saxony's *Libellus* and the legend of Peter Ferrand had dwelt on this preaching and provided details. Constantine's legend also does not dwell on the role of important figures such as Fulk, Diego, and Innocent III, whose ideas had nevertheless contributed greatly to the formation of the nascent order. Constantine's "simplistic" version of events was to have a major influence on later Dominican historiography.

The account of the mission of the first friars in 1217, as reported in the legend of Constantine, does not recall or mention the political circumstances of this event, such as the struggle against the Albigensians. Instead, it skips ahead to a vision Dominic had at St. Peter's Basilica in Rome. Saint Peter and Saint Paul appeared to him and exhorted him to the apostolic mission: "Go and preach, since you have been chosen by God for this ministry."[45]

Constantine was not the only one to present Dominic as the sole founder of the order. The chapter celebrated in Valencia in 1259 decided that in the legend of Dominic, the name of Diego should be replaced each time with that of Dominic, beginning with the episode in which Diego, bishop of Osma, founds the monastery of the nuns of Prouille.[46] The legend of Constantine of Orvieto is also the

---

one year; on the following June 24, in the bull *Meminibus,* he recalled the decrees of the previous bull, *Quo vos*, to the attention of both orders.

45. Constantine of Orvieto, *Legenda*, 25; Bériou-Hodel, 889.

46. *Acta Capitulorum, I,* MOPH 3, p. 98.

first to mention Dominic's ecstasies during mass at the moment of the elevation of the consecrated host.[47]

The legend of Constantine of Orvieto has thus effectively introduced into historiography the image of a saint as an inspired founder and effective miracle worker, benefiting from a private revelation.

Humbert of Romans

The last legend of Dominic is linked to the name of Humbert of Romans. Its writing is a part of the final phase in the formation of the official image of the saint. In 1254, Humbert was elected Master of the Order at the Chapter of Buda and was charged with completing the liturgical reform initiated by his predecessor, John the Teutonic. The chapters of 1255 and 1256 authorized this new liturgy, and a manuscript was prepared from 1256 to 1259 from the archetype just approved by the order as a reference to be kept in the convent of Saint-Jacques in Paris. This manuscript, now kept in Santa Sabina, is known by the misnomer "prototype."[48] It was during its preparation that the liturgical commission headed by Humbert produced the last official version of the legend of Dominic. The Chapter of 1260 celebrated in Strasbourg gave its official approval to this legend.[49]

It is not difficult to see a parallel here with the *Legenda maior* of St. Francis, also written by the Minister General of the Order, Bonaventure.[50] Both authors emphasized in their respective prologues the

47. Constantine of Orvieto, *Legenda*, 61; Bériou-Hodel, 919: "Frequently, when the Lord's body was raised during Mass, he was enraptured into an ecstasy as if he were seeing the incarnate Christ present, and for this reason for a long time he did not hear Mass with the others."

48. See *Acta Capitulorum, I*, MOPH 3, pp. 73–78. See the volume by Leonard Boyle, Pierre-Marie Gy, and Pawel Krupa, eds., *The Origins of the Dominican Liturgy*.

49. *Acta Capitulorum, I*, MOPH 3, p. 105; Bériou-Hodel, 1448: "The Master orders that the friars use the *Legend* of Blessed Dominic which has been inserted in the lectionary and that henceforth the other legends should not be copied."

50. The *Legenda maior* acquired such an official dimension that in 1266 the Paris chapter of the Franciscans ordered the destruction of all other biographies, including the one written by Thomas of Celano. The capitulars thus intended to impose Bonaventure's vision of Francis and to avoid the risks inherent in the earlier legends, which were too divergent from this vision.

universal role of the two founders in salvation history. However, unlike Bonaventure, Humbert did not claim to offer a new image of Dominic, nor did his order need one.

In terms of content, the legend is a compilation of the previous two. Regarding the events surrounding 1215, Humbert thus takes up many of the points of Peter Ferrand's text; for example, he gives an account of the activity of the first friars in Toulouse. The remaining text presents a new stage in the process of the refinement of Dominic's image, more and more in conformity with the ideal of the holy founder and the perfect intercessor. The legend of Humbert of Romans concludes the list of official legends of St. Dominic. The time of the writing of the legend is marked by a conflict with the secular clergy and universities who were questioning the very legitimacy of the mendicant orders. The rivalry of the Friars Preachers with the Friars Minor at this time in history came to an end when they realized that a common enemy was threatening them. Humbert of Romans and his Franciscan counterpart, the Minister General John of Parma, addressed an encyclical letter in 1255 to the members of both orders urging them to practice fraternal charity toward each other.

Other Collections of Saint Dominic's Miracles

During the conflict with the secular clergy, the General Chapter of 1255 encouraged the friars to collect new miracles of St. Dominic and St. Peter of Verona (Peter Martyr), the latter having been canonized in 1253.[51]

The second wave of the mendicant quarrel occurred in the years 1266 to 1275. The question of the legitimacy of the pastoral action of the mendicant orders was at the heart of this new conflict.[52] In

51. On the conflicts with the seculars, see C. Hugh Lawrence, *The Friars: The Impact of the Early Mendicant Orders on Western Society* (Longman, 1994).

52. For an analysis of the quarrel, see Yves Congar, "Les aspects ecclésiologiques de la querelle entre mendiants et séculiers dans la seconde moitié du XIIIe siècle et le début du XIVe," in *Archives d'Histoire doctrinale et littéraire du Moyen Âge* 36 (1961): 35–151. See also Michel-Marie Dufeil, *Guillaume de Saint-Amour et la polémique universitaire parisienne (1250–1259)* (Picard, 1972); Jean-Pierre Torrell, "Séculiers et mendiants ou Thomas d'Aquin au naturel," *Revue des Sciences Religieuses* 67, no. 2 (1993): 19–40.

1254, the position of the secular clergy and the University of Paris had been strengthened by Innocent IV's publication of the bull *Etsi animarum*, which abolished the preaching and confessional privileges of the mendicants. However, these measures were abrogated the following year by the new pope, Alexander IV, with the bull *Quasi lignum vitae*. But the danger was not over. In 1256, William of Saint-Amour published a treatise in Paris entitled *De periculis novissimorum temporum* (*On the Dangers of the Latter Times*), which questioned the legitimacy of mendicants to exercise a pastoral ministry, which in his opinion remained the prerogative of the secular clergy.

Two important measures were adopted at the General Chapter of 1255 and reiterated the following year. One concerned the compilation of reports of miracles linked to the two saints of the order, the task of which fell to the priors of the convents of Bologna and Milan, where the saints' tombs were located. The other called for the creation of a sort of collective hagiography, the gathering of edifying stories about the members of the order. The task of organizing these texts fell to the Master of the Order, Humbert of Romans. The second project led to the publication of the *Liber vitae fratrum* (*The Lives of the Brethren*). The collections of the miracles of Dominic and Peter of Verona were intended to perpetuate their cults. The recognition of the sanctity of a life, whether official or not, required the existence of an authentic legend but also the widest possible repertoire of accounts testifying to the saint's ability to perform miracles. In addition to the two collections of texts, the general chapters used other means to promote the cult of the two Dominican saints, both within and outside the order.[53]

There is only indirect evidence of the existence of these collections of miracles. Simon Tugwell concludes from the manuscript

53. Confraternities were established under the patronage of these saints in several cities. In 1247, the Roman provincial chapter ordered all confraternities to possess an image of St. Dominic and to introduce his feast into the local calendar. The General Chapter of Budapest in 1254 urged the friars to celebrate the feasts of the two saints of the order and to include the names of Dominic and Peter of Verona in their liturgical calendars. The same chapter ordered that the feast of the martyr Peter of Verona be elevated to *totum duplex*. The chapters of 1254–1256 introduced Dominic's name into the formula of the vow of profession, a decision ratified by the next three chapters.

tradition of the *Vitae fratrum* that such collections must have existed. James of Voragine probably drew from a Bolognese collection, among other sources, while the legend of St. Peter Martyr composed by Thomas Agni of Lentino is probably based on a collection preserved in Milan.[54] A new appeal for the collection of miracles was made later, in 1289, to the General Chapter of Trier, by the Spaniard Muño of Zamora, then Master of the Order. This request no longer mentions either Milan or Bologna, thus the collections of miracles that had been composed there had probably already been forgotten.

Muño of Zamora had likely planned to write a life of Dominic, but at the same time Dietrich of Apolda, a German Dominican friar, began on his own initiative to write a kind of biography of Dominic entitled *Book on the Life, Death and Miracles of St. Dominic and on the Order He Founded.*[55] In 1288, he had already collected important materials, for example, the acts of the first canonization process in Bologna, making him the first hagiographer to put them to use. Shortly after he began his work, he received a letter from the Master Muño officially entrusting him with the task of writing a new life of St. Dominic.[56]

Behind this work to establish a new collection of miracles and write a new legend, Simon Tugwell sees an echo of the election to the papal throne in 1288 of Jerome of Ascoli, a Franciscan cardinal who took the name Nicholas IV. The new pope had previously opposed Muño of Zamora. The first signs of a conflict between the pontiff and the Order of Preachers were seen in 1289, when Nicholas IV approved the rule of the Franciscan penitents, declaring St. Francis to be their founder, while the approval of the same rule for

54. Simon Tugwell, *Miracula sancti Dominici*, MOPH 26, pp. 40–41.

55. The only French edition available is Thierry d'Apolda, *Livre sur la vie et la mort de saint Dominique*, translated and annotated by Amédée Curé, Paris (Œuvre de Saint-Paul, 1887). See, however, Bériou-Hodel, 983–98.

56. This request probably arrived around 1288. The legend of Dietrich does not therefore contain any elements that could result from the 1289 enquiry. It is also possible that this investigation was unsuccessful. We do not know whether Muño of Zamora had a similar project concerning the legend of St. Peter of Verona. On the legend of Dietrich, see Berthold Altaner, *Der heilige Dominikus*, 170ff.

the Dominicans was refused.[57] This conflict led to the fall of Muño of Zamora, and Nicholas IV tried to have him dismissed by the Chapter of 1290.[58] This maneuver was unsuccessful, and the pope deposed Muño from office in 1291.[59] The investigation into the miracles of 1289 may have had a connection with these events.

The chapter celebrated in London in 1314 under the generalate of Berenger of Landorre led to another effort to collect accounts of miracles.[60] As in the previous case, the capitular request was not motivated solely by the desire to increase the veneration of Dominican saints but also reflected a new and difficult situation experienced by the Order of Preachers.[61] The historical context is well known. The death of Emperor Henry VII in the vicinity of Siena in 1313 had given rise to suspicions of assassination, which mainly implicated his confessor, the Dominican Bernard of Montepulciano. Although the latter's innocence was proven, malicious rumors continued to circulate, leading to a real persecution of the Order of Preachers, especially in the Germanic world. It is clear from these circumstances that a new crop of Dominic's miracles could help to restore the prestige of the order.

The investigation conducted in 1314 made it possible to compile two collections of miracles, drawn up by order of Master Berenger.

57. The rule for Franciscan tertiaries had been rewritten by Caro around 1284; Muño of Zamora did the same in 1285 for the penitents linked to the Order of Preachers, which might have seemed an infringement on Franciscan interests. Rejected by the pope, this rule was approved only in 1405 thanks to the efforts of Thomas of Siena.

58. See William A. Hinnebusch, *The History of the Dominican Order: I. Origins and Growth to 1500* (Alba House, 1966), 224–29.

59. Muño's deposition is also likely related to a conflictual relationship between the former provincial of Spain with ecclesiastical authorities. Cf. Peter Linehan, *The Ladies of Zamora* (Pennsylvania State University Press, 1997).

60. See *Acta Capitulorum Generalium Ordinis Praedicatorum, II*, ed. B. M. Reichert, MOPH 4, p. 73.

61. The seriousness of the situation is shown by other capitular decisions such as the prescription of weekly Marian litanies and votive masses, as well as votive masses to St. Dominic. In 1315, a votive mass to St. Peter Martyr was fixed every fortnight. In the period 1318 to 1320, an invocation to St. Peter Martyr was added to the celebration of Vespers.

Of the nineteen miracles of St. Dominic, only a few can be considered truly new. Two miracles that took place in Hungary in the monastery of Érsomlyó are worth mentioning: both stories are related to the water in which the first class relic of St. Dominic's finger, kept in this monastery, was soaked. This water, poured into both the mouths of one sick and one dead man, respectively, led to the healing of the former and the resurrection of the latter.

It is uncertain to what extent the investigation carried out at the request of Berenger of Landorre had a positive outcome. In fact, only one manuscript survives of the material he had collected. Some of this material was later taken up by hagiographers, but the scarcity of information testifies to the difficulties in promoting the cults of Saint Dominic and Saint Peter of Verona. Local pilgrimages linked to a specific place were more likely to succeed. The cult of the Dominican saints could only spread when the attitude of the laity toward the Order of Preachers was favorable to this diffusion. By the time of the investigations into the miracles of 1289 and 1314, the paradigm had changed: it was no longer a question of rearticulating the legends of the Saint, as the legitimacy of the order was no longer in question.[62] What the leaders of the order were looking for were new miracles for preaching that would have the effect of moving the faithful in great numbers.

We have attempted to show how the order turned to its saints in times of crisis. The Preachers desired to advance the causes of their altar-bound brethren, not only to encourage local cults but also the interests of the order so that it could weather challenging times. As Simon Tugwell summarizes:

> It is not surprising that the General Chapter and the Master of the Order should have been engaged in developing the legend and updating the *miracula* of its saints precisely when the Order was facing all sorts of crises: in 1245, when rivalry with the Franciscans became particularly dangerous; in the 1250s, when

62. The Council of Lyon II in 1274 praised the Franciscans and Dominicans for their services to the church. The other mendicant orders received less favorable treatment. See Giuseppe Alberigo, ed., *Les Conciles œcuméniques: Les décrets* (Éd. du Cerf, 1994), 678–81.

the hostility of secular priests had threatened the Order by affecting its *raison d'être*; in 1289, when the Order had experienced its first serious confrontation with the papacy; and finally in 1314, when malicious rumors threatened to turn the Empire and its supporters against the order.[63]

63. Simon Tugwell, *Miracula sancti Dominici*, MOPH 26, *Introduction*, p. 57.

Part II

THE DOMINICAN WAY

Chapter 3

The Mission of the Preachers

The Dominican message is the Gospel. It is not the Order of Preachers' property, yet the church has entrusted the order with the Gospel as a special mission, "that at the name of Jesus every knee should bend, of those in heaven, on earth, and under the earth" (Phil 2:10). Dominicans are not alone in transmitting the good news of salvation, but they are among those who are exclusively dedicated to this task, having developed their own way of doing so over eight centuries of the Dominican adventure. The Dominican message is therefore not a matter of dusty archives but of the path St. Dominic opened for his followers in the thirteenth century, an ever-new path we may describe as both our heredity and heritage.

Heredity biologically conditions what we are. The history of the Order of Preachers is the unfolding over time of the preaching and founding grace that Dominic enjoyed. In the same way that St. Paul considers the church as a body, the Order of Preachers within this church can be considered as a living organism that has constantly added new members and has transmitted to them a genetic patrimony of unprecedented richness. The formula of religious profession, which has been used in the order since the thirteenth century, is a commitment not only to God and the Virgin Mary but also to Saint Dominic and to the Master of the Order who succeeded him. Through this profession, a man or woman really becomes a Dominican. It is a new identity, not simply a label that can be removed when one no longer wants it. Religious profession makes one a kinsman, consanguine of St. Dominic, and every member of the order knows this. Through his profession, he participates in a genetic patrimony that includes the Dominican form of life in common, a form of prayer (common and personal), but also assiduous study—and all this at the exclusive service of the preaching of the Word of God. The Preachers' heredity disposes them to their mission.

However, a second image must complement that of heredity: the notion of inheritance. The first term evokes biology, the second is a matter of law and history. The Dominican heritage is immense. It is made up of all the actions, good or bad, of those who have gone before us. Lest this heritage become dusty, like an old museum no one visits, each generation must reexamine it. Careful historical research allows us to do so, while prudence and respect must guide us. This examination is a chance to receive anew our Dominican heritage and pursue our mission.

The Mission of the Preachers

The *raison d'être* of St Dominic's life, the mission of the Order of Preachers, is the preaching of the Gospel message in response to the Lord's command: "Go therefore and make disciples of all nations, baptizing them in the name of the Father, and of the Son, and of the Holy Spirit, and teaching them to observe all that I have commanded you" (Mt 28:19–20). In his *Treatise on Preaching,* Humbert of Romans (Master of the Order from 1254 to 1263), argues rather dryly for this primacy of preaching when he says:

> Jesus Christ, in the whole time He spent upon earth, celebrated Mass but once, at the Last Supper; moreover, it is not said that He heard one confession; He administered the Sacraments rarely and to a small number; He never devoted Himself to the recitation of the canonical Office; and one can make the same observation about all the rest, except for preaching and prayer. It is also worthy of note that when He began to preach He spent more time in that than in prayer.[1]

What other vocation can the apostles of Christ claim? St. Paul went so far as to place preaching at the top of his concerns: the apostle thanks God that he baptized few people, saying that he was sent not to baptize but to evangelize (cf. 1 Cor 1:17).

1. Humbert of Romans, *Treatise on Preaching,* IV.xx, ed. Walter Conlon, OP (Newman Press, 1951), 86.

The testimonies gathered for his canonization process bear abundant witness to the fact that Dominic was a man of the Word. As one of his travelling companions, Friar Ventura of Verona, explains: "In going along the road Dominic wished that the Word of God be proposed by himself or others to nearly all who accompanied him. . . . Moreover, Dominic always wished to dispute, talk or read about God or to pray while journeying. When traveling he celebrated Mass almost every day if he found a church."[2] Brother Stephen of Lombardy adds that Brother Dominic "carefully prepared himself and was unremitting in his preaching. His words were so moving that most of the time he stirred himself and his listeners to tears. He [the witness] never heard a man whose words so moved the brethren to compunction and tears. And it was his custom to speak always of God or with God."[3] This adage, *de Deo vel cum Deo*, taken from the life of St. Stephen of Grandmont, has taken hold in the order.[4]

Saving Souls

"It is known that our Order was founded, from the beginning, especially for preaching and the salvation of souls."[5] Beginning in 1220 and up until today, this statement is found in all editions of the Dominican *Constitutions*. It is the institutional response given by St. Dominic to the double evangelical precept of the love of God and neighbor: "Dominic thirsted ardently for the salvation of souls with a zeal that was unparalleled," noted a witness at the canonization process.[6] Jordan of Saxony added in the *Libellus*: "For his part, brother Dominic, with all his energy and with passionate zeal, set himself to win

2. *Acta canonizationis*, Bologna, 3; Francis C. Lehner, OP, ed., *Saint Dominic: Biographical Documents* (The Thomist Press, 1964), 101.

3. *Acta canonizationis*, Bologna, 37; Lehner, 125.

4. Concerning the adage, see Bériou-Hodel, 734n1: the Latin formula *de Deo vel cum Deo*, "to speak of God or with God," which is found in the ancient constitutions of the Order of Preachers, is borrowed from Stephen of Muret. A French hermit trained at the school of the Calabrian Solitaries, he founded the Order of Grandmont in the tenth century.

5. *The Primitive Constitutions of the Order of Friars Preachers*, prologue, in Lehner, *Saint Dominic: Biographical Documents*.

6. *Acta canonizationis*, Toulouse, 18; Lehner, 143.

all the souls he could for Christ. His heart was full of an extraordinary, almost incredible, yearning for the salvation of everyone."[7] Seven centuries later, Father Humbert Clérissac (1864–1914) dared to speak of the order's mission as a search for truth coupled with an immense hunt for souls:

> God is the hunter, the apostles the huntsmen; the prayers of the saints thrill through the air like a noble hunting song; on all sides are seen rebel and timid souls fleeing from the approach of divine grace; the pack breaks forth and the cry goes up as they give tongue. Who would not wish to join the hounds of St. Dominic?[8]

In expressing himself in this way, the French theologian took up a medieval image first spun by Humbert of Romans:

> Preachers, like keen huntsmen, seek sinners of all kinds, souls yet untamed which they wish to offer as a banquet to the Lord. He is as pleased to see this prize on His table as the noblemen of the earth are with tasty venison. Do we not read in Genesis that Isaac ate with pleasure the kill of Esau? (Gen 25:28.) The pleasure that God takes in this hunt for souls is such that He prompts preachers to devote themselves to it, speaking to them as Isaac spoke to his son: "Take thy weapons, thy quiver and bow, and go abroad; and when thou has taken something by hunting, make me savory meat thereof, that I may eat: and my soul may bless thee before God" (Gen 27:3–4).[9]

Only a life-threatening challenge can merit such ardor.

What is the challenge that calls for this ardor? It is the battle for the Kingdom of God. The Christian knows that he is fighting with Jesus against the ancient enemy of the human race, yet the disproportion between his forces and those of the adversary is a source of

7. Jordan of Saxony, *Libellus*, 34, trans. Simon Tugwell (Dominican Publications, 1982), 9.

8. Humbert Clérissac, *The Spirit of Saint Dominic* (Burns, Oates, & Washbourne, 1939; reprint, Cluny Media, 2015), 15.

9. Humbert de Romans, *Treatise on Preaching*, I.iii, 11.

anxiety and sorrow. The abundant tears Dominic shed for the salvation of souls did not arise from a sensitivity overexcited by the misfortunes of the times: error and lies, war and disease, injustice and ignorance. They bear witness to a deep compassion for their neighbors, especially for sinners. From the time of his youth in Palencia, recalls Jordan of Saxony, "God had given him a special grace to weep for sinners and for the afflicted and oppressed; he bore their distress in the inmost shrine of his compassion, and the warm sympathy he felt for them in his heart spilled over in the tears which flowed from his eyes."[10] The abbot of St. Paul's told the canonical investigators of 1233 that he "saw no one so frequent in prayer or so easily moved to tears."[11] But these tears were not shed for himself. It was for others that Dominic wept, and it was this singular grace of weeping for others and giving himself to them that he wanted to communicate to his own. An anecdote in the *Lives of the Brethren* bears witness to this:

> Having often observed Brother Bertrand to grieve bitterly at the remembrance of his own sins, [Dominic] forbade him to weep so much for his own transgressions, but would have him to grieve over the unrepented sins of others. So efficacious were his words, that from that hour the brother wept copiously for others, but could no longer do so for himself even when he wished it.[12]

This personal testimony is in line with that of the Abbot of St. Paul's, William Peyre, who said that when Dominic was at prayer, "he could be heard on all sides saying: 'O Lord, be merciful to Thy People. What will sinners do?' In this manner he spent sleepless nights weeping and bewailing the sins of others."[13]

The salvation brought by Christ opens the way to the forgiveness of sins. Dominic was therefore assiduous not only in the ministry of

10. Jordan of Saxony, *Libellus*, 12; Tugwell, 3.

11. *Acta canonizationis*, Toulouse, 18; Lehner, 144.

12. *Lives of the Brethren of the Order of Preachers*, II.xix, trans. Placid Conway, OP (Burnes, Oates, and Washbourne, 1924), 66. This religious is Brother Bertrand of Garrigue.

13. *Acta canonizationis*, Toulouse, 18; Lehner, 144.

preaching but also in that of sacramental confession, as some witnesses recalled during the canonization process. His second successor at the head of the Order, St. Raymond of Peñafort, was also one of the masters of moral theology and canon law of his time.[14] As a student and then professor in Bologna, he worked specifically to train priests for the ministry of penance. For Humbert of Romans, Dominic's fourth successor, fruitful preaching is accompanied by conversions. If the preacher refuses to listen to confessions, he becomes like the lazy peasant who does not take the trouble to reap what he has sown before, "for it is by preaching that one sows and by confession that one gathers the fruits. As Isaiah said: '*Sow and reap*' (Is 37:30)."[15] The joy of salvation can already be tasted in forgiveness.

A Fraternal Order

By no means is preaching a solitary adventure, the affair of an isolated individual. Rather, it is born and built up within an order composed of men and women, nuns and Friars Preachers, clerics, and laity. Note, in particular, the originality of the *feminine* dimension in the Order of Preachers. It is closely linked to the life of Saint Dominic. His whole life and his itinerary were woven from numerous relationships with women marked by affection, respect, and friendship: first of all, his mother Jane and then the sisters of Prouille, Madrid, and St. Sisto in Rome. They also included the hostesses who welcomed him into their homes during his itinerant preaching in the South of France and who, during the process of canonization, were so precise in their concrete details about his sleeping arrangements, his clothes, and his way of eating. Among them, Guillielma, wife of Elias Martin, explains that she wove a hair shirt for him. "She knows and believes . . . that he was a virgin," the report adds, and as a well-informed housewife, she sees fit to specify that she shared a meagre meal with him "on more than twenty occasions." Guillielma remembers that

14. André Vauchez, "Raimundo de Penyafort, saint," in *Bibliotheca Sanctorum*, vol. 11 (Città Nuova Editrice, 1968), col. 16–24.

15. Humbert de Romans, *Treatise on Preaching*, VII.xliii, 153. On Humbert de Romans, see Marie-Humbert Vicaire, s.v., *Dictionnaire de spiritualité*, vol. 7, 1969, col. 1108–16.

when he was ill, he refused the bed that his traveling companions prepared for him and lay down on the floor, as was his habit.[16] Two other witnesses, Tolosana Rogueza and the nun of Sainte-Croix-Volvestre, Beceda, also affirmed that they wove him rough hairshirts. The latter's words express her affection but also her admiring attention toward her holy visitor. Beceda said that she:

> collected cow-tails to make a hair shirt for him and for Lord Fulk, the bishop of Toulouse. She never heard him speak an idle word although they were close friends. And when she prepared his bed, he did not use it; indeed, in the morning she found it in the same condition as she had left it. Even when he was sick, he did this. Moreover, she frequently found him sleeping without blankets on the ground and would cover him. When she returned, she found him, either standing or prostrate on the ground, praying. She took great pains on his behalf. She declared, too, that, on the more than twenty occasions that he ate in the house where she lived, he took at most two eggs, even though much more food had been set out for him.[17]

Another woman holds a special place in the history of the foundation of the Preachers: Diana d'Andalò, foundress of the monastery of Bologna, who loved Brother Dominic "with all the affection of her spirit." She attracted to the order "many noble ladies and prominent matrons of the city" to the point of suffering violence from her family, who wanted to prevent her from following Dominic by embracing the religious life. When faced with her parents' refusal, she tried to take the habit in the monastery of Ronzano, not far from Bologna, but her relatives rushed to take her home by force: "They took her out so brutally that they broke a rib and she retained a mark from this fracture until the day she died." It was only after Dominic's death that she was finally able to join the nuns in Bologna, but not without having to flee from her home during the night.[18]

16 *Process of Canonization*, Toulouse, 15; Lehner, 142.

17. *Acta canonizationis*, Toulouse, 16–17; Lehner, 142–43.

18. *Analecta Sacri Ordinis Praedicatorum* 1 (1893), 181–84. Edition by Hyacinthe-Marie Cormier of the *Chronicle of Saint Agnes of Bologna*, 4. See also the

This fruitful bond of fraternity between Dominican brothers and sisters has never ceased to manifest itself over the centuries. In the years following St. Dominic's death, Jordan of Saxony and Diana d'Andalò were both strengthened for their mission through their mutual friendship, which is well-known thanks to Jordan's letters that testified to their trusting and fraternal relationship.[19]

In the fourteenth century, in the Rhine Valley, the Dominican mysticism of Meister Eckhart, Henry Suso, and John Tauler was clarified through their contact with numerous female communities. The part played by the *cura monialium*, that is, the way these friars accompanied the order's monastic communities by writing vernacular religious literature, was very important. As one historian has pointed out, "Treatises and sermons by Eckhart, Suso, Tauler were written for educated nuns, curious about high spirituality. Adolf Harnack does not overstate the case when he describes the spiritual movement that was spreading in the nuns' convents as a real 'source of living ideas.'"[20] At the time of the pope's stay in Avignon, Catherine of Siena and Raymond of Capua developed exemplary and demanding fraternal ties, which are well known thanks to the letters they exchanged.[21] Catherine was not a nun but a *mantellata* totally consecrated to God, although she was strongly involved in the city. Her influence proved decisive for the reform of the order, to which she contributed by restoring an impetus that had been hampered by the crises of the fourteenth century and, perhaps, also by a certain gentrification linked to the continuous Dominican expansion during 150 years of existence. In the centuries that followed, close collaboration between brothers and sisters was still evident in missionary undertakings: everything from foreign missions, as in Iraq or Brazil, to missions in Christian countries,

---

French translation by Bériou-Hodel, 556–60, based on the provisional edition provided by Simon Tugwell.

19. *Beati Iordani de Saxonia epistulae*, ed. Angelus Walz, MOPH 23 (Institutum Historicum Fratrum Praedicatorum, 1951).

20. Jules Augustin Bizet, "Henri Suso (Heinrich Seuse; Blessed)," *Dictionnaire de Spiritualité*, vol. 7, col. 242.

21. S. Caterina da Sienna, *Le lettere*, ed. Umberto Meattini (Edizioni Paoline, 1987).

such as the one that Blessed Jean-Joseph Lataste carried out in the nineteenth century in women's prisons, which led to the foundation of the congregation of the Dominican Sisters of Bethany and the fraternities claiming the same spirit of Christian charity.[22]

However, if we stick to the question of monasteries, difficulties arose from the very beginning of the order. Conflicts arose in the thirteenth century between the bishop of Zamora and the monastery of Dominican nuns, and the friars attempted to intervene. The incident gives an idea of the difficulties created by the initiatives of the Dominicans in the medieval world.[23]

As Marie-Humbert Vicaire recalls, Dominican female monastic life:

> did not formally begin until 1267, when the pope placed under the jurisdiction of the order all the female monasteries founded by the Friars Preachers: Prouille (1207), Madrid (1218–1220) and San Sisto in Rome, which were all incorporated into the Order. As other monasteries had followed the example of the previous ones, the Order, after agreeing to incorporate them, tried to limit their number in 1239; then, in 1246, to avoid the administrative burden and finally in 1252 to refuse it for all but the two main ones, before the agreement with the papacy intervened in 1267.[24]

22. The question of the historical collaboration between the brothers and sisters of the Order of Preachers is still largely undeveloped. For the foundation of Bethany and the history of Father Lataste's preaching to women prisoners, see Jean-Marie Gueullette, *"Ces femmes qui étaient mes sœurs. . ." Vie du père Lataste apôtre des prisons (1832–1869)* (Éd. du Cerf, 2012).

23. Peter Linehan, *The Ladies of Zamora* (Pennsylvania State University Press, 1997), 16: "In a critique as scathing as any penned by the Order's secular opponents, Humbert [of Romans] impressed upon the Dominican sisters the need for threefold protection ('triplex custodia'). As well as such feeble protection as enclosure itself afforded, they must be guarded against all manner of social intercourse, even conversations at the window. Also—and in the case of the Ladies of Zamora this was a prophetic warning—they must be guarded against the friars charged with their spiritual case."

24. See Valerio Ferrua and Humbert Vicaire, *San Domenico e i suoi frati,* presentazione di Enzo Bianchi, "Ritorno alle fonti" (Piero Gribaudi editore, 1984), 41.

The nuns' legislation postdates St. Dominic, since it was largely the work of Humbert of Romans, who imposed it on all the monasteries in 1259, thus replacing the various observances that had gone before.

There are few written records of what constituted for St. Dominic the essence of his religious life. There is no trace of Prouille's first legislation, but some elements shed light on the Madrid foundation's functioning and spirit. The foundation of the monastery must have taken place in the first months of 1219, before Dominic went to Paris.[25] It was probably from Bologna, on the occasion of the first general chapter celebrated in 1220, that Dominic wrote a letter for the nuns of Madrid that he entrusted to his brother Mannes, who was charged with directing, visiting, and correcting the monastery. When he addressed his sisters, Dominic did not speak as to little girls treated like minors, adopting a condescending tone. He made it very clear that he did not want the prioress to be able to be removed without the consent of a majority of the nuns. He also demanded that the power to receive or admit candidates into the community be reserved to the prioress and her council.[26] As Nicole Bériou and Bernard Hodel point out, Dominic showed concern for organizing the daily life of the nuns with "realism and flexibility," without sacrificing anything to the demands of the spiritual battles waged in the cloisters.[27] In the extraordinary series of miracles recounted by Sister Cecilia, who witnessed them, and that were written down several decades later by one of her companions, Sister Angelica, we do not find any trace of Dominic's personal influence on the constitutions of the nuns,[28] but we do discern certain traits of the saint in his relationship with the nuns: he exercises authority by defending, ordering, requesting, deciding, but he also appears as a spiritual master whose

25. Bériou-Hodel, 79.

26. Simon Tugwell, "St Dominic's Letter to the Nuns of Madrid," AFP 56 (1986): 12–13.

27. Bériou-Hodel, 81.

28. On the Institutions of San Sisto of Rome, see Bériou-Hodel, 571–73: they borrow from the Rule of Saint Benedict, the customs of Cîteaux, and quote the Rule of Saint Augustine, but they also have recourse to the institutions of Sempringham and the statutes of Prémontré.

preaching fascinates his audience, and as a spiritual man whose fight against the devil is one with the nuns' own spiritual combat.[29]

One of the secrets of this happy fraternal relationship between men and women was perhaps revealed in Dominic's final confession as he was dying. He confessed to the friars who assisted him that he had always remained a virgin, adding, however, that he had found more pleasure in the conversation of young women than in that of old women.[30] This double confession embarrassed later generations. During the General Chapter of 1242 celebrated in Bologna, the friars, in a sort of inverted modesty, demanded that this trait be removed from his legend, that is, from the praise of his virtues.[31] This public testimony of Dominic is, however, of the greatest interest. If he remained a virgin and chaste, and if he insisted on affirming this at the time of his death, it is undoubtedly because he had a very high idea and conception of the fraternity founded on Christ. As St. Paul teaches: "There is neither Jew nor Greek, there is neither slave nor free, there is neither male nor female; for you are all one in Christ Jesus" (Gal 3:38). For those who love the kingdom, there are only brothers and sisters called to sit for eternity at the table of the same Father. The Dominican Order is a prophetic witness of this dimension of the goodness to come. Nuns and friars do not divide up the roles: contemplation for the nuns, action for the friars. Within a single family, both are engaged in the same struggle but in different modes.

A Life Given in Poverty

Without a doubt, a fraternal spirit animates and characterizes the Order of Preachers, and this spirit has been present from the beginning. We see this especially in the desire for unanimity within the community. The fourth paragraph of the Fundamental Constitution of the Order clearly recalls this: "Sharing the Apostles' mission, we

29. Bériou-Hodel, 505.

30. Peter Ferrand, *Légende de saint Dominique*, 42; Bériou-Hodel, 843.

31. *Acta capitulorum generalium ordinis Praedicatorum*, vol. 1. Nicole Bériou and Bernard Hodel note the following point: "Such a confidence of Dominic could imply that he had not attained the absolute perfection expected of a saint" (Bériou-Hodel, 1444n2).

also follow their way of life, in the form devised by Saint Dominic. We do our best to live of one accord the common life, observing faithfully celebration of the liturgy, especially the Eucharist and the divine office, diligent in study and constant in regular observance."[32]

In 1216, Dominic and his followers chose to adopt the Rule of St. Augustine. This decision should not seem strange or anecdotal. This rule of religious life indicates from the beginning what the goal of religious life in community is to be: "To live harmoniously in the house and to have one heart and one soul seeking God."[33] In his commentary on the *Constitutions*, Humbert of Romans emphasizes that "a precept of the rule commands us to have one heart and one mind in the Lord."[34] The whole community thus moves forward with one heart toward a common goal: the salvation of souls. As the second paragraph of the Fundamental Constitution makes clear:

> The Order of Friars Preachers, founded by St. Dominic, "is known to have been established, from the beginning, for preaching and the salvation of souls, specifically." Our brothers, therefore, as the founder prescribed, "should everywhere behave uprightly and religiously, as men intent on procuring their own and other people's salvation; they should behave as gospel men, following in the footsteps of the Savior, speaking to God or of God, among themselves or with their neighbors."[35]

If it is lived with this required unanimity, fraternal life prepares the preachers of the Eternal Word for their mission by giving them mutual support. A collection of the *Lives of the Brethren* compiled by

32. *The Book of Constitutions and Ordinations of the Brothers of the Order of Preachers* (Dominican Publications, 2012), 39.

33. "Primum, propter quod in unum estis congregati ut unanimes habitetis in domo et sit vobis anima una et cor unum in Deo" (*Regula ad servos Dei*, 1, 2), trans. in *Constitutions*, 25.

34. Humbert of Romans, *Expositio super Constitutiones Fratrum Praedicatorum: Prologus*, in *Opera de Vita Regulari* II, 3; English-language version: *Commentary on the Dominican Constitutions*, trans. Albert Judy, OP (Chicago, 2018), http://www.domcentral.org/study/humbertconstitution.pdf.

35. *Constitutions*, 39.

Gerard de Frachet[36] reports a saying by Jordan of Saxony according to which the fervent religious must imitate the cantor in the choir who raises the tone when the voices of the brothers tend to drop:

> When the fervent religious finds that idle words are creeping into his conversation, he ought to bring in appropriately some story or spiritual maxim, and so ward off in time what might prove hurtful. In the same way when we see that through the weakness of the flesh we are gradually slipping down, not merely in speech, but in our common fervor, we ought mutually to uplift one another.[37]

When questioned in the canonization process, Friar Paul of Venice, Dominic's travelling companion in the latter part of his life, says:

> He never remembers having heard Dominic speak any detraction or flattery, or any idle or malicious word. On the contrary, when they were traveling, he noticed that he either prayed or preached, or devoted himself to mental prayer and meditation on God. . . . Master Dominic used to say to the witness himself and to the others who were with him, "Go on ahead and let us meditate on Our Savior." The witness then used to hear him groaning and sighing. Wherever the master was, he always spoke either with God or of God, strongly urged his brothers to do this and had the practice written into the legislation of the Friars Preachers.[38]

Attention to others, even in the smallest details, is another benefit of fraternity. When on the road, the Father of the Preachers imposed on himself exhausting fasts, yet he made his brothers eat because of the pain of the journey: "When they had to stop for a meal or for the night, he did not insist on his will, but followed the wishes of his brothers who were with him. And if he were badly treated, he showed

36. On the *Vitae Fratrum*, see Simon Tugwell, "L'évolution des *vitae fratrum*: Résumé des conclusions provisoires [Summary of provisional conclusions]," *Cahiers de Fanjeaux* 36 (2001): 415–18; Bériou-Hodel, 391–92, 1067–68.

37. *Lives of the Brethren*, III.xxxxi; Placid, 126.

38. *Acta canonizationis*, Bologna, 41; Lehner, 129.

greater signs of joy than if he were served well."[39] When, on the other hand, during the mission in the South, he made exceptions to his ascetic diet, it was always "for the sake of the brethren or other company," as a witness explains: He "took nothing but bread and wine.... Yet he always wanted others to have as much as the means of the house would permit."[40] Fraternal delicacy governed his attitude, without weakness or stiffness. "During the daytime nobody was more sociable and happy with his brethren and companions," notes Jordan of Saxony.[41] And since fraternity is cultivated with gestures, Sr. Cecilia of the monastery of San Sisto recounts that in 1219, "Blessed Dominic returned from a trip to Spain bringing each of the sisters a wooden spoon as a gift."[42] In the same Roman community, he shared a full cup of wine with the nuns, encouraging them, "Drink up, my daughters," without any petty fear. "In all there were one hundred and four sisters and each of them took as much as she wanted of the wine; yet the cup remained full, as though new wine were continually being poured into it."[43] This was no mere wine-tasting; Dominic and the nuns were tasting together the joy of being saved.

Consecrated to preach the truth of salvation, preachers are also called, both in community and individually, to embrace poverty. Itinerant preaching requires travel. The first *Constitutions* states that the friars "shall neither receive nor carry with them any gold, silver, money or gifts, but only food, clothing, books, and other necessary objects."[44] But there is more. Many witnesses agree on the importance Dominic gave to poverty. As Jordan writes in the *Libellus*: "He was a true lover of poverty, and he always wore cheap clothes. He confined himself to a very modest allowance of food and drink, avoiding all luxuries. He was quite content with very simple food, so firm was his bodily self-control, and he drank wine so austerely diluted that, though it satisfied his bodily needs, it never blunted his fine, sensitive

39. *Acta canonizationis*, Bologna, 22; Lehner, 112.

40. *Acta canonizationis*, Toulouse, 18; Lehner, 143.

41. Jordan of Saxony, *Libellus*, 104; Tugwell, 26.

42. Sister Cecilia, *Miracula S. Dominici*, 10; Lehner, 178.

43. Sister Cecilia, *Miracula S. Dominici*, 6; Lehner, 172.

44. Antonin H. Thomas, *De oudste Constituties*, 364 [Dist. II, ch. 31]; Lehner, 24.

spirit."[45] Friar Amizo of Milan, a witness for the canonization process, states that Dominic had:

> an ardent zeal for regular observance. His great love for poverty showed itself, not only in his own food and clothing and that of the brethren of his Order, but even in the buildings and churches of the brethren, the liturgy and the ornamentation of ecclesiastical vestments. He was most diligent about this, and took great care all his life to prevent the brethren from using rich and silken vestments in the churches, either for themselves or for the altars. Except for the chalices, he allowed them to have no gold or silver utensils.[46]

A friar named Rodolfo, who knew Dominic in Bologna, adds that:

> he was a great lover of poverty and exhorted the brethren to practice this virtue. And he knows because, when Brother Dominic arrived at Bologna, Lord Odoric Galliciani wanted to give the brethren property worth over five hundred Bolognese pounds. The deed had already been drawn up in the presence of the Lord Bishop of Bologna, but Dominic tore up the contract. He did not want to have that property or any other wealth, but to live poorly, wholly dependent on alms. If they had enough in the house to support them for the day, they were not to accept anything else on that day, or send anyone out for alms.[47]

This same friar, procurator of the convent of Bologna—that is to say, in charge of providing for the needs of the community—took advantage of an absence of Dominic to raise the cells of the friars "the length of an arm." On the Master's return, he was reproached for this work: "He rebuked Rodolfo and the other brethren many times, saying to them: 'So soon you want to abandon poverty and build great palaces!' Hence, he ordered them to stop the work. It remained unfinished while he lived."[48]

45. Jordan of Saxony, *Libellus*, 108; Tugwell, 27.
46. *Acta canonizationis*, Bologna, 17; Lehner, 110.
47. *Acta canonizationis*, Bologna, 32; Lehner, 121.
48. *Acta canonizationis*, Bologna, 38; Lehner, 126.

Dominic wanted to live on alms not only to ensure the life of the convents but also to provide for the daily needs of the friars. Brother Paul of Venice recalls that he:

> wore an extremely ragged habit, and when he got outside the villages and towns he used to take off his shoes and travel barefoot. . . . He sometimes saw the blessed Dominic himself going from door to door, begging alms and receiving a piece of bread like any pauper. Once when he was begging at Dugliolo, some man gave him a whole loaf of bread. Father Dominic received it on his knees, in great humility and devotion. The witness often heard Dominic express his desire to the brethren that they live by begging.[49]

But this provision did not last long, nor did the rules limiting the height of Dominican churches. The Parisian poet Rutebeuf, the hungry juggler, may have admired the nascent mendicant orders, but he was no longer satisfied with what the Dominicans had become in the middle of the thirteenth century: "The Jacobins came into the world dressed in white and black robes; in them abound all the virtues, whoever will believe it. If by their dress they are pure and clean, you know very well, it is the truth that a wolf, under a closed cloak, would look like a priest." So the poet promises himself not to give them a penny, not even "the skin of an apple!" How can we trust men who without taking responsibility for anyone, demand to be maintained?[50]

If poverty was so important to Dominic, it was because it made fraternal communion and free preaching possible: mendicants had nothing to sell and could not seduce their contemporaries like fairground merchants. It detaches the preacher from the inessential and makes it possible to give freely a Gospel that has been received freely. The rule of the brothers, the customs implemented in Toulouse from 1215 onward, and then the first *Constitutions* adopted at the general chapters of 1220 and 1221 had no aim other than to maintain fraternity in the service of the mission in a climate of poverty. In the first *Constitutions* of the order, grave faults against poverty, those concerning the

49. *Acta canonizationis*, Bologna, 42; Lehner, 130.

50. Rutebeuf, *Œuvres complètes*, vol. 1 (Picard, 1977), 209–11.

personal appropriation of goods unduly given, were subjected to the same penalties as faults of the flesh. Indeed, it is a very grave fault, penanced by temporary deprivation of communion, of the kiss of peace and of preaching for "the brother who secretly accepts something which he is forbidden to receive. . . . In the terms of Blessed Augustine, he is to be condemned by the judgment made about a thief. It is the same in the case of the brother who falls into a sin of the flesh, which we deem should be punished more severely than the others."[51]

According to Brother Rodolfo:

> He observed the Rule and the customs of the Friars Preachers with perfect exactitude, as to himself and for others, in their clothing, food and drink, the fasts, and in everything else. . . . He wished them to have modest houses and poor clothing. Even the vestments in church were not to be made of silk; his desire was that they be of buckram or some other cheap cloth.[52]

The common life and the poverty that accompanied it disposed hearts to receive God's gifts. On entering the order, each brother is asked the question: "What do you desire?" He is invited to answer: "God's mercy and yours." The brother recognizes that he is fallible, but he knows that he can count on God's presence and on his brothers' support. This double assurance is the source of a profound joy that recalls that of the first Pentecost. Likewise, the medieval account of the vestition of Brother Roland of Cremona by Reginald of Orleans bears witness to this joy:

> He came alone, intoxicated with the spirit of God, and without more ado sought to be admitted into the Order. . . . Brother Guala, the sacristan, rang the bell, which weighed but twenty imperial pounds, while the brethren joined in the *Veni Creator*. As they sang, with voices half choked with sobbings of joy, the people flocked in, and a crowd of men, women, and children filled the church. The whole town was thrown into an uproar at the news.[53]

51. Thomas, *De oudste Constituties*, 336–37 [Dist. I, ch. 23]; Lehner, 229–30.
52. *Acta canonizationis*, Bologna, 31, 32; Lehner, 120–21.
53. *Lives of the Brethren*, I.v; Placid, 16–17.

Praying Alone and in Choir

Prayer was the foundation of St. Dominic's life: liturgical prayer, but also personal prayer. Friar Ventura of Verona, called to testify at the canonization process, attested that:

> when traveling he celebrated Mass almost every day if he found a church. When he sang Mass, he shed many tears, as the witness himself saw it happen. If there was a church at the lodging, he always went to pray there. Almost always while he was outside the priory, when he heard the first stroke of the matins bell from the monasteries, he used to arise and rouse the friars; with great devotion he celebrated the whole night and day Office at the prescribed hours so that he omitted nothing.[54]

In the opinion of William of Montferrat, who was his travelling companion or *socius* in the last period of his life, Dominic "spent more time in prayer than in sleep."[55] Moreover, according to Brother Stephen:

> After the brethren had finished Compline and their common prayers, he would then send them to the dormitory and usually remain himself in church to pray. During the night, his prayer affected him so strongly that he would burst into groans and exclamations. Brothers sleeping nearby were awakened and some were moved to tears. Most of the time he would stay up to pray until Matins. He nevertheless remained for the Office, and would walk around each side of the choir, exhorting and encouraging them to sing devoutly and on key. Thus he dedicated the night to prayer, so that he never remembers having seen him sleeping in a bed, although a regular place was prepared for him.[56]

A booklet distributed at the end of the thirteenth century presented and illustrated nine bodily postures Dominic adopted in his

54. *Acta canonizationis*, Bologna, 3; Lehner, 101.
55. *Acta canonizationis*, Bologna, 13; Lehner, 108.
56. *Acta canonizationis*, Bologna, 37; Lehner, 125.

personal prayer.[57] The friars' curiosity led them to watch their founder's movements and listen to his groans. "The 'bodily modes' of St. Dominic's prayer have a double reality, vocal and gestural," writes the historian Jean-Claude Schmitt.[58] The soul and the body in fact act on each other: "The soul makes the members of the body work so that [the soul] may be carried with greater devotion to God, so that the soul, by setting the body in motion, moves away from the body and comes to be, sometimes in ecstasy like Paul, sometimes in agony like the Savior, sometimes in the transport of the spirit like the prophet David."[59] As Schmitt rightly notes:

> St. Dominic's prayer is not only linked to the "rationalist," patristic and scholastic current, but to the Davidic, prophetic, hagiographic and mystical model. His devotion reproduces "that of the saints of the Old and New Testaments": like them, St. Dominic was animated during his lifetime by a spiritual force that drew tears from his body and subtracted it from his will.[60]

Four attitudes particularly express the virtue of humility: Dominic, facing the altar surmounted by a crucifix, bows deeply and then rises; he prostrates his whole self, face to the earth; he scourges himself with an iron chain; he genuflects repeatedly. Three other attitudes insist on the offering of his life: he prays with his hands open, in the position of the *orant*; or with his arms in a cross; or finally with his arms raised, forming an arrow toward heaven. Finally, two last modes present Dominic seated in front of a writing table, reading and meditating, "recollecting himself in himself and fixing himself in the presence of God."[61] And finally, as if he has drawn strength and courage from study and prayer, he is represented on

57. The text of *The Nine Ways of Prayer of Saint Dominic* was written by an unknown friar, probably from Bologna in the period 1274 to 1290. The latest edition was given by Simon Tugwell in AFP 83 (2013): 37–56.

58. Jean-Claude Schmitt, *La Raison des gestes dans l'Occident médiéval* (Gallimard, 1990), 310.

59. "De modo orandi corporaliter sancti Dominici," AFP 83 (2013): 41.

60. Schmitt, *La Raison des gestes dans l'Occident médiéval*, 310.

61. *The Nine Ways of Prayer of Saint Dominic*, ed. Simon Tugwell (Dominican Publications, 1978), eighth way; Tugwell, 42.

the road, in the presence of a companion, going his own way, praying, walking, and feeding the fire of his charity by meditating on Scripture. At least some of these ways of praying served a pedagogical purpose. The four modes in which prayer is expressed by bowing and genuflecting were taught to the novices and transmitted to the brothers. Humbert of Romans gives evidence of this in his commentary on the *Constitutions of the Order of Preachers*, in which he devotes an entire chapter to "inclinations," distinguishing six forms that range from a simple inclination of the upper body, in a standing position, to the prostration of the whole body called the *venia*. In all cases, Humbert reminds us, the heart must follow the movement of the body.[62] This is an essential dimension of Christian prayer, especially in the monastic tradition.

Dominic's prayer was also accompanied by various penances. The violence and frequency of his disciplinary blows—he often drew blood—have troubled many commentators. Sister Catherine Aubin, a Dominican theologian, even asks the question, "Is this a way of praying?" in a book entitled *Praying with One's Body* [*Prier avec son corps*].[63] The author bases her answer, which is positive, on contributions from biblical theology and anthropology. The suffering servant of Isaiah gives his back to those who beat him and his face to those who pluck his beard, she notes (Is 50:6). But there is still something else. One can understand these gestures only with a lively awareness of what was at stake. St. Dominic had this awareness, haunted as he was by the image of Christ voluntarily entering into his Passion. Eternal salvation is not a bonus after earthly life, or a supplement for the soul; it is a question of life or death, and at the end of the day, it is the only question that is worth asking. Dominic, therefore, begged the Lord "that God would grant him true charity, which would be effective in caring for and winning the salvation of men; he thought he would only really be a member of Christ's Body when he could spend himself utterly with all his strength in the winning of souls, just as the Lord Jesus Christ,

62. Humbert de Romans, *Expositio in Constitutiones*, in *Opera de vita regulari*, ed. Joachim Joseph Berthier, vol. 2 (Marietti, 1956), 160–71, especially 167.

63. Catherine Aubin, *Prier avec son corps à la manière de saint Dominique* (Éd. du Cerf, 2005), 79.

the Savior of us all, gave himself up entirely for our salvation."[64] The object of his prayer was therefore the love of God, the treasure of charity, which he wished to offer to his neighbor.

One of the unique characteristics of the order took shape as the itinerant preachers sought to join personal prayer with prayer in common. It was no longer possible for itinerant preachers to continue to celebrate the office as did monks or canons. Efforts were made early on to achieve a certain uniformity, while the movement of the friars according to their mission and assignments made them subject to diverse local customs. It was under the government of Humbert of Romans, between 1254 and 1256, that Dominican liturgical practices were essentially fixed. One result of this work can be found in the work that has come to be known as the "Prototype" (1254) and which is preserved in the archives of the order in the convent of Santa Sabina in Rome.[65]

The Dominican liturgy, born of these reflections, is one of the ancient Latin liturgies that St. Pius V allowed to survive alongside the Roman liturgy after the Council of Trent.[66] Its distinctive elements are the calendar, a number of gestures, several liturgical pericopes, and seven offices whose antiphons and responsories are written in a rhymed poetic style. It is a type of Romano-Gallican liturgy of the thirteenth century but differs in some respects from the contemporary liturgies of Paris and Lyon. The musical text of the Dominican liturgy is closely related to that of the Cistercians. It is indebted to them, for example, for the suppression of the *caudae*, or melodic repetitions. Over the course of centuries, there have been similarities with the Roman liturgy, especially in the seventeenth and twentieth centuries, after the Second Vatican Council. At the general chapters of

64. Jordan of Saxony, *Libellus*, 13; Tugwell, 3.

65. *Aux origines de la liturgie dominicaine: le manuscrit Santa Sabina XIV L1*, ed. Leonard E. Boyle and Pierre-Marie Gy, with the collaboration of Pawel Krupa (CNRS—École Française de Rome, 2004).

66. For the question of the Dominican liturgy, see William R. Bonniwell, *A History of the Dominican Liturgy: 1215–1945* (J.-F. Wagner, 1945). See also the publications of the Liturgy Commission of the Order of Preachers. This development on the Dominican liturgy is indebted to a careful reading of Father Innocent Smith.

1968 and 1971, the superiors of the order took stock of new pastoral requirements. Feeling that the Dominican Rite did not express a specific spirituality but was the result of outdated historical circumstances, they chose to fully adopt the Roman Rite, both for the Liturgy of the Hours and for the missal, while preserving an abundant liturgical calendar and proper. The latter, enriched by numerous beatifications and canonizations, was revised in 1971 and again in 2019. In adopting the Roman Rite, the Dominicans were nevertheless eager to retain a number of chants proper to their tradition and elements of the ritual for the mass and the office. The celebration of Compline, the Sacrament of the Sick, and certain processions for the Feast of the Presentation or Holy Week thus draw on the treasure of the Dominican liturgy.

"Our Weapons Are Our Books"

While the chapters of other orders prior to the thirteenth century (Grandmont, the Carthusians, Cîteaux, and even the customs of the Canons Regular) paid only secondary attention to study, the annual chapters of the Preachers never ceased to emphasize its importance, excellence, and necessity. At every turn, they remind all, even the oldest, of their duty to apply themselves assiduously and forcefully to it. If we are to believe the testimony of Brother John of Spain, Dominic sent the first companions from Toulouse to Paris "to study, preach, and found a priory."[67] Dietrich of Apolda concurs in a hagiographic account, noting that after his return from Rome in 1216, Dominic outlined in two words the duties of his first companions gathered in Toulouse: "Let them study, and let them preach." The Latin phrase sounds like a watchword: *Ut studerent et praedicarent.*[68] In the commentary on the Rule of Saint Augustine that he wrote for the brothers, Humbert of Romans declares the need to test the novices' capacity for study. He does not rule out the possibility of dismissing those who proved insufficient. These half-preachers would put themselves in danger

67. *Acta canonizationis*, Bologna, 26; Lehner, 115.

68. Thierry d'Apolda, *Livre sur la vie et la mort de saint Dominique*, II.lxxi, trans. Amédée Curé (Librairie catholique internationale de l'œuvre de Saint-Paul, 1887), 106.

and put souls at risk: the weakness of the adversary makes the wicked bold. Without sufficient knowledge on the part of its members, the order could be despised, and the enemies of God and the Church would take glory from it.[69]

In order to train the new religious, a system of studies was set up early on: it included a conventual level, with the lector as a home teacher; a provincial level, with a center of studies (or *studium*); and an international level with *studia generalia*, the most prestigious in the Middle Ages being Saint-Jacques in Paris and San Domenico in Bologna, as well as those of Cologne in the Rhine valley and Oxford on the other side of the Channel. Over the course of the centuries, other universities or other centers of specialization were founded by the Dominicans, such as Salamanca, Manila, Fribourg, Jerusalem, Rome, Bogota, Washington, D.C., etc. These institutions continue, in a certain way, the work of the medieval foundations. But study does not only concern teachers and students. Conceived as a duty of their calling by the Preachers, it extends well beyond the time of the first training, and all are subject to it. The historian Célestin Douais notes that "it was as if with regret that the Chapter of the Province of Toulouse in 1336 exempted the religious who had been professed for fifty years from attending the convent's classes."[70]

To fulfill this obligation of their life, Dominicans have always given special care to their libraries. Over the centuries, biblical editions, *summae* of all kinds, volumes of philosophy and theology, sermons, and chronicles have come to constitute precious collections, and these treasures are a luxury of Dominican convents. Humbert of Romans devotes an entire chapter of a treatise on the employment of the friars to the role of the librarian and the functioning of the library.[71] Using warlike rhetoric, he notes: "The holy books provide the Friar Preacher with weapons for defense and attack. Every convent is a fortress always under siege. The books are, for the soldiers

69. Humbert de Romans, *Expositio Regulae beati Augustini*, in *Opera de vita regulari*, ed. Joachim Joseph Berthier, vol. 1 (Marietti, 1956), c. CXLIII, 433–35.

70. Célestin Douais, *Essai sur l'organisation des études dans l'ordre des frères prêcheurs au treizième et quatorzième siècle* (Privat, 1884), 12.

71. Humbert de Romans, *Instructiones de Officiis Ordinis*, in *De vita Regulari*, vol. 2 (Marietti, 1956), c. XIII, 263–67.

of this place, always under attack by the spirit of evil, the water from which they drink, the food with which they repair their lost strength, the weapons with which they victoriously repel the attack."[72] As a chapter held in 1288 in Avignon stated: "Since our weapons are books, and since, without books, no one exposes himself without risk to preaching and listening to confessions, we warn the priors and the other brothers to work to multiply the books in the common library."[73] As Humbert of Romans affirms in his *Treatise on Preaching*, the Dominican apprentice must devote himself to the study of books with a real desire to assimilate what he can discover there:

> Observe that, granted the grace of preaching well is a special gift of God, nevertheless it demands from the preacher full application to the study of whatever is needed for the proper execution of his office. . . . Moreover, St. Jerome, while explaining the text of the prophet, Ezekiel, 'Eat this book' (Ezek 3:1), points out that the preacher must nourish his heart with the words of God and must meditate attentively on them before delivering them to the people.[74]

The Grace of Preaching

The common life, ardent prayer, long study—all this is indispensable for leading the life of a preacher, but these sefforts are not enough. Brother Stephen of Bourbon, a famous Dominican preacher of the thirteenth century, tells the story of a great personage, "an excellent preacher in Paris," who was congratulated for the excellence of his sermons and assured that he could glorify God for being so learned. Flattered, the preacher failed to attribute this gift to God's glory, explaining: "I must give thanks to my bedside lamp by which I have watched so much that I have reached this excellence in science."

72. Humbert de Romans, *Commentaire de la Règle de saint Augustin*, quoted by Célestin Douais, *Essai sur l'organisation des études dans l'ordre des frères prêcheurs au treizième et quatorzième siècle*, 47.

73. Célestin Douais, *Acta capitulorum provincialium ordinis fratrum Praedicatorum: Première province de Provence, province romaine, province d'Espagne, 1239–1302* (Privat, 1894), 319 [Première province de Provence, chapitre d'Avignon, 1288].

74. Humbert de Romans, *Treatise on Preaching*, I.vi, 31–32.

Immediately, explains Stephen of Bourbon, he lost his memory and knowledge.[75]

The *Primitive Constitutions* provides that the brothers judged fit for preaching must undergo an examination before beginning to exercise this function. The examiners, in fact, must inquire not only into the reality of the efforts made by the religious they are questioning but also into "the graces which God has conferred upon their preaching."[76] The prior, that is, the superior, must then decide whether the candidate should persevere in study or practice preaching with more advanced brothers, or whether he is immediately suitable and useful to exercise the office of preaching. As the *Constitutions* states: "The office of preacher may be exercised by one who has listened to [theology] lectures for a year, provided there is no danger of scandal likely to arise from the preaching."[77] Preaching, then, is not the mere fruit of good preparation; the preacher is never ready for his mission. No one, except Christ and his apostles, is capable of being a preacher; only the grace of God can call one to this office. A brother is first called to follow Christ as a disciple, then he is sent to preach the Gospel; the readiness and obedience of the disciple must remain in the heart of the apostle.

In his *Treatise on Preaching*, Humbert of Romans notes several difficulties associated with the office of preaching. In the first place, there are few capable preachers: "In the early days of the Church a small number of Apostles, trained for their particular mission, was enough to convert the entire world; but present-day preachers, in spite of their numbers, make only mediocre gains." Secondly, he adds, it is necessary to be called to this ministry: "All have seen, and, indeed, still frequently see, very learned priests who, in spite of serious application to the task, have never been able to attain success in preaching. . . . It is by repeated playing on his instrument that a harpist becomes master of it. But the gift of a preacher is quite different. His virtue is a special gift which only God can grant."[78]

75. Albert Lecoy de la Marche, *Anecdotes historiques, légendes et apologues tirées du recueil inédit d'Étienne de Bourbon, dominicain du XIIIe siècle* (Renouard, 1877), 247.

76. *Primitive Constitutions*, II.xx; Lehner, 242.

77. *Primitive Constitutions*, II.xxxi; Lehner, 246.

78. Humbert de Romans, *Treatise on Preaching*, I.vi, 29–30.

The office of preacher, therefore, has a charismatic dimension. One is a preacher by the grace of God. The master of preaching is the Holy Spirit. For Humbert of Romans, the sum of personal efforts, prayer, and ascetic work is vain if there is not a mysterious and personal call from God, accepted by a Christian and then recognized and validated by the church that sends him on mission. In Bologna in 1219, Dominic encouraged the friars' spirit of adventure, testing their confidence by sending a novice to preach in his home town of Piacenza. Friar Buonviso was a doctor of canon law, which guaranteed a certain gravity in his speech, but he had not studied theology. He claimed that he would not know how to preach and "tried to excuse himself because of his inexperience." Dominic, however, persuaded him to leave, telling him not to worry: "Go confidently for the Lord will be with you, and He will put the words in your mouth."[79] At the canonization process, the friar recounted that the Lord gave him such a preaching grace that he gained three new members to the order!

Looking further back, we see that the historical circumstances of the order's earliest days forced the friars to clarify from where their preaching derived its authority. They were not, strictly speaking, pastors in charge of souls. For some Christians at the end of the twelfth century, preaching was charismatic. Its authority came directly from the Holy Spirit. In particular, some followers of Waldo claimed a right and even a duty to preach for all, including the laity, relying among other things on quotations from the fathers of the church. In a Waldensian *Enchiridion* quoted by Simon Tugwell:

> Chrysostom is cited as saying: Just as the priest is under an obligation to preach the truth which he has heard from God, so the layman is under an obligation freely to preach the truth which he has heard from the priests." Gregory is also cited as saying, "Be careful not to hide the talent you have received from God, or you will be tormented in Hell. Hence St. Paul: 'Woe to me if I do not preach'(1 Cor 9:16)."[80]

79. *Acta canonizationis*, Bologna, 24; Lehner, 114.

80. Giovanni Gonnet, *Enchiridion Fontium Valdensium* (Torre Pellice, 1958), 59–60, quoted in Simon Tugwell, *The Way of the Preacher* (Darton, Longman & Todd Ltd., 1979), 122.

But contrary to these advocates of a purely charismatic preaching, religious of the twelfth century insisted on the role of the canonical mission to accredit the preaching. When he preached in the Toulouse region, St. Bernard of Clairvaux relied on the quotation from St. Paul, "How can they preach if they have not been sent?" (Rom 10:15), in order to prevent the reception of a preacher who had not been mandated by the pope or the local bishop: "These foreign preachers have neither the appearance of piety nor the spirit of it; in order to better hide the venom of their doctrines, they wrap their profane novelties in expressions that are all divine; beware of them as true poisoners, and consider them to be rapacious wolves even though they hide under the skins of sheep."[81]

For St. Dominic and his followers, it was not a question of choosing one or the other of these two contradictory options. The *gratia praedicationis* imposes a difficult balance on the order: the first mandate of preaching comes from God, but it is up to the order to discern it and to frame it by means of a way of life. As the *Didache* already pointed out, a true prophet cannot be greedy.[82] He wants to gain souls, not wealth. Stephen of Bourbon tells the story of a cleric who, after praising the humility of the Savior on Palm Sunday, was retiring on a superb horse when an old woman asked him: "Is this, Master, the ass you spoke of and the Savior who rode her?"[83] The church needed exemplary preachers whose competence was not simply reduced to a legal mandate, nor was it seen as arising from ascetic or charismatic qualities.[84] The brethren saw themselves as members of the same company, the same college, called to work together to win souls. On the day of judgment, Humbert explains, the apostles will have to give an account of the grace that has been given to them: "What fruit shall we then show for our labors?" he

81. Saint Bernard, *Ep* 242, 3, in *Œuvres complètes de saint Bernard*, traduites en français par les abbés Dion et Charpentier, nouvelle édition, vol. 1 (Vivès, 1887), 344–45.

82. *The Teaching of the Twelve Apostles (Didache)*, 11, 3.

83. Quoted in Albert Lecoy de la Marche, *La chaire française au Moyen Age spécialement au* XIIIe *siècle d'après les manuscrits contemporains* (Didier et Cie, 1868), 38.

84. See Tugwell, *The Way of the Preacher*, 38.

asks, and then replies, borrowing from St. Gregory, "Before the Supreme Judge 'Peter will appear with converted Judea, Paul leading, so to speak, the entire world; then Andrew with Achaia, John with Asia, Thomas with India. What shall we say, we unfortunate ones, who after the business has been confided to our care, shall appear before the Lord with empty hands.'"[85]

At the Heart of the Church

The Father of Preachers resolutely placed his life and action at the heart of the church, *in medio Ecclesiae.* In was, in truth, the only way to carry out his apostolic mission toward dissidents, heretics, and pagans. The Order of Preachers was the result of a slow and patient work of response and adaptation to the needs of the times and of the church. Dominic carried out this work in collaboration with popes Innocent III, Honorius III, Gregory IX, and numerous bishops, among whom Diego of Osma and Fulk of Toulouse stand out, as they were linked to Dominic by a close and trusting friendship. But Dominic, for his part, did not accept the episcopate when it was offered to him three times. "He preferred living with his brethren in poverty to being a bishop."[86] It would be wrong, however, to see this as contempt for the episcopal office; he was keenly aware of his place as a cooperator of the bishops. The early *Constitutions* of the order forbade the friars to preach without a mandate: "When our brethren enter the diocese of any bishop to preach, they shall, if possible, first call on that bishop and, according to his advice, reap the harvest they intend. As long as they are present in his diocese, they shall devotedly obey him in all things that are not against the Order."[87]

The first words of the Proper of the Mass of St. Dominic, therefore, celebrate him biblically as being placed *in medio Ecclesiae*, that is,

85. Humbert de Romans, *Treatise on Preaching*, VII.xxxi, 115.

86. Brother John of Spain gives this testimony: "Two or three times he was selected for the episcopacy, but always refused." He then specifies that these were the bishoprics of Béziers and Comminges. See *Acta canonizationis*, Bologna, 28; Lehner, 117.

87. *Primitive Constitutions*, II.xxxii; Lehner, 247.

in the middle, or rather in the heart, of the church.[88] This place does not prevent the Father of the Preachers and the first generations of friars from reaching the frontiers of Christianity and even going beyond them. The work accomplished by the Florentine Dominican Riccoldo de Monte di Croce in a dozen years, from 1288 to 1300, bears witness to this, among other examples: mandated by Pope Nicholas IV for the mission in the East, Riccoldo lived in Iraq for almost ten years. After the fall of St. John of Acre, he fell victim to the reversal of the political and religious situation. Arrested and enslaved, he considered himself a poor "camel driver of Christ," wandering the Middle East. After escaping, he returned to Italy and wrote strong and poignant accounts in which he evoked the customs of those he met: Muslim populations, but also Tartars and Mongols.[89] It is understandable that Saint Dominic, who was at the origin of such a missionary impulse, is presented by the liturgy as a new and true athlete of the Lord:

> He trod the world beneath his feet,
> Forward to strenuous toil he pressed,
> He stripped himself the foe to meet,
> By Christ's strong grace upheld and blessed.[90]

To be an apostle, one must be fully of the church.

The mendicant order's privileged links with the papacy made these religious the privileged agents of papal action, beyond the limits of dioceses and traditional communities. The service of the church was also manifested in the doctrinal help given to the sovereign pon-

88. "In medio Ecclesiae aperuit os eius" (Sir 15:5): "In the midst of the congregation [wisdom] opens his mouth" (*Jerusalem Bible* translation). The Introit of the Mass, the piece that bears the name of Office in the Dominican liturgy, begins with these words.

89. Jean-Marie Mérigoux, "L'ouvrage d'un frère prêcheur florentin en Orient à la fin du XIIIe siècle: Le *Contra legem Saracenorum* de Riccoldo de Monte di Croce," *Memorie domenicane* 17 (1986): 1–144; Emilio Panella, "Ricerche su Riccoldo da Monte di Croce," AFP 58 (1988): 5–85.

90. Liturgical Offices for the Feasts of St. Dominic, English translation in *The Hymns of the Dominican Missal and Breviary*, ed. Aquinas Byrnes, OP (B. Herder Book Co., 1943), 405. This is the hymn *Novus athleta Domini.*

tiffs, from the institution of the masters of the sacred palace to that of the theologian of the pontifical house. Dominican participation was also decisive in many synods, especially during the ecumenical Council of Trent or the two Vatican councils. In a sermon on St. Dominic, a thirteenth-century preacher glosses a well-known verse from the Song of Songs, "Let the fragrance of your breath be like apples" (cf. Song 7:9), and he then compares the preacher to "the mouth of holy Church, through which she teaches and corrects her children."[91] The religious family of the saint buried in Bologna has no other vocation.

91. First Sermon of Pelagius the Lesser for the Feast of St. Dominic, translated and kindly provided by Bernard Hodel. The *Jerusalem Bible* translates: "the fragrance of your breath, [let it be] that of apples" (Song 7:9).

Chapter 4

A Summary of Dominican Heritage

Dante Alighieri's *Divine Comedy* had a special place for Dominic and those belonging to his order. The poet writes of the Order of Preachers that "one is fattened in the good, provided one is not lost." He rejoices that from the Dominican torrent flow many streams "which water the Catholic garden and make its shrubs more perennial" (*Paradiso* X, 96 and XII, 103). Eight centuries since its founding, the Dominican adventure has amassed an immense and rich patrimony, of which it is possible only to summarize.

Dominic, Father of a Family

After the dispersion of Dominic's first companions in 1217, the order experienced rapid growth. Writing to Diana d'Andalò in 1224 after the feast of Easter, Jordan of Saxony tells her that since Advent, "about forty novices joined the Order, of whom many are Masters, others are well-lettered, and of many others again we have high hopes."[1] Humbert of Romans, already a Master of Arts, and Hugh of Saint-Cher, a bachelor of theology, were to be part of this group. According to Thomas de Cantimpré, Jordan, the champion of vocations, received up to sixty young men at once, but the quality was not always equal to the quantity, and according to this author, a general chapter reproached him for this fishing for young men "of such short knowledge that many of them, in spite of long practice, could hardly, as I was told, read a single reading at the Matins service."[2] If one believes the account in the *Lives of the Brethren*, "He

1. Jordan of Saxony, *To Heaven with Diana! A Study of Jordan of Saxony and Diana d'Andalo with a translation of the Letters of Jordan by Gerald Vann, OP* (Henry Regnery Company, 1960), 75 (letter IX).

2. Thomas de Cantimpré, *Les exemples du Livre des abeilles: Une vision médiévale*, presentation, translation, and commentary by Henri Platelle (Brepols, 1997), 138 [c. XIX, exemplum 91].

would often have a number of habits made in advance, feeling sure that our Lord would not be long in sending him subjects to wear them, a result which came about directly he resumed his preaching: nay, it often happened that so many thronged in at one time that habits could not be provided as fast as they were required."[3] It is therefore not surprising that the number of Dominicans by 1303 was estimated at nearly ten thousand. For the friars of the fifteenth century, the discovery of America, the New World, opened new opportunities for the order, and at the beginning of the eighteenth century, there were more than twenty thousand preachers. Decimated by the French Revolution and the hostility toward religious life that accompanied it, the order struggled to regain strength, although it did regain momentum in the nineteenth century. By the end of the Catholic crisis of the 1960s and 1970s, the number of Friars Preachers stabilized at around six thousand, spread over some forty provinces.[4]

If the long process of founding the order began in Prouille in 1206, the story of the definitive incorporation of the nuns into the family of St. Dominic underwent many developments in the thirteenth century and has since experienced many twists and turns. The Dominicans were reluctant to accept the care of the nuns (*cura monialium*). This fraternal yoke seemed too heavy for them, and only by the authority of the popes and the constancy of the nuns was the matter finally settled. Like the friars directly under the authority of the Master of the Order, the nuns do not constitute a secondary class, a parallel to the feminine order of the Friars Preachers; they are constitutive of the order in the same way as the friars. As the order expanded, new monasteries were founded as well. When consulted by the energetic Diana d'Andalò about the possibility of a female foundation in Bologna, when the friars were only beginning to gain footing in the city, Dominic replied: "It is absolutely necessary,

3. *Lives of the Brethren*, part IV, chap.11, trans. Bede Jarrett, OP (Blackfriars Publications, 1955).

4. Statistics of the order published by Angelus Walz in his *Compendium historiae Ordinis Praedicatorum* (Angelicum, 1948). For the second half of the twentieth century, see the annual statistics published in the journal *Analecta Sacri Ordinis Praedicatorum*.

brothers, that the house of the ladies be built, even if it were necessary that our house be left to wait."[5]

From the very beginning of preaching in the Lauragais, lay people were associated with the sisters of Prouille and with Dominic's first companions. The first known names are those of a couple, Ermengarde Godolina and her husband, Sans Gasc, who on August 8, 1207, "of good heart and according to their free will," gave themselves and all their goods "to the Lord God, to the Blessed Mary, to all the Saints of God, to holy preaching, to the Lord Dominic of Osma and to all the brothers and sisters, those who are now and those who will be in the future."[6] The link of the laity with the order then took on diverse forms from the thirteenth to the twentieth century. When they began to build conventual churches, the Dominicans imagined having large naves for the faithful, as is the case not only in the Jacobin church in Toulouse but also in Florence or Bologna in Italy, in Friesach in Austria, or in Krakow in Poland. Crowds of men and women wishing to lead a life of penance yet remaining in the world imitated the practices of the regular conventual life. A Dominican historian, Father Gilles Gérard Meersseman, was able to reconstruct the involvement of lay people with the Preachers in the city of Florence at the beginning of the order. Pious Tuscan merchants and bankers had been moved by the sermons against usury preached by the sons of St. Francis and St. Dominic; they wished to repair the wrongs caused by usurers to their impoverished clients, and they founded *case di misericordia*. When the mendicant orders settled in the city, the first communities of religious were welcomed in these places, since they were poor by vocation. It was after stopping in one of these houses that the Dominicans, who arrived in Florence in the summer of 1219 led by John of Salerno, were installed in the new district of Santa Maria Novella. It was necessary to live there, but the Dominican *Constitutions* forbade the possession of property. The

5. ASOP 1 (1893): 181–84. Edition by Hyacinthe-Marie Cormier of the *Chronicle of Saint Agnes of Bologna*, 4. See also the French translation by Nicole Bériou and Bernard Hodel, 558, based on the provisional edition by Simon Tugwell.

6. Charter of May 15, 1211, *Monumenta diplomatica*, 11; Bériou-Hodel, 489–90.

Florentine financiers quickly found a way: "Since the Preachers were poor, there was only to give these goods to a charitable institution so that the latter could use the income for the maintenance of the friars as it helped other poor people. The founders and then benefactors thus became Confreres of Penance."[7] In 1285, the Master of the Order, Muño of Zamora, laid down the elements of a rule of life for these faithful, which was used by laymen living in the world, within the Order of Penance of St. Dominic. It was later also used by women who, from the sixteenth century onward, grouped together in communities, led an apostolic type of religious life. These women, sometimes referred to as Daughters of Charity, and later the female religious congregations proper, dedicated to teaching and hospitality, originated here. Nuns and friars of the Order of Preachers, lay people, Daughters of Charity and Dominican sisters, and members of secular institutes all recognize themselves as belonging to the same spiritual family.

At the very end of his life, and not without some bitterness, Father Lacordaire confided to his friend Charles de Montalembert that "in the foundation or regeneration of a religious Order, there are always three categories: the saints, the fools, and the mediocre people."[8] Thanks to God, the first category was not lacking in the Order of Preachers, whether in the ranks of the nuns, the friars, or the laity. Several hundred saints and blessed constitute the most precious treasure of the Dominican heritage. In a directory published in 2016 under the title *El año dominicano*, Father José A. Martínez Puche listed eighty-three canonized saints, 287 blessed, twenty-five venerable, and 119 servants of God in the liturgical calendar or in the files of the General Postulator of the Order of Preachers, without forgetting 306 martyrs who have been canonized or whose process of canonization is underway.[9] The number is considerable, as is

7. Gilles Gérard Meersseman, *Dossier de l'Ordre de la Pénitence au XIIIe siècle* (Éd. Universitaires, 1982²), 11–12.

8. Charles de Montalembert, *Catholicisme et liberté: Correspondance inédite avec le P. Lacordaire, Mgr de Mérode et A. de Falloux (1852–1870)* (Éd. du Cerf, 1970), 201. Montalembert reports a conversation he had with Lacordaire on September 27, 1861; the latter died on November 21, 1861.

9. José A. Martínez Puche, *El año dominicano* (Edibesa, 2016), 9–16.

the variety of forms of sanctity among them. What do St. Thomas Aquinas († 1274), the Angelic Doctor and rigorous scholar, and St. Martin de Porres († 1639), the mystical and charitable doorkeeper of the convent in Lima, Peru, have in common? How can we compare St. Catherine of Siena († 1380), Doctor of the Church and prophetess in her time, with St. Zdislava of Lemberk († 1252), wealthy aristocrat, mother of a family and mother of the poor? In more recent times, what do Blessed Pier Giorgio Frassati († 1925), a fervent, boisterous, and joyfully lay student, and Blessed Hyacinthe-Marie Cormier († 1916), a tireless and unassuming servant of his order, have in common? The "broad and fragrant" spirituality of St. Dominic can be adapted to various paths of holiness: the gift the life of our brother, Pierre Claverie, Bishop of Oran, which was taken from him when he was assassinated in Algeria in 1996; the art of the cultivated painter, Blessed Fra Angelico († 1455), which spurred this religious to make his own life a masterpiece; the commitment to the service of the city for Giorgio La Pira († 1977), lay academic, mayor of Florence, and tireless promoter of peace initiatives in the world. What unifies all these figures is the fact that they followed the path opened to them by the Father of the Preachers: to espouse the Word of God, to contemplate it, and to pass on the fruits of this contemplation to their contemporaries.

Nothing is less dull and repetitive than a history of Dominican sanctity. The quaint frequently rubs shoulders with the sublime. The friar Anthony Neyrot provides a fine example of this at the beginning of the fifteenth century. Born in Rivoli, near Turin, around 1423, and initiated into Dominican life by St. Antoninus in the convent of San Marco in Florence, Brother Anthony had experienced apostolic successes without much effort. The result for this young priest was that he became too greatly attached to these moments of excitement. Shortly afterward, in the absence of adventure, this Northern Italian wanted to go to Sicily. His ship was captured by pirates, and he was deported as a slave to Tunisia. He was then only twenty-five years old. His love of Christ was not strong: to regain his freedom, he abjured his faith, got married, and even started to translate the Koran into Latin. Fortunately, his story does not end there. Italian merchants told him of the death of Antoninus, the holy Archbishop of Florence in 1459. Remembering the man who had guided him and invited him to follow St. Dominic, he realized his fault, sought a priest, and resolved to make public his return to the Catholic faith. With his head shaved and wearing the Dominican habit, he presented himself on Palm Sunday of 1460 before the King of Tunis to bear witness to Christ. The renegade who had returned to the faith was imprisoned, tortured, maimed, and then stoned to death. His executioners tried to burn his body, and his remains were thrown in the garbage. What was left of his body, hidden by Christians as precious relics, were taken to Rivoli. His cult as a Blessed was approved in 1767.[10]

Across the Atlantic, the first Saint of the New World, Rose of Lima, was not to be outdone in Dominican fervor.[11] Born in 1586 in Lima, Peru, to a Spanish officer father and a Peruvian mother, Isabella de Flores received the nickname of Rose from a servant, and the name remained with her on account of her beauty. As a child, fascinated by an image of the *Ecce Homo*, she took a vow of virginity and set out to follow in the footsteps of St. Catherine of Siena. Dressed in the order's habit, she took the name Rose of St. Mary in 1606 and became a tertiary. From then on, she divided her days between long periods of solitary prayer, strange penances, and works of mercy, particularly with indigenous people, abandoned children, and the elderly. When questioned by the Inquisition, which was concerned by her ecstasies and her austerity, they found nothing to reproach her faith. This young woman, who wore a crown of thorns under her veil, lived in a tool shed at the edge of a garden and slept on a mattress made of pottery shards. She had no other desire than to accompany Christ as closely as possible in his Passion in order to give the world the charity that does not pass away. Does not this life mirror that of Mary Magdalene, who the Dominicans venerate as "the apostle of the apostles"? Exhausted by her asceticism and admired by those who tasted the benefits of her friendship with God, Rose of Lima died on August 24, 1617. Beatified some fifty years later, this younger sister of St.

10. Gian Ludovico Masetti Zannini, "Neyrot (Neirotti, Niger), Antonio," *Biblioteca sanctorum*, vol. 9 (Città Nuova Editrice, 1967), col. 841–43.

11. Niccolò del Re, "Rosa, da Lima," *Biblioteca sanctorum*, vol. 9 (Città Nuova Editrice, 1967), col. 396–400.

Catherine of Siena and St. Catherine of Ricci, and elder sister of Blessed Agnes of Langeac, was canonized in 1671.

At the time when the cult of Rose of Lima was flourishing, a young French woman, Marie Poussepin, born in Dourdan in 1653 and animated by an apostolic spirit, succeeded in combining the efficiency of a captain of industry and the love of the poorest of the poor and led the active life of charity, enlivened by her Dominican commitment. Living for nearly fifty years in Sainville, a tiny village in the Beauce region of France, with few opportunities for its idle inhabitants, this woman of faith, endowed with a great amount of the virtue of prudence, undertook to give work to those who had none. In this way, she contributed to the growth of the Kingdom of God there, where the Lord had placed her. Marie Poussepin's holiness was achieved by giving herself fully to both practical and spiritual tasks: the training of very poor young men to make stockings as a trade, the enlivening of her parish, and the teaching of catechism for which she set up small schools that provided primary education. All of this she did in addition to care of the sick. By gathering companions around her, this religious pioneer intended to create a community of Dominican women leading an apostolic life without enclosure. However, the Dominican Sisters of the Presentation of Tours, the congregation founded by this daughter of St. Dominic, this sister of St. Catherine of Siena, would not be fully joined to the Order of Preachers until 1959! Thus, an important international and missionary development was to confirm the intuitions of this good and holy Dominican worker, who died in 1744 at the age of ninety after a life of active charity.[12] She was beatified in 1994.

In contemporary Italy, a radiant figure of holiness stands out in the twentieth century, receiving recognition well beyond national borders. Pier Giorgio Frassati was born on April 6, 1901, in Turin, where his father had founded a liberal daily newspaper, *La Stampa*, before pursuing a successful political career.[13] This entrepreneur considered

12. Madeleine Saint-Jean, "Poussepin (Marie)," *Catholicisme*, vol. 11 (Letouzey et Ané, 1988), col. 694–96.

13. Cristina Siccardi, *Pier Giorgio Frassati* (Edizioni San Paolo, 2002); [in France, Artège, 2010].

his son timid. From childhood, Pier Giorgio took to heart the suffering of others. For him, studies were difficult, but he worked hard to become an engineer and thus put himself at the service of the working class. At the age of seventeen, he received Communion every day and was involved in the St. Vincent de Paul Society and Catholic Action while he gathered his close friends to help the needy in Turin. Taking the Gospel seriously, he obtained hospital beds, placements in schools, and accommodations for those in need. An accomplished sportsman, he also led his friends on hikes in the mountains, inviting them to action as well as to contemplation. Photographs show him feasting with his friends with a glass in hand and a jester's hat on his head, or climbing the Alps in search of arduous climbs and breathtaking summits; these images do not fully reveal his greatest joys or his most successful climbs. It was toward God that he climbed, joyfully and at great speed, following St. Dominic. In 1922, Pier Giorgio entered a Dominican lay fraternity, where he chose to place himself under the patronage of Brother Jerome Savonarola. He could be seen in the streets of Turin with his rosary in his hand, ready to do good. At the age of twenty-four, he contracted fulminant poliomyelitis and died in less than a week. On the day of his funeral, a large crowd of strangers from all walks of life witnessed to the scope of his charity. Pier Giorgio Frassati was beatified by the Holy Father John Paul II on May 20, 1990.

In a famous chapter of the *Dialogue* of St. Catherine, the saint of Siena relates an original vision of St. Dominic. She sees him as a proven sailor who leads his crew to a safe harbor:

> Now look at the ship of your father Dominic, My beloved Son: he ordered it most perfectly, wishing that his sons should apply themselves only to My honor and the salvation of souls, with the light of science, which light he laid as his principal foundation, not, however, on that account, being deprived of true and voluntary poverty, but having it also. And as a sign that he had it truly, and that the contrary displeased him, he left as an heirloom to his sons his curse and Mine, if they should hold any possessions, either privately or in community, as a sign that he had chosen for his spouse Queen Poverty . . . he has rigged his ship with the three ropes of obedience, continence, and true

> poverty; he made it a royal ship, not obliging his subjects under pain of mortal sin, and illuminated by Me the true light, he provided for those who should be less perfect, for though all who observe the order are perfect in kind, yet one possesses a higher degree of perfection than another, yet all perfect or imperfect live well in this ship.[14]

The diversity of Dominican saints verifies the words of this Sienese saint: it is good to live under the guidance of St. Dominic, who worked and prayed so that his religion, that is to say, his religious family, would be "very large, very joyful, very fragrant: a true garden of delights."[15]

Theology as a Science

In the time of St. Dominic, Europe experienced a real revolution in the field of knowledge. In Paris, Cologne, Oxford, Bologna, Naples, and Palencia, schools were opened at the end of the twelfth and beginning of the thirteenth century. Given an abundance of new ideas, a great deal of work was being carried out in these schools and done according to new methods. This theology of the schools, or scholastic theology, differed not only from monastic theology (such as that practiced by Bernard of Clairvaux) but also from other forms of understanding the faith (such as that of the mystics). One of its characteristics and novelties was that it was presented as a science. In a famous text, Peter Cantor explains:

> The work on Holy Scripture consists of three things: reading, debating, and preaching (*legere*, *disputare*, *praedicare*). Reading is like the foundation, the substratum of all the rest, by which one produces all that is useful. Discussion is like the wall of the building: nothing can be fully understood, nothing can be faithfully preached without the text first having been torn apart by the teeth of discussion. All of the above is at the service of

14. Catherine of Siena, OP, *The Dialogue*, trans. Suzanne Noffke, OP, The Classics of Western Spirituality (Paulist Press, 1980), chap. 158.

15. Catherine of Siena, OP, *The Dialogue*, 340.

> preaching: it is the roof that preserves the faithful from the fires and storms of vices. It is therefore after having read Holy Scripture and after having examined in it what may be difficult . . . that one must preach.[16]

This is the program that the Preachers set out to implement.

According to the Dominican perspective, it is not enough to know the scriptures. One must also allow oneself to be transformed by the Word of God. In St. Dominic's time, a method of investigating reality was forged for this purpose in the university context: scholasticism, a method often caricatured but essentially revolutionary. This way of researching and teaching was born of the tension of holding together all the truths of scripture and understanding them in relation to the affirmations of reason. Questions arose to which answers had to be given that preserved the mean between allowing heresy to develop or falling into fideism—that unshakable, naive faith, which is only a vague credulity, more worrisome than reassuring if one is not naive. Saint Thomas Aquinas was renowned in this new quest for truth and wrote a set of philosophical and theological works that ranks high among Dominican treasures. The philosophers Jacques Maritain († 1973) and Étienne Gilson († 1978), among many others, have experienced the inexhaustible richness of Thomistic intuitions in our time. Father Raymond-Léopold Bruckberger, known for his films, writings, and adventures, delivered a convincing tribute to St. Thomas that does justice to the working method of the *Summa Theologica*:

> "Does God exist?—It seems not! *An Deus sit?—Videtur quod non!*" The tone is set once and for all, and will be maintained throughout this immense interrogation, this quest for truth—as there was the quest for the Grail—that constitutes the *Summa Theologica*. Yes, the textbook of my youth is a book of adventure. Honor to Thomas Aquinas, rectifier of wrongs, knight without fear and without reproach to questioning, who gives all objections a full chance, and who fights only with an uncov-

16. The text, taken from the *Verbum abbreviatum* of Peter Cantor, is quoted by Gilbert Dahan, *L'Occident médiéval lecteur de l'Écriture*, "Cahier Évangile, supplément 116" (Éd. du Cerf, 2001), 16.

> ered face. Nothing is more opposed to Thomas Aquinas than the *larvatus prodeo*[17] of Descartes and so many modern thinkers. Today we call "masters" not those who encourage us to question, but those who force upon others their unconditional affirmations or negations. [Saint Thomas] knows that the intellectual act ends and finds its own fruitfulness only in judgment; but the answer, always proposed, never imposed, comes only after the questioning, after the objection, like the sowing after the ploughing. And the field of sowing is never more extensive than that of ploughing. Shame on him who affirms or denies, without any prior questioning! . . . "Does God exist?—It seems not!" This is the very beginning of the *Summa*. But everything is like that from A to Z. Thomas does not take a step, I say not one, without putting his foot on a question.[18]

An undisputed master of theological studies because of the power and clarity of his synthesis, Thomas Aquinas was not the only theologian of note in the medieval period, but he played an essential role in the development of university studies. His legacy has been one of the most valuable of the Dominican inheritance, but there were other Dominican masters of great importance who preceded him or were his contemporaries. Among them we may mention the biblical scholar Hugh of Saint-Cher († 1263), the master of the first biblical concordance and editor of *postillae* (collections) of patristic commentaries assembled for the purpose of preaching. We may also recall the theologian Albert the Great († 1280), whose intellectual openness, particularly toward the work of Aristotle, was to prove decisive for his student, Thomas. The master of Cologne helped to distinguish philosophy from theology more clearly. Moreover, his theological insights related to the intellect were the beginning of the future discoveries of the Rhineland Mystics. Finally, we can mention Raymond of Peñafort († 1275), author of a widely used moral and

17. *Larvatus prodeo* could be translated as "I advance masked." This is the expression Descartes applies to himself in a fragment of his work from 1619 to 1620.

18. Raymond-Léopold Bruckberger, *Le monde renversé: Pour quoi je vis* (Éd. du Cerf, 1971), 86–89.

canonical work, *Summa de paenitentia*, the influence of which was considerable and bears witness to the role played by the Dominicans in the dissemination of the sacrament of penance.

If these Dominican authors are of great importance, the place occupied by St. Thomas remains unique. The catalog of the works of Thomas Aquinas published by Father Gilles Emery is about forty pages long and mentions the main translations of the Neapolitan Master's books.[19] Listed first are the three syntheses that make up the *Commentary on the Sentences* by Peter Lombard, the university evaluation that allowed him to pursue a teaching career, followed by the *Summa Contra Gentiles* and the *Summa Theologiae*. Then came the *Disputed Questions* and the biblical commentaries, which constituted the core of the Master's teaching, and finally several dozen works of polemics, treatises, expert opinions, and *Opuscules* (minor works), some of them highly developed. These testify to the theologian's active interest in the issues of his day: defending the right of religious to live by begging or to teach at the university, or taking an interest in the movement of the heart or in the nature of political regimes, which are also matters of theological reflection. Thomas did not shy away from the requests of religious or civil dignitaries, or even of the simple brothers. As a son of St. Dominic, he was likewise a preacher of important sermons, several of which have been preserved, and a mystic who worked to sing the glory of the Incarnate Word, notably by composing the Office for *Corpus Christi* to honor the Eucharist. In saying the *Tantum ergo*, the faithful throughout the world place on their lips and in their hearts the words of one of the greatest Christian theologians of all time.

The importance of the work of St. Thomas is not, however, primarily due to its quantity. As one of the best contemporary experts on Thomas, Father Jean-Pierre Torrell, explains, the work of the Dominican theologian developed along three main lines.[20] The first

19. A brief catalogue of the works of St. Thomas first compiled by Gilles Emery and subsequently updated can be found in Jean-Pierre Torrell, OP, *Saint Thomas Aquinas*, vol. 1, *The Person and His Work*, 3rd ed., trans. Matthew K. Minerd and Robert Royal (The Catholic University of America Press, 2023), 383–436. This third English edition of Torrell's biography supersedes the prior two.

20. Jean-Pierre Torrell, *Saint Thomas Aquinas: Spiritual Master,* trans. Robert Royal (The Catholic University of America Press, 1996), 2–3.

is the speculative dimension for which he is especially renowned. It is that of the intelligence of the faith, that is, the effort to understand everything that is believed through revelation, set out by the professions of this same faith, and expressed in the catechism. This line of thought has been followed by the commentators of St. Thomas, among the best known of which are the Frenchman John Capreolus in the fifteenth century, the Italian Thomas de Vio, known as Cajetan, in the sixteenth century, and the Spaniard John of St. Thomas in the seventeenth century. But Thomas also practiced another line of study that we would today call historical-positive. As a commentator on scripture, he never ceased gathering material from the fathers of the church who had carefully studied it before him, but he was also interested in the history of the councils. As Jean-Pierre Torrell notes, it is certainly this line, transformed into positive theology, that has been the most developed, leading to notable progress in exegesis, patristics, and church history up to our time. Finally, Thomas took a perspective in his theological work that can be described as mystical.[21]

What we call theology is far from the leisure and pleasure of a Christian intellectual for St. Thomas; rather, it is a privileged way to enter into the mystery of God and of our vocation: to live the filial vocation of the children of God. What we call theology, and what St. Thomas calls *sacra doctrina*, is in fact a science that is at once speculative and practical. By relating two truths, one of which, better known, plays the role of explanatory principle, and the other that of explained conclusion, Thomas presents the whole of revealed truth "in a coherent synthesis which reproduces in a human mode something of the intelligibility of the divine plan for the world and in the history of salvation."[22] This presentation necessarily leads to the search for life in God, in a relationship of knowledge and love with him, in communion with all the faithful. One might be frightened by this requirement, but the scientific rigor, the precision, and the tech-

21. Torrell, *Saint Thomas Aquinas*, 3.

22. Jean-Pierre Torrell, "Thomas Aquinas," *Dictionnaire critique de théologie*, under the direction of Jean-Yves Lacoste, 3rd ed., revised and expanded by Olivier Riaudel and Jean-Yves Lacoste, "Quadrige" (Presses Universitaires de France, 2007), 1393.

nicality of the lexicon did not alter the beauty of expression and the spirituality of the discourse in St. Thomas. Alain Michel noted:

> Like all the scholastics, he sought to establish a language of the absolute. This undoubtedly requires determination, but an open mind and clarity are also necessary. One has the impression, when reading Thomas, of encountering the same virtues and the same difficulties as in a figure of Johann Sebastian Bach: power of abstraction, extreme penetration of sensitivity.[23]

A century after St. Thomas Aquinas, Meister Eckhart († 1328), followed by John Tauler († 1361), studied the ways in which the deification of man is achieved by establishing the link between the incarnation of the word and the indwelling of the Trinity in the soul. Blessed Henry Suso († 1365) faced the mystery of Christ's suffering humanity and drew from it a doctrine of the abnegation of one's own will.

The science of God was not reserved in the Order of Preachers to academics with diplomas. St. Catherine of Siena († 1380), for example, led a life of penance and prayer rich in mystical experiences and apostolic daring. She could not write, or could barely write, but dictated to those around her the words of her *Dialogue* of love with God. Her insights into the church and Christ, religious orders and Christian obedience expressed through powerful images, constitute a sure doctrine. Mariette Canévet, a specialist in the fathers of the church, has, for example, highlighted the originality with which St. Catherine of Siena conceived spiritual discernment. Distinguishing in the human soul three powers: memory, intelligence, and will, Catherine affirms that when free will chooses evil by turning away from God, then the three powers are affected because of their unity.[24] As the Sienese saint explains: "Understanding is deluded at the sight of [worldly pleasures], and the will in loving them (for it loves with it

23. Alain Michel, *Théologiens et Mystiques au Moyen Âge: La Poétique de Dieu, Ve-XVe siècles*, Choix présenté et traduit du latin par Alain Michel (Gallimard, 1997), 67.

24. Mariette Canévet, *Le discernement spirituel à travers les âges* (Éd. du Cerf, 2014), 166–78.

should not love), and the memory in holding on to them."[25] "Thus," comments Canévet, "if the love we have for God unifies the powers, conversely the love for sensible realities scatters in a frantic race that never satisfies."[26] God is One in Three Persons; he who approaches him is called to interior unification. Paul VI understood what light St. Catherine of Siena brought to the understanding of the Christian mystery, and he proclaimed her a Doctor of the Church on October 4, 1970.

The Rosary, a Dominican Prayer

Jordan of Saxony, the first successor of St. Dominic, concludes his account of the origins of the Order of Preachers by recounting the ordeal of a certain novice, Brother Bernard of Bologna, at the beginning of the thirteenth century. The unfortunate man, subjected to diabolical temptations, was stirring up trouble and ill-will in the community. Master Jordan finally discovered the adversary's game:

> This cruel harassment of Brother Bernard was the first occasion that moved us to establish the custom of singing the *Salve Regina* after compline at Bologna. . . . How many tears of devotion have sprung from this holy praise of God's venerable Mother? How many hearts of those who sang or listened has it not melted, how often has it not softened bitterness and installed fervor in its place? . . . A certain man, both religious and trustworthy, has told me that, in spirit, he often saw the Mother of our Lord prostrate before her Son praying for the security of the whole Order, as the friars were singing: "Turn, then, most gracious advocate, thine eyes of mercy toward us."[27]

The Marian devotion of Dominic and his first companions cannot be doubted. The contemplation of the divine mysteries, strengthened by study and cultivated in prayer, was built on the

25. Cf. Catherine of Siena, *Dialogue*, The Classics of Western Spirituality edition, chap. 51, 104.

26. Canévet, *Le discernement spirituel à travers les âges*, 169.

27. Jordan of Saxony, *Libellus*, 120; Lehner, 82.

preacher's great love for the Virgin Mary. Dominic and his first companions were the first witnesses to this. The *Lives of the Brethren*, written a few decades after Dominic's death, abounds in the maternal interventions of the Virgin with her Son. The Rule of Muño of Zamora, written for the members of the Order of Penance, prescribes that those who cannot read should recite a certain number of *Our Fathers* accompanied by an equal number of *Hail Marys.*[28] Many friars, praying personally, were accustomed to greeting the Virgin, especially before her altars and images. The repetition of the *Hail Mary* was in fact accompanied by bows, genuflections, and prostrations that were repeated a certain number of times, generally a multiple of ten: fifty times, a hundred times. Blessed Romeo of Livia († 1261), who had known St. Dominic personally, was buried, according to the testimony of Bernard Gui, still holding in his hand the knotted cord that he used to count the thousand *Hail Marys* with which he used to greet the Blessed Virgin every day.[29] From the fifteenth century onward, Dominic's name became attached to the devotion of the rosary, which consisted of meditating on scripture through the alternating recitation of the *Lord's Prayer* and ten *Hail Marys.*[30] The word rosary was used in the Middle Ages to designate a collection or chain of texts. When the word is applied to the prayer repeating the Gospel greeting, it evokes a garland of roses with which the Virgin Mary is crowned. These flowers are, in reality, each of the prayers that the believer recites to meditate on the mysteries of Christ's life, uniting his prayer with that of Christ's Mother. This prayer undoubtedly has its immediate origin in the milieu of the hermits of the Rhine valley. A German Carthusian, Adolphus of Essen († 1439), practiced the regular recitation of fifty *Hail Marys* even before he entered the monastery. He tried, beyond the repeated words of the angelic salutation, to fix his attention on Jesus himself. A few

28. "Regula Fratrum et Sororum Ordinis de Penitentia Beati Dominici," in Gilles Gérard Meersseman, *Dossier de l'Ordre de la Pénitence au* XIII*e* siècle, 147 [c. VI, 15–20].

29. Cf. *Maria: Études sur la Sainte Vierge*, ed. Hubert du Manoir SJ, vol. 2 (Beauchesne, 1952), 747–48.

30. Rigorous historical clarification by André Duval, "Rosaire," *Dictionnaire de spiritualité*, vol. 13 (Beauchesne, 1988), col. 937–80.

years later, when he became prior of his Carthusian monastery, he used this method to help Brother Dominic of Prussia († 1460) to get out of the state of sadness in which the latter found himself. Dominic had the idea of dividing the life of Jesus into fifty stages and wrote several series of short phrases to extend and particularize each *Hail Mary*. Since in the Flemish countries the Psalter of Mary, composed of 150 *Hail Marys*, was practiced, Dominic of Prussia tripled the number of his short phrases, or *clausulae*, to correspond to the Gospels of the Infancy, the Passion, and the Resurrection and what followed from it. The mysteries thus contemplated formed groups of five and were described as joyful, sorrowful, or glorious according to the stages of the Lord's life to which they referred. The Annunciation to Mary opens the cycle of joyful mysteries; the Coronation of the Virgin into Heaven closes that of the glorious mysteries. The meditation of each mystery is followed by the recitation of ten *Hail Marys*, which are preceded by an *Our Father*. Each series—also called the rosary—is composed of five mysteries. The threefold series of joyful, sorrowful, and glorious mysteries was established in the fifteenth century. The Luminous Mysteries complete the list of episodes in the life of Christ that the rosary proposes for meditation, and this latter set was introduced by the Holy Father John Paul II in his apostolic letter *Rosarium Virginis Mariae* (2002).

The rosary might have remained a predominantly monastic practice if a Dominican had not undertaken to promote it. Born around 1428, Brother Alain de la Roche was active in the convents of Lille, Douai, and Ghent. As an enthusiastic and innovative preacher of the psalter of the Virgin Mary, Brother Alain was aware of the Carthusian development of Marian devotion and made the recitation of this psalter the main obligation of the confraternity of the Virgin and St. Dominic that he founded in Douai in 1470.[31] The confreres undertook to meet regularly in a chapel of the conventual church to pray together in this manner. The success was immediate, and ten years later, the Dominicans claimed a monopoly on the establishment of

31. For the work of Alain de la Roche, see *Beato Alano della Rupe, Il Salterio di Gesù e di Maria: Genesi, storia e rivelazioni del santissimo Rosario. Opere complete del beato Alano della Rupe*, ed. Don Roberto Paola (Ancilla Editrice, 2006).

these confraternities. In Germany, Italy, and France, groups of the faithful were formed. An image was created for the places where they prayed in this way in which the Virgin Mary was usually depicted giving the rosary to St. Dominic. We have gone from Dominic the Carthusian to Dominic the preacher! The idea that St. Dominic was the founder of the rosary confraternities was thus encouraged by this image. Pious legends were spread by the Dominicans to justify these representations: the Virgin is said to have given the rosary to the father of the Preachers in the forest of Bouconne, near Toulouse. Pope Pius V, although a Dominican, spoke of this as a pious belief, but his successor, Gregory XIII, fully accepted the Dominican origin of the rosary in the bull of 1573 and instituted its liturgical feast on October 7 in thanksgiving for the victory won at Lepanto over the Turks by the Christian princes on October 7, 1571.[32] St. Catherine of Siena, considered to be the instigator and patroness of the Dominican reform, was often depicted from the seventeenth century onward as a parallel and feminine complement to St. Dominic in representations of the giving of the rosary.

Three elements have contributed to the worldwide diffusion of the rosary until our day. First, this prayer is associated with a small object, which can be made of the most humble or most noble materials—prisoners have made them out of breadcrumbs or cardboard. The object is so discreet and reassuring that it is slipped into one's pocket and may be placed into the hands of the deceased. The Dominicans, followed by many religious orders, made it part of their habit. Second, the rosary is simple and universal. It includes the basic Christian prayers: *The Creed*, *Our Father*, *Hail Mary*, *Glory be to the Father*. It is based on the best-known episodes in the life of Jesus and is a prayer for lay people as well as clerics. It can be prayed alone or in groups, in a church, and while working or walking. In Japan and Brazil, Christian communities that had just been evangelized only to be abandoned to their fate were able to transmit the rudi-

32. *Bullarium Ordinis Fratrum Praedicatorum* (Romae, 1733), vol. 5, 318. Concerning the history of the Rosary and its spirituality, see Albert Énard, *Le Rosaire: Prier avec Marie*, preface by Mgr Pierre Plateau (Éd. du Cerf, 1987); *Il rosario: teologia, storia, spiritualità*, ed. Riccardo Barile (Edizioni San Domenico, 2011).

ments of Christian instruction by using this method. Finally, the Dominicans were able to promote this devotion with firmness and efficiency in every age. In the nineteenth century, the felicitous invention of the Living Rosary by Pauline Jaricot of Lyon was the cause of a vigorous revival on the part of the Order of Preachers due to its success. The Perpetual Rosary succeeded the Living Rosary. The apparitions at Lourdes in 1858 led, fifty years later, to the creation of a Dominican Rosary pilgrimage. Marian magazines were born, with hundreds of thousands of copies printed: *La Couronne de Marie* and the *Revue du Rosaire* in France, *The Rosary Magazine* in England, *Il Rosario e la Nuova Pompei* in Italy, *El Rosario* in Spain, etc. In France in the 1950s, a laywoman, Paulette Couvreur, and Father Joseph Eyquem established Rosary Teams: missionary groups of Marian prayer meeting in the homes of participants. In Italy, at the heart of the twentieth century, Father Enrico Rossetti gave new impetus and life to the *Rosarianti* association in a moving speech to children, adolescents, and young people.

In 1952, the same year he was awarded the Nobel Prize for Literature, the French writer François Mauriac testified to the ever-renewed popularity of the rosary from the fifteenth to the twentieth century:

> It is in its most humble aspect that the devotion of the rosary touches me. . . . Every Christian, especially in times of temptation, if he is determined not to give in to it, recites the Rosary, just as a swimmer who is out of his depths is no longer aware of the imperceptible movement of his hands, so the Christian who has recourse to the rosary no longer knows that his lips are moving: he is no longer carrying his prayer, it is his prayer that carries him. He entrusts himself to this monotonous flow of words; each *Hail Mary* is the little wave that brings him closer to the land.
>
> Devotion to the Rosary manifests itself in an even humbler form: this object in my pocket, this chain, this pile of black beads that the Christian clutches when things go wrong. I have not parted with this rosary for twenty years: the one I held during an operation when my life was at stake and I had to be kept awake. One of my hands was clutching the little rosary as

> if it were alive. There is nothing superstitious about this transfer by the Christian of an infinite reality into a material that signifies it. . . . Even the beautiful spirits, if they wish to remain pure, know well that at certain times the most humble means are the best: they do not ignore any buoy; they cling to that chain which the Church throws them, linking them to a whole immense cooperative of prayers which takes no account of death, which associates in an uninterrupted supplication the militant Church with the suffering Church; they allow themselves to be carried by this tide not to the highest dwelling place, but to the door where the prodigal Son, whom we all are, waits with bare feet, hungry, shivering, for the Father to open the door for him.[33]

Democracy and Dominican Life

In a book entitled *To Govern is to Serve*, Jacques Dalarun notes that "medieval religious communities served as a laboratory for the development of modern 'governance.'"[34] Contemporary democracy has, in fact, inherited an electoral parlance forged in convents. The words "poll," "scrutiny," "suffrage," and "ballot" belong to the Dominican vocabulary. Five centuries before the moral lessons of the Enlightenment, the Preachers developed a wisdom in governing that was destined to preserve the unity of the order while allowing for the active participation of each of its members. This sage form of government also provided the Dominicans with the means to remain faithful to their founding inspiration while adapting to changes in culture and times. At each new stage of their history, the Preachers felt the need to hear, as if for the first time, the good news of the Gospel. Thus the *raison d'être* of the Dominicans is as valid in the twenty-first century as it was in the thirteenth. But as an institutional structure, the order could have missed the mark and proved inadequate over time. The internal organization of the Preachers, which is completely original, has played and continues to play an important

33. Henri-Dominique Laval, *Le Rosaire ou les trois mystères de la rose*, préface by François Mauriac (Plon, 1952) [unpaginated].

34. Jacques Dalarun, *Gouverner, c'est servir: Essai de démocratie médiévale* (Alma, 2013), 15.

role in the success of the ongoing renewal of the order through the ages. Before exploring the current governmental structure and its implications, we must try to explain this by first recalling the genesis of this organization.[35]

When Dominic and his brothers who were gathered in Toulouse turned to Pope Innocent III in 1215 to ask for confirmation of their community, the pope demanded—before any recognition—that they base the principles of the young foundation on an already approved rule. The religious enthusiasm of the early thirteenth century and the many abuses that had resulted (i.e., questioning the authority of the pope, deviation from sound Catholic doctrine) had led the Holy See to warn Christians against the groups of unchecked preachers who were roaming the roads and towns. Therefore, the friars turned to the rule of St. Augustine. This choice was not arbitrary, and neither was the way it was made. According to Jordan of Saxony, companion and first successor of St. Dominic as Master of the Order, the rule of St. Augustine was not imposed by the founder but chosen by all the first friars.[36] Moreover, this rule indicates from the beginning what the purpose of life in the communities would be: "First of all, why are you gathered together if not to dwell together in unanimity, being one heart and one soul in God?" Dominican democracy can only be understood in relation to this search for unanimity, and thus it stands out from modern democracies that only understand this mode of government as a balance of power between a majority and a minority, a balance of power that must be developed by all means for the greater benefit of the majority of the people. Humbert of Romans, the fifth Master of the Order, indicates, in commenting on the *Constitutions*, that "unity of hearts is a precept."[37] The whole community must therefore move with one heart toward this common goal: the salvation of souls. It is from this rule that the Dominican *Constitutions*,

35. This chapter is based on a historical and canonical study by Father Vincent Tierny, OP, kindly made available to us. We would like to thank him warmly for this. One may also refer to Gert Melville, *Le comunità religiose nel Medioevo: Storia e modelli di vita* (Morcelliana, 2020), 245–55.

36. Jordan of Saxony, *Libellus*, 41; Bériou-Hodel, 629–30.

37. Humbert de Romans, *Expositio in Constitutiones*, in *Opera de vita regulari*, ed. Joachim Joseph Berthier, vol. 2 (Marietti, 1956), 3.

initially called customs,[38] were drawn up. Between 1216 and 1236, as foundations multiplied throughout Europe, vocations poured in and forced the first friars to provide the order with well-structured legislation. The regular meetings of the general chapters during these years allowed these first *Constitutions* to be drawn up and amended.

Although Pope Honorius III had given Dominic himself full powers to organize the order in the first years of its existence, the holy founder convened the first General Chapter in Bologna for Pentecost 1220. He did so in a particular frame of mind. A friar who was present tells us: "This friar Dominic used to say: 'I deserve to be deposed, because I am useless and slack,' and he humbled himself greatly in everything. As the friars did not want to depose him, it seemed good to this friar Dominic that definitors should be instituted who would have power, as much over himself as over the others and over the whole chapter, to rule, define and order as long as the chapter lasted."[39] It was clear to Dominic that the responsibility for the order did not belong to him alone but was to be shared by the friars themselves, who would appoint delegates from each community to participate in the general chapters. After St. Dominic, three Masters of the Order worked to shape the *Constitutions* and give them their definitive shape: Jordan of Saxony (1222–1237), who translated Dominic's intuitions, Raymond of Peñafort (1238–1240), who ordered the *Constitutions* in a manner that was more in line with logic and law, and Humbert of Romans (1254–1263), who brought out the spirit of the *Constitutions* through his commentaries. For a more precise view of the first *Constitutions*, it is necessary to refer to the legislation resulting from the Most General Chapter of 1236 held in Paris under the authority of Brother Jordan of Saxony. A "Most General Chapter" (*capitulum generalissimum* in Latin) is organized and "celebrated," according to Dominican terminology, following an extraor-

38. Jordan of Saxony mentions the "stricter customs on food and fasts, on beds and woollens" inherited in part from the Premonstratensians. The full text of these *Constitutions* no longer exists. See Jordan of Saxony, *Libellus*, 42; Bériou-Hodel, 630. See also Antonin H. Thomas, *De oudste Constituties van de Dominicanen*, Bibliothèque de la Revue d'histoire ecclésiastique 42 (Leuven, 1965).

39. *Acta canonizationis*, Bologna, 33, Deposition of Brother Rodolfo; Bériou-Hodel, 730.

dinary procedure. The text of this legislation can still be consulted by deciphering the *Codex of Rodez* kept in the general archives of the order, in the convent of Santa Sabina in Rome.[40] It is the source of all the constitutional legislation of the order.[41]

The first organization of the order is linked to its division into provinces. A province is, in principle, a geographical territory that groups together a certain number of convents and houses (as of 2021, the order had about forty provinces). A province is erected according to three criteria: a sufficient number of brothers and convents, a territory distinct from that of the other provinces, and the capacity to ensure the religious and intellectual formation of the "sons" it is able to receive. The provinces enjoy a strong autonomy and play an important role in the government of the order through the provincial chapters, which elect the provincial priors and the definitors who will participate in the general chapters.

At the top of the hierarchy of Dominican norms, we find a supreme juridical body composed of both the general chapter and the Master of the Order, successor of St. Dominic. The general chapter and the Master of the Order have authority over all the provinces that make up the order. The norms of government are in the form of *Constitutions*, or ordinances, both of which impose general norms on the entire order, with the distinction made regarding the degree of importance and permanence. For a decree to be incorporated into the *Constitution*, it must first have been approved by three successive general chapters. In the present state of Dominican legislation, this means that it can only really become constitutional after nine years. During these nine years, both the provincials and the definitors (who represent their communities of origin) have had the opportunity to vote at one of the general chapters and are thus made coresponsible for the decisions reached. Ordinances are equally binding but can be modified or abrogated by a single general chapter.

40. See Dominicus Planzer, "De Codice Ruthenensi miscellaneo in Tabulario Ordinis Praedicatorum asservato," AFP 5 (1935): 5–123; Thomas, *De oudste Constituties*.

41. *Liber Constitutionum et Ordinationum Fratrum Ordinis Praedicatorum* (Curia generalitia, 2018).

All these norms are binding according to a principle laid down by St. Dominic himself and later solemnly proclaimed, according to which the laws and *Constitutions* do not oblige the friars under pain of sin but of sanction, wanting the friars to assume them in light of divine wisdom.[42] In a famous passage in his commentary on the *Constitutions*, Humbert of Romans states that St. Dominic declared himself ready to erase the handwritten text of his rules with a small knife, as one would erase parchment to correct an error, rather than see the friars fail to observe this principle of the obligation of the laws *ad poenam tantum*, that is, only to be punished by sanction, not under pain of sin.[43] This is explained by the apostolic vocation of the friars, whose preaching mission is not always compatible with the demands of regular observance:

> It is necessary to be perfectly at ease to give priority to charity over observance when necessary. Then, far from having committed a sin, one has accomplished a virtuous act. But the concern for regularity requires an external sanction for this external failure.[44]

It is not a question of dispensing with Dominican laws for oneself and for one's personal comfort. This would be a scandalous attitude on the part of religious who are solemnly committed by vow. The obedience mentioned in the formula of profession, including chastity and poverty, cannot be a pious vow that would not entail any consequences. The *Constitutions* give superiors the power to dispense with the regular observances of the order for a just cause, especially in favor of study, preaching, or the good of souls. It is clear that the Dominican *Constitutions* was established around the proper end of the mission of the Preachers: preaching for the salvation of souls. It is in relation to this goal that the laws of the order are elaborated.

42. *Liber Constitutionum et Ordinationum*, no. 281, 81: "Leges nostrae et ordinationes superiorum non obligant fratres ad culpam sed ad pœnam, nisi propter praeceptum vel contemptum."

43. Humbert de Romans, *Expositio in Constitutiones*, c. XIV, 46.

44. Pie-Raymond Régamey, *Un ordre ancien dans le monde actuel: Les dominicains*, Cahiers Saint-Jacques, 25 (Paris, 1958), 20.

Having sketched the broad outlines of the organization of the government of the order, it is also necessary to understand its coherence. As we know, a democratic system can suffer from serious drawbacks: instability, lowering of standards, lack of dynamism, etc. Why be attached to such a fragile system and how, if at all, can we make it produce results?

The Belgian sociologist Léo Moulin has devoted several studies to religious law. It was he who popularized the image of the Dominican *Constitutions* as a "cathedral of constitutional law."[45] According to his analysis, the system for the elaboration of the *Constitutions*, with the three successive general chapters (a series composed of a chapter of definitors, then a chapter of provincials, and finally an elective chapter composed of provincials and a greater number of definitors), allows for a distribution of the legislative function among several assemblies. This pluricameralism gave great stability to the law, but it also allowed for the development of a real democracy since the assemblies were made up of different friars who had to deal with the same texts each time. A regular turnover in the brothers participating in the legislation of the order inevitably takes place. It is impossible, in principle, for a group of friars to "settle down" for long periods to govern the order.

An axiom from Roman law was used by Pope Innocent III and later canonized in 1298 by Pope Boniface VIII in the so-called *Regulae iuris* of the *Corpus Iuris Canonici*: "What concerns everyone must be approved by everyone."[46] Its field of application has often been discussed. The fact is that Dominican legislation presents, in particular, an application in the law of religious. It is not a question of denying superiors a certain authority but of allowing each part of the order to participate in its government. How does this translate into practice? First of all, by the participation of each of the prov-

45. Léo Moulin, *Le monde vivant des religieux: Dominicains—Jésuites—Bénédictins* (Calmann-Lévy, 1964).

46. On the adage "Quod omnes tangit, ab omnibus tractari et approbari debet," see the article by Yves Congar, *Revue historique de droit français et étranger* 35 (1958): 210–59. The axiom "Necesse est omnes suam auctoritatem praestare, ut, quod omnes similiter tangit, ab omnibus comprobetur" goes back to the Code of Justinian.

inces in the general chapters through their provincial priors and their elected definitors. Each entity of the order is affected by the decisions that are made during the general chapters, so each one must be able to make its voice heard, regardless of the number of members of the province or its geographical location. The same applies at the provincial level. During the chapters that take place every four years, each convent sends to the assembly its prior and one or more delegates, known by the Latin word *socius*, that is, companion or ally, in order to make the decisions that are necessary for the smooth running of the province. And at the conventual level, each professed brother must actively participate in the chapter. What concerns each level of the order is therefore discussed and approved or rejected by all. Moreover, in elections, the numerical majority wins the vote; no other element, for example, seniority in the order, is taken into account. Regulation is exercised through what the Dominican historian William Hinnebusch has called two parallel and balanced chains of power: a downward chain of command, which includes the Master General, the provincial priors, and the conventual priors exercising authority over the friars by means of commands, formal precepts, dispensations, confirmations or cancellations of elections, and canonical visitations. On the other hand, an ascending chain of control of authority is exercised by the communities through the frequent election of superiors (every three years for the conventual priors, every four years for the provincials, and every nine years for the Master of the Order) as well as through representation at the provincial and general chapters allowing the exercise of legislative power.[47] These two chains complement each other: each friar can feel responsible, but the authority of the Master of the Order, the prior provincial, and the conventual prior also guarantees the unity of each entity and the proper functioning of the institutions.

This Dominican organization bears witness to a certain optimism. It is the belief that each brother can and will invest himself in the growth of the order by seeking the common good, not only his

47. William A. Hinnebusch, *The Dominicans: A Short History* (Alba House, 1975).

own good.[48] On entering the order, each one is asked the question: "What do you desire?" He or she is invited to answer: "God's mercy and yours." The religious recognizes that he or she is fallible but trusts the community to which he or she belongs. The unity aimed for in this model of democratic government can only be achieved with God's help. The Holy Spirit is the inexhaustible source of the brothers' and sisters' desire for unity. Before each chapter, before each election of superiors, the Holy Spirit is invoked in prayer during the Eucharistic celebration, so that he may be at work as the members of the chapter meet. This is the condition for this mode of government not to become rigid but rather to continue to bear fruit in the order so that the Dominicans may continue contemplating and to announce to the world what they have contemplated.

Praedicatores Inquisitores: The Shameful Part of the Heritage?

When St. Dominic died in Bologna, the Order of Preachers was already founded and had spread throughout Europe. What we call the Inquisition, in the singular and with a capital "I," did not yet exist. Its history, however, accompanies that of the Dominicans, and one would be accused of partiality, not without reason, if he refrained from mentioning it when drawing up a summary, even an abbreviated one, of the order's heritage. This task is not without difficulty, so strong is the popular imagination of this institution. For most of our contemporaries, an inquisitor is a *serial killer* from the Middle Ages dressed in black and white, cruel, and fanatical, essentially the character of "Bernardo Gui," played with talent by F. Murray Abraham in Jean-Jacques Annaud's film *The Name of the Rose*.[49] But there are great differences between this film and the true story.

The Inquisition began in the thirteenth century as a judicial procedure that allowed the judge, even without an accuser, to open an investigation (*inquisitio*) into a person whose faith was suspect,

48. For the required optimism, see Philippe Toxé, "L'esprit et la lettre du droit de la famille dominicaine," *Mémoire dominicaine* 13, no. 2 (1998): 13–15.

49. Jean-Jacques Annaud's successful film *The Name of the Rose* dates from 1986 and is based on the theme of Umberto Eco's famous 1980 Italian novel.

to hear witnesses, and to pronounce a sentence. Around 1230, the Inquisition came to mean an ecclesiastical court of exception, working in cooperation with the civil authority, usually by delegation or by papal order.[50] The Order of Preachers was young and susceptible to ecclesiastical demands; its members were capable of conducting a written procedure. The Dominicans, as well as the Franciscans and secular priests, were invited by the papacy to collaborate in the office for the repression of heresy. St. Dominic died in 1221, before the foundation of the Inquisition, but his sons became and remained, in the eyes of many, "instruments of ecclesiastical power and even agents of political propaganda in the service of the Holy See."[51] The Dominicans, moreover, contributed to this association through a deliberate anachronism by claiming Dominic as the first inquisitor from the beginning of the fourteenth century. This baseless claim was repeated until the eighteenth century. In 1666, Father Vincenzo Maria Fontana entitled a chapter of his *Sacrum theatrum dominicanum* "*S. Pater Dominicus Primus in Ecclesia Inquisitor.*"[52] In order to affirm this, he did not hesitate to draw on the most varied authors: the medieval Dominicans Bernard Gui and Nicolas Eymeric, the Spanish Jesuit Sebastian Salelles, the poet Dante Alighieri, and Pope Sixtus V.

From the beginning of the institution in the thirteenth century, the inquisitors, in particular the Dominican inquisitors, met with sporadic resistance, as witnessed by the attacks on the judges of Avignonet in 1242 and on Brother Peter of Verona in 1252. (The latter, canonized as a martyr in 1253, was the second saint of the Order of Preachers.) The Catholic population, however, does not seem to have contested the validity of the Inquisition. As the medievalist Charles de La Roncière wrote: "At the end of the fifteenth century . . . no one seems to me to have been able to judge and explicitly denounce

50. Laurent Albaret, "Les Prêcheurs et l'Inquisition: L'ordre des Prêcheurs et son histoire en France méridionale," *Cahiers de Fanjeaux* 36 (2001): 319–41.

51. The expression is by André Vauchez, quoted by Albaret, "Les Prêcheurs et l'Inquisition," 337.

52. Vincentius Maria Fontana, *Sacrum theatrum dominicanum* (Romae: Ex Typographia Nicolai Angeli Tinassii, 1666), Pars tertia, caput I, "De inquisitoribus sanguine laureatis," 498.

. . . the Inquisition as an abuse."[53] There is no questioning of the Inquisition as an institution, especially since the church itself has not ceased, since the censure of Robert le Bougre, to repress its excesses.[54] The question of the philosophical and theological basis of the Inquisition was not really debated until the eighteenth century, with the exception of Erasmus, who was perhaps the first to denounce the contradiction between the actions of the clerics and the teaching of the Gospel.[55] In the Middle Ages, any spiritual divergence was perceived as an extremely serious matter: offending the church of God offended God himself and compromised the common salvation. It was a sort of crime of divine treason. The offence of heresy was felt to be a diabolical undertaking, and it follows that the clerics gradually built up an increasingly negative response to it.

As a result, the historiography of the eighteenth century saw two types of works in opposition. Without batting an eyelid, pious and traditional writers repeated the legend of Dominic as the first inquisitor and that the brothers naturally followed in the founder's supposed footsteps. Father Charles-Louis Richard, a Parisian Dominican and author of a monumental *Dictionnaire universel . . . des sciences ecclésiastiques*, thus asserted in 1760 that "Innocent III and Honorius III named Saint Dominic the first Inquisitor General; and twelve years after his death, in 1233, Gregory IX named two friars of his Order to exercise the same office." In the face of these typical accounts, the French Enlightenment saw the development of a narrative that was radically critical of the Inquisition to the point of rejecting Dominic and the Dominicans at the same time.

The most famous example of this is offered by Voltaire. Virulent and talented, the philosopher launched the polemic of numbers by

53. Charles de La Roncière, "L'Inquisition a-t-elle été perçue comme un abus au Moyen Âge," in *Inquisition et Pouvoir*, ed. Gabriel Audisio (Publications de l'université de Provence, 2004), 24.

54. The first inquisitor of Northern France, the Dominican Robert le Bougre, was deposed and sentenced to life imprisonment in 1239 for abuse of power and notorious injustice.

55. Erasmus, *Contra sanctam haereticorum Inquisitionem*, title IV, objection 22, in *Opera omnia*, vol. IX (Leiden), col. 1054D–1055D.

accusing the Inquisition of having condemned "more than a hundred thousand so-called sorcerers . . . and a greater number of immolated heretics."[56] Statistics were used to impress people, while appealing to the "scientific" emphasis of this period. In his *Traité de l'intolérance*, Voltaire harshly condemned the methods of the Holy Office, and in his poem *La Pucelle*, he placed St. Dominic in hell. Published in 1769, the article "Inquisition" in the *Philosophical Dictionary* begins with the words: "The Inquisition is, as is well known, an admirable and entirely Christian invention to make the Pope and the monks more powerful and to make a whole people hypocritical."[57] The author concludes his description of the *auto-da-fé* with the following words: "They sing, Mass is said, and men are killed." After such charges, described with such talent, Dominic and his followers seemed definitively doomed to opprobrium, especially since the Voltairian critique was taken up in the article on the Inquisition in the *Encyclopaedia* written by the Chevalier de Jaucourt. Also, in 1778, on the eve of the revolution, Mirabeau published a poem in twelve songs in Amsterdam entitled *Guzmanade ou l'établissement de l'Inquisition*. A new penal philosophy had taken the opposite view of the real nature of the Inquisition, so much so that the Dominicans were carried away with it.

In 1839, after the revolutionary break in France, Father Lacordaire, a young Parisian priest already famous for his oratorical talent and his gifts as a polemicist understood that his project of living in France as a Dominican required an explanation of the phenomenon of the Inquisition to public opinion. Before entering the novitiate in Italy, he published a *Mémoire pour le rétablissement en France de l'Ordre des Frères Prêcheurs*, which was intended, among other things, to combat preconceived ideas about the Inquisition. In a long letter addressed to Dom Guéranger in 1839, founder of the Benedictine abbey of Solesmes, the novice Lacordaire described his point of view:

> I entered the Order of St. Dominic only after having studied and understood its nature, which seemed to me to be absolutely opposed to the popular opinion that has been formed of it.

56. Voltaire, *Commentaire sur le Traité des délits et des peines*, in *Œuvres*, "Bibliothèque de la Pléiade" (Gallimard, 1961), 785.

57. Voltaire, *Dictionnaire philosophique* (Garnier, 1951), 746–49.

> There are few learned men in France who do not regard St. Dominic and the Dominicans as burners of men, as an order founded to defend the Church by iron and fire. If it were so, I would never have given him even the nail of my little finger.... No doubt he was not a nineteenth-century liberal, but . . . he understood the inadequacy of force to save the Church, and the need to have recourse to an apostolic regeneration. . . . It was this peaceful view that made him what he was and what he is. . . . I therefore bring to the restoration of order in France the spirit of poverty, gentleness and unction of St. Dominic; the profound persuasion that the apostolic spirit is the only true bulwark of the Church, and that force, a secondary and unfortunate means, is never more than the effect of a legitimate need for defense, in which the Church must temper the ardor of its own people much more than it must excite it. The Inquisition is over. . . . We must therefore leave to the past what is past, and draw from the ruins that which is immortal in its nature, that is to say, the spirit of Jesus Christ, the spirit of grace and love. If God grants me the grace, I will leave the Order of St. Dominic in the reputation of the sweetest order in the world.[58]

The enterprise of Lacordaire was only partially successful. In the violent polemics that arose in France from the time of the Third Republic, the black legend of the Inquisition found new vigor: politicians, authors of dictionaries, playwrights, historians, authors of school textbooks, painters, and caricaturists associated Catholicism with inquisitorial barbarity. Freethinkers, rationalists, and atheists were not the only ones to associate Christianity with judicial arbitrariness; some Catholic preachers and polemicists praised the legitimate violence exercised by the Inquisition. In the heat of the controversy, the memory of the gentle face of St. Dominic and his sons often hardened into a grimace, and St. Dominic and the French Dominicans were held jointly responsible for this crime. The *Grand Dictionnaire*

58. Henri-Dominique Lacordaire to Dom Guéranger, La Quercia, August 10, 1839, in Henri-Dominique Lacordaire, *Correspondance: Répertoire. Tome 1. 1816–1839*, ed. Guy Bedouelle and Christoph-Alois Martin (Éd. du Cerf, 2001), 1116–17.

Universel du XIXe siècle offers a particularly interesting case in point. This freethinking, anticlerical monument built by Pierre Larousse and a whole team anonymously grouped around him developed the theme of the Catholic Inquisition with entries that aroused the readers' horror and reprobation.[59]

The nineteenth century saw the death of the Inquisition as had been historically known. It even lost its name in 1908, when Pope Pius X reformed the Roman Curia. The word disappeared from the vocabulary of the Roman dicasteries, and the surviving congregation of the Holy Office devoted itself mainly to the examination and possible condemnation of works or doctrines judged to be dangerous in relation to orthodoxy or morality. In this capacity, it intervened in theological disputes during the twentieth century, such as those linked to the Modernist crisis. Despite its transformation, the institution was no less contested. On November 8, 1963, Cardinal Frings, Archbishop of Cologne, intervened in the aula of the Second Vatican Council by remarking during the discussion of the scheme on the church, that a clear distinction had to be made between administrative and judicial procedures. This, he said, applies to all the Roman congregations, including the Holy Office, "whose way of proceeding in many things is not up to the standard of our time." No one, he added, can be condemned without first being heard, nor without having the means to defend himself and to correct himself.[60] In this perspective, the Holy Office underwent a radical reform in 1965, although Dominican religious continued to collaborate closely with the new Congregation for the Doctrine of the Faith as advisors.

In this new institutional context, from the very end of the nineteenth and beginning of the twentieth century, a new effort to reread the documents and draw new conclusions appeared among historians,

59. According to research generously shared with us by the lexicologist Isabelle Turcan (University of Nancy II/University of Lorraine), there are no less than 622 occurrences of the word Inquisition in Pierre Larousse's *Grand Dictionnaire*, 155 of the word inquisitor (singular), and 105 of the word inquisitors (plural); more than sixty articles establish a link between the Dominicans and the Inquisition.

60. *Il Concilio Vaticano II. Cronache del Concilio Vaticano II*, ed. Giovanni Caprile, vol. 3 (Ed. La Civiltà Cattolica, 1966), 212.

especially thanks to the work of Henry Charles Lea.[61] This scholarly work stimulated the study of Catholic historians. In France, Célestin Douais, a Dominican tertiary and an editor of the work of Bernard Gui, had already published a study on *Les Albigeois* in 1879, and the lay academic Jean Guiraud undertook a *Histoire de l'Inquisition du Moyen Âge* (1935–1938). Their impact was not as great as that of Lea's work, probably because of their desire to put the Inquisition into context, and because it was more difficult to get public opinion to accept a nuanced presentation, but these authors helped to open the way for the real historiographical and theological turning point that took place in the years 1970 to 1975, which led to a more serene, though sometimes severe, perspective of the reality of the Inquisition. This effort at objectivity was made possible by a very large number of academic works, both Catholic and non-Catholic, which sought to make the texts speak for themselves and which abandoned an apologetic assessment. The *Cahiers de Fanjeaux,* the result of colloquia organized since 1965 in the Lauragais, have greatly contributed to this work. The attention paid to the archives and the return to the sources has led to a relative consensus on the reality of the Inquisition. In an important article from 1988, the Italian Adriano Prosperi summarized this evolution by speaking of a "new image" of the Inquisition among historians,[62] believing that the demonizing stereotype shaped by literature, under the impact of the Reformation and especially the Enlightenment, as well as its romantic fascination, have practically disappeared among professional historians. The discovery of the totalitarian systems of the twentieth century has made it possible to perceive, by comparison, the differences in the justice systems of contemporary dictatorships and the Inquisition. The rules of the latter were harsh, as was the case for the entire judicial system of the time, but they were also precise and objective. Adriano Prosperi called for an examination not only of the victims but also of the inquisitorial phenomenon itself, paying attention to the aims of the Inqui-

61. *History of the Inquisition of Spain* (Macmillan, 1906–1907). It is, to this day, with its translations, a reference work on this subject, constantly republished.

62. Adriano Prosperi, "L'Inquisizione: verso una nuova immagine," *Critica storica* 5 (1988): 119–45.

sition, an approach that had previously been neglected by the romantic analysis of the judicial system. In 1998, ten years after that article, the same researcher, analyzing the opening of the archives of the Holy Office, confirmed the reorientation of the historical perspective, attributing it to the new attitude of the church toward its past. He underlined the novelty represented by the church's adherence to the process of historical research.[63] The Dominicans participated in the movement encouraged by Pope John Paul II; between 2002 and 2009, four international university colloquia questioned the role of the Dominicans in the Inquisition but also in the Iberian Peninsula and its colonies in the modern period, and in its multiple intellectual or artistic representations. This joint movement was marked by the unprecedented act of St. John Paul II on March 12, 2000. Together with seven collaborators from the Roman Curia, the pontiff made seven requests for forgiveness to God on behalf of the Christian people. The second request concerned the faults committed in the service of the truth. Cardinal Ratzinger, "Recognizing that men of the Church, in the name of faith and morals, have sometimes resorted to non-evangelical methods in carrying out their duty to defend the truth," invited us to pray that each of Christ's faithful "may know how to imitate the gentle and humble Lord Jesus." The Holy Father then addressed this prayer to God:

> Lord, God of all men, in certain periods of history Christians have sometimes indulged in intolerant methods and have not observed the great commandment of love, thus sullying the face of the Church, your Bride. Show mercy to your sinful children and accept our firm intention to seek and promote the

63. Adriano Prosperi, "L'inquisizione nella storia. I caratteri originali di una controversia secolare," reprinted in *L'Inquisizione romana: Letture e ricerche* (Edizioni di storia e letteratura, 2003), 94: "Oggi, la discussione sull'inquisizione è di nuovo aperta: ma lo è per la prima volta non come scontro tra scelte religiose ed ecclesiastiche diverse o come contrasto di interpretazioni nel mondo degli studi storici, ma come riflessione della Chiesa cattolica su se stessa e sul suo passato" ["Today, the discussion on the Inquisition is open again: but it is open for the first time not as a clash between different religious and ecclesiastical choices or as a contrast of interpretations in the world of historical studies, but as a reflection of the Catholic Church on herself and on her past"].

> truth in the sweetness of charity, knowing well that the truth is imposed only by virtue of the truth itself.[64]

It is now better understood that medieval justice was hard on the victims and that the medieval Inquisition undoubtedly played, for a time at least, a role in regulating violence. For its part, the church better understood that if truth had rights, so did people; if it is legitimate for the church to oppose what it deems to be errors, it must do so with "the weapons of light" evoked by St. Paul in the Epistle to the Romans, not by using weapons of war.

The Grace of Hearing One's Own Century

There has been no shortage of counter-testimonies and inadequacies given by Dominicans over the centuries, right up to our own time. St. Paul wrote: "We believe, and therefore we speak" (2 Cor 4:13). Lack of faith and the selfish pleasure of listening to one's own words have too often harmed the message of the Gospel, but the grace of St. Dominic has not disappeared. It may have seemed less visible, but new movements have caused it to reappear. Spiritual and apostolic revivals in the Order of Preachers were often linked to the action of determined women: the nuns of the Rhine Valley in the fourteenth century provided a significant example. Rheinland mysticism was largely the result of the encounter between professional theologians, who were responsible for accompanying the nuns and their female audience. Master Eckhart, for example, was responsible for delivering teachings in seventy-five convents of Dominican nuns, to laywomen linked to the order in Alsace and Switzerland, and in eighty-five *beguinages* in Strasbourg, where about a thousand women were gathered.

The fervent atmosphere of these monasteries is revealed in a copy of the *Vies des sœurs*, short notes written at the beginning of the fourteenth century by Sister Catherine de Gueberschwihr, a nun who had been raised "since her childhood" in the monastery of Saint-Jean-Baptiste d'Unterlinden, in Colmar. According to the historian of these nuns, Sister Élie Cails, the work evokes monastic life as the antechamber to Paradise:

64. "Confession des fautes et demande de pardon [Confession of Faults and Request for Forgiveness]," *Documentation catholique* 2223 (April 2, 2000): 331.

> "Everything takes place most often in an atmosphere of joy, light, and radiant beauty. They sometimes perceive sweet harmonies. (Who can say if it is not the choir of angels?) and they enjoy an extraordinary peace which the visionaries say is indescribable."

The mystery of the incarnation is at the heart of their life of contemplation. During the Christmas service, the heavenly Father says to one of the thirty-nine nuns mentioned in the book: "This is my beloved Son, open your heart" and "I forgive all men for the sake of my beloved Son." Another hears the Father say to her: "I am your end. When you die, you will be united to me without delay."[65] These nuns, as well as the nuns of Prato in Italy, Langeac in France, or of Avignon in the Comtat Venaissin, knew how to revive the theological hope of the brothers and the faithful around them.

In the fourteenth century, the great figure of St. Catherine of Siena stood out as a model in a totally different way. She led the order in a renewal crowned with many examples of holiness: Blessed Raymond of Capua († 1399), John Dominici († 1419), St. Antoninus of Florence († 1459), and Fra Angelico († 1455) stood out among many others. A mystic by grace and doctrinally sound, she grasped in her contemplation of the divine mysteries that God is the one who is and that we are those who are not. Discovering God as Unchanging Being and First Truth, she understood in faith that this double knowledge generates in us a love that is the image in us of substantial love: seen in an ardent charity for God and for neighbor. This unique and double charity testifies in favor of the evangelical truth of the way opened by Catherine in the *Dialogue*:[66] "He who does not love his brother whom he sees, cannot love the God he does not see" (1 Jn 4:20). Catherine's abundant correspondence and her boundless apostolic activity, which did not discriminate between persons, bear witness to the greatness of her love for God and for mankind.

On another continent, a few decades later, the impetus received by the order at the time of the discovery of the New World was

65. Sister Élie Cails, *Un monastère dominicain au Moyen Âge: Les débuts d'Unterlinden* (Éd. du Cerf, 2013), 69–70.

66. See "Frères prêcheurs," *Dictionnaire de spiritualité*, vol. 5 (Beauchesne, 1964), col. 1439–40.

accompanied by radical and far-reaching choices, as witnessed by the sermon delivered by Antonio de Montesinos in December 1511 in the young Spanish colony of Santo Domingo, in the heart of the Antilles Archipelago discovered by Christopher Columbus a few years earlier. Horrified by the attitude of the colonists toward the natives, the Dominican preacher, supported by his community, addressed the settlers with urgent pastoral demands: "And what care do you take to instruct the Indians in our religion so that they may know God our creator, so that they may be baptized, so that they may hear Mass, so that they may observe Sundays and other obligations? Are they not men? Are they not human beings? Shouldn't you love them as yourselves?"[67] His appeal was heard by Bartolomé de Las Casas and undertaken with energy and effectiveness familiar to us in the life of this future saint. Las Casas's *History of the Indies*, which has become a classic source of colonial history, shows a friendship for the indigenous people that does not shy away from controversy. The Dominican theologian Francisco de Vitoria († 1546), for his part, took a more academic approach to the same problems, opening the way to numerous theological and juridical renewals. What is important here is that the discovery of a new continent not only led the Order of Preachers to enlarge its field of evangelization but to also deepen its vocation. America was for Montesinos and his followers not only a place where they had to gain a foothold; there they discovered brothers and sisters invited to share with them the joy of the Kingdom of God. The canonizations of Rose of Lima († 1617), Martin de Porres († 1639), and John Macias († 1645) attest to an authentic evangelical witness given by the Dominicans on the American continent.

A religious order dies when it is no longer ultimately relevant to its time. However beautiful its history, it does not have the promise of eternal life. Father Pierre Mandonnet once noted that institutions

> enter into decadence as they no longer adapt to the great vital elements of the environments in which they are immersed. When their preoccupations and objectives are no longer those

67. See, for example, Alvaro Huerga, *Bartolomé de Las Casas: Vie et œuvres* (Éd. du Cerf, 2005), 56. The summary of the homily is published by Las Casas himself in his *History of the Indies.*

> of their time, when they live with outdated intellectual formulas and activities, they can remain as venerable witnesses of another age, the time of their prosperity is over: they lack a principle of adaptation to their environment, a *sine qua non* of any intense vitality, whether it be of the organism or of a social body.[68]

To be in tune with the times, however, is not to be *of* this world. The right place for the apostle is to be *in* the world without being *of* the world. He cannot carry out his mission of evangelization by extricating himself from the world, yet he must not be implicated in its wanderings. St. Peter went to Antioch and then to Rome, the capital of the Roman Empire; St. Paul moreover, went to Athens and perhaps to Spain. Both were put to death in the capital of the empire. In their footsteps, the Dominicans must frequent the cities of their time without abandoning any of them, even if it means death. The brothers and sisters do this, even today. Blessed Pierre Claverie, bishop of Oran in Algeria, gave his life for the witness of the Gospel in 1996. Every continent could provide such examples for the twentieth century.

Thanks be to God that throughout its eight centuries of history, reforms have allowed the Dominican tree to continue to grow and bear fruit. A beautiful image of this capacity for renewal is offered by the career of Father Lacordaire in France at a time when it was imagined that Dominican life had been totally eradicated. Henri Lacordaire returned to the Catholic faith in 1823. He was twenty-one years old, and following his First Communion, he had ceased all religious practice. His vocation to the priesthood arose with his conversion. In a long letter addressed in 1825 to one of his childhood friends, Victor Ladey, Lacordaire described the drama of his journey from the perspective of a twenty-three-year-old:

> We are like those honest people who would perform a boring play of which they know nothing. This is the man without religion. He makes self-interest or self-love the principle of all his actions depending on whether he has a more or less elevated soul; time passes; old age arrives, he sees death more closely, he

68. Pierre Mandonnet, "Comptes rendus," *Revue thomiste* 2 (1894), 430.

> does not understand it any more than he does life; he awaits the blow with regret, with anxiety. . . . He dies; God knows the rest.[69]

In this sad situation, faith in God changes everything: Lacordaire discovered first of all the act of goodness that God had performed in giving him life; he also learned to want the good of others: "Man is a social being destined to exert a salutary or harmful influence on his fellow men. . . . Each one is Fénelon or Voltaire, the one making virtue amiable to others, the other embellishing vice, the one saving the world and the other losing it."[70] Lacordaire loved his time and could not want anything other than to bring it to love God. "I dare to say that I have received from God the grace to listen to this century which I have loved so much," he wrote to his friend Madame Swetchine in 1836.[71] After a Dominican novitiate in Italy, he returned in 1841 to preach in France. This lover of Christ had already fought for freedom: freedom of education, freedom of the press, freedom of religious orders, freedom of self-determination of peoples, etc. He also increasingly demanded freedom for the church, apart from the state, freedom to wear publicly the black and white habit of the preachers, and freedom to live as a religious, at the risk of scandal. In the wake of Lacordaire, the Order of Preachers was able to be reborn, regain its original unity, and strengthen France before spreading widely on an international level. In his *Letter on the Holy See*, published in 1838, Father Lacordaire wrote: "He who has life gives it, he who has love spreads it, he who has the secret tells it to all!" Preaching, like charity, urges the one who is called to it. In short, the Christian faith changes everything, including the way we look at the world. "Once a Christian," he explained shortly before his death:

> The world did not fade away in my eyes; it grows with me. Instead of a vain and passing theater of deceived or satisfied ambitions, I saw in it a great sick person who needed help, an

69. Henri Lacordaire to Victor Ladey, August 20, 1825, in Lacordaire, *Correspondance*, 162–63.

70. Lacordaire to Ladey.

71. Letter from Lacordaire to Madame Swetchine, December 21, 1836, in *Correspondance du R. P. Lacordaire et de Madame Swetchine*, published by Comte de Falloux (Didier et Cie, 1864), 102.

> illustrious misfortune made up of all the misfortunes of the past and future centuries, and I saw nothing comparable to the happiness of serving it under the eye of God with the Gospel and the Cross of His Son.[72]

To move from unbelief to faith, to see the world as it is, and to lead it toward what it is called to, preachers are needed.

In 2019, an elective General Chapter of the Dominicans celebrated in the young province of Vietnam elected as successor to St. Dominic a son of the young province of the Philippines. The Dominican history in these two countries is centuries old, and the order can be proud of having founded in Manila, in 1611, the oldest university in Asia, but it took this double event to showcase the impressive dynamism of these two provinces of the Order of Preachers that achieved provincial autonomy around the 1970s. In America, Europe, and Africa, renewals and developments are also taking place. Since the time of Leo XIII, the Dominicans have endeavored to cultivate in the heart of the church a heritage of St. Thomas Aquinas, whose fruitfulness, far from being exhausted, continues to bear fruit at the *Angelicum* in Rome and the University of Fribourg, as well as in the faculties of theology and the study centers of the provinces. In 1890, Father Marie-Joseph Lagrange founded, from a modest Dominican establishment, a French Biblical and Archaeological School in Jerusalem. A few years later, in 1928, a Dominican laywoman, the novelist Sigrid Undset, received the Nobel Prize for Literature. After leading the reconstruction of a Europe devastated by the Second World War, the Belgian Dominican Dominique Pire, who was awarded the Nobel Prize in 1958, founded the "Islands of Peace." In the same spirit, Giorgio La Pira, a Dominican layman, academic, and mayor of the city of Florence, multiplied his international travels to preach peace between nations. By promoting justice and peace as well as teaching theology, by teaching their contemporaries to pray as well as praying for them, brothers and sisters of the Order of Preachers continue the work of St. Dominic. "The Kingdom of Heaven is at hand" (Mt 10:7). It is the Dominican mission to proclaim this good news, "on the way."

72. "Testament de Lacordaire," *Mémoire dominicaine* 4 (1994): 247–48.

Part III

THE IMAGE OF THE FOUNDER

CHAPTER 5

Faces and Gestures of Saint Dominic

*Claire Rousseau**

NO ONE CAN IDENTIFY WITH CERTAINTY which was the first portrait of Dominic, but the most likely candidate for the oldest representation of the saint now seems to be that of a panel kept in the Fogg Art Museum in Cambridge, Massachusetts, which was created for a convent church. It reflects an emphasis on not just the physical features described by Sister Cecilia of Rome but the dignity of the founder who was elevated to the rank of saint and the closeness of a brother. Appearing without specific attributes save for a book, often associated with the founders,[1] the iconography of the friar was progressively enriched and quickly gave way to images that portrayed scenes of his life.[2] Without a doubt, this fragment of the panel comes from the central part of an altarpiece depicting Dominic standing, of which the side panels must have shown scenes of his

* A portion of this chapter was prepared with the assistance of Coralie Machabert.

1. See, for example, the triptych of the Florentine school of the late thirteenth century, preserved at New Haven, Connecticut, Yale University (Gallery of Fine Arts, Jarves Collection, 1871. 4, 22.9 × 25.7 cm, closed; 39 cm, open). On the central panel, a *Virgin and Child* is framed by the figures of St. Francis on the right and St. Dominic on the left. The saints are haloed, and Dominic holds a closed book in his hand.

2. The panel would have been originally executed for the Dominican church in Siena. It has been repainted several times, probably beginning as early as 1270, and thus its original characteristics are difficult to access and require the use of X-rays. However, specialists believe that the panel is from 1240, or even 1235. For guidance, see the views published in *The Art Bulletin*: Carmen Gómez Moreno, Elizabeth H. Jones, Millard Meiss, and Arthur K. Wheelock. Jr., "A Sienese Saint Dominic Modernized Twice in the Thirteenth Century," *The Art Bulletin* 51 (1969): 363–66.

life,[3] and this model was used repeatedly from the fourteenth century onward to decorate reredos and altar fronts.[4] These works show the need felt by the order to accompany the depiction of the saint and his attributes with scenes from his life in the manner of many historiated icons[5] of the medieval period. Hans Belting remarks:

> Its shorthand scenes could be understood only if they had been memorized from texts. Their sequence followed the liturgical plan by which the *vita* was read, being sometimes divided into sections of appropriate length. The figure at the center, not always a full-length standing figure, offered itself for veneration, as it was displaying the saint's visual appearance. The scenes supplemented the physical portrait with the ethical portrait of an exemplary life and with divine approbation in the form of miracles.[6]

Certain evocations of the events of Dominic's life highlight his holiness through deeds; others speak of the charism of the father of an order in full expansion. There is no formal list from the curia that states how he is to be represented. The number and subjects of the scenes vary not only according to the available space and its structure but also to the message that the patrons wanted to promote. The Order of Preachers, however, has always been conscious, through the individual figure of Dominic and the memory of his life, of depicting something of the order itself, its foundation, its own nature, and its history.[7] Each episode in the life of the saint is extended to the whole order, from the thirteenth century to today.

3. The *Arca*, the tomb of Dominic in Bologna, is another example of the valor illustrated in scenes from the life of the saint. The monument was originally commissioned to Nicola Pisano, who completed it in 1267.

4. See the painting by Giovanni da Tarento (c. 1305), the altar front in the church of San Michele di Tamarità in Litera (1300–1320), and the retable by Francesco Traini (1344–1345).

5. Historiated: (of an initial letter in an illuminated manuscript) decorated with designs representing scenes from the text.

6. Hans Belting, "The Madonnas of Siena: The Image in Urban Life," in *Likeness and Presence: A History of the Image Before the Era of* Art, trans. Edmund Jephcott (University of Chicago Press, 1994), 380.

7. See the analyses of Dominique Donadieu-Rigaut, *Penser en images les ordres religieux (XIIe–XVe siècles)* (Arguments, 2005).

More generally, images fulfill different functions. Paintings, altarpieces substitute for the absence of relics and offer in the choirs of convents and monasteries a rereading of the path to follow. The lessons of liturgical illuminated manuscripts are reserved for cantors or readers of lessons at office. The frescoes in the cloisters and even in the cells enlarge one's vision and transform communities into places where the exercise of memory is actualized in prayer, study, and mission. Devotion can be expressed in the sprinkling of holy water and in adorning statues with flowers, statues that one can venerate and touch. Since the thirteenth century, books in which images of the founder's life or his ways of praying (*De modo orandi*) also played a specific role, and the invention of the printing press later amplified their importance.[8] All forms of plastic art were employed: painting, drawing, engraving, stained glass, bas relief and three-dimensional sculpture, ceramics, enameling, gold and silvers work, embroidery, polychrome wax molding, etc. Some of the materials used were precious, coming from far away, while others were drawn more modestly from local resources.

The emergence of artwork in which Dominic was the subject follows the geographical expansion of the order in Europe, Asia, Africa, and the New World, as well as the foundation of new communities and the restoration of those destroyed by earthquakes, human violence, fires, or abandonment. From generation to generation, men and women, Dominicans or not, paid a vibrant tribute to Saint Dominic with their talents. Even though the most prestigious works, such as the constantly enriched *Arca*, arouse admiration, more modest productions such as the series of small images to be slipped into a prayer book should not be neglected, because they attest to the same desire to venerate the Father of the Preachers and to entrust to him the present and the future of the order.

The emotion and devotion, both individual and collective, evoked by the representations of St. Dominic are always vivid. The intrinsic characteristics of a work of art, however, are not sufficient

8. By way of example, see the *Libellus de instructione et consolatione novitiorum* (c. 1300; Toulouse, Bibliothèque Municipale, ms. 418) and the various manuscripts known as the Ways of Prayer of St. Dominic kept at Bologna, the Vatican, Madrid, etc.

when it comes to understanding a message that requires the indispensable mediation of those who deliver its meaning. This has always been true and is even more so today, particularly in the most secularized countries. However beautiful it may be, Dominic's image itself says nothing of his person. Even if the spectator before a canvas depicting the child being resuscitated can perceive his miracle-working, few manage to decipher the character of St. Dominic. Many of the works now kept in museums or libraries have lost their function and meaning. In this respect, histories and art historians play a fundamental role as interpreters of such art. By retracing the history of these works, honoring their artistic qualities, and placing them in the context of the narratives of the saint's life, they give them a new significance and make them intelligible *libelli* again. It is the responsibility of the members of the order to pragmatically convert the multivoiced lessons into something understandable for the wider public.

The portraits of Dominic make him present where his relics cannot be. Fra Angelico (c. 1400–55), artist and prior, was acutely aware of this, and he was inspired to adorn the walls of the cells and corridors of the convent of San Marco with frescoes in which Dominic is often depicted. But his compositions do not draw the gaze to the saint himself. Instead, they establish him as a guide for souls, he who through studying, praying, and preaching had no other desire than to lead each person to Christ. The softness of Dominic's features under the brush of John of Fiesole, the charm of an embroidery, the strength of an angular sculpture, and the fascinating goldsmith's work adorning the reliquary for his skull must ever serve to remind us of Dominic's ardor for the salvation of souls. What single work could give an account of his zeal?

Dominic's Holy Childhood

To emphasize the holiness of a founder, hagiographers often have recourse to similar symbols and stories. For example, these may indicate that holiness is a gift from God, granted even before the birth of the child. In 1649 and 1650, the young Friar Balthazar-Thomas Moncornet painted fifteen scenes on the ceiling of the chapel in Toulouse that was built at the back of the house in which St. Dominic established the first community of friars there. The second of these

Balthazar-Thomas Moncornet, OP (1630–1716), *The Signs Announcing Dominic's Holiness*, 1649–1650. Oil on wood. Toulouse, France, Bruno de Solages Amphitheatre. Photo credit: Fr. Dominique-Benoit Jean-Luc, OP

scenes shows the astonishment of Dominic's family before this baby marked with a star on its forehead: he is depicted surrounded by bees and preferring to sleep on the floor rather than in his cradle (see Peter Ferrand's *Legend of St. Dominic*, §4–5). These signs speak as much for Dominic's personal sanctity as for that of his order. Dominic, as Gregory IX and the liturgy of the order expressed it, was a star destined to make the divine science shine forth and to announce the coming of Christ in glory. His privileged mode of action was the word, of which the bees are the symbol. Through penance, his life was ordered from his earliest years to this essential end: to make known to men their salvation. These signs make Dominic's charisma apparent and trace a path for the members of his order: to work for salvation by fruitful preaching and a life ordered according to the demands of the Gospel, and God, from heaven, will bless each one as he did the child Dominic.

Selling Books in Palencia

The Dominican Joannes Nys, master of novices in the convent of Antwerp, commissioned numerous prints for the spiritual formation of young religious. In 1611, he had an illustrated life of St. Dominic in thirty-two plates engraved as well as a portrait which he dedicated to Agostino Galamini, Master of the Order (1608–1612). In the pages of the booklet, each of the engravings is titled and captioned in Latin. The work concludes with short notes written in the vernacular, sometimes in French, sometimes in Flemish. From then on, copies were engraved and published in Paris. The scenes were the basis of reproductions using different media: oil on copper, small earthenware dogs for monastic stoves, etc. The Palencia representation above is the third plate. In the foreground on the left, one sees Dominic selling his books, while the background reveals the motive of this action: to help those in need, which is a response to the evangelical counsels. All that is missing from this plate is the third reason for the action given in Jordan of Saxony's *Libellus* (§7): to arouse the charity of others through the example of this gesture. The young student's relinquishing of his books, which were indispensable for study, inaugurated what would characterize the rest of his life: a particular disposition of heart and mind to respond in concrete acts to the spiritual or material distress he encountered. The foundation of the order is born of this same compassionate and unique charisma.

Disputation in Montreal

Although the historical facts of this incident have been contested, the scene of the miracle of the fire in Fanjeaux is thought to have occurred not far from Prouille, in Aude. This miracle was decisive in St. Dominic's mission of evangelization. In 1207, following a dispute between Dominic and heretics in the neighboring village of Montreal, the holy preacher's *libellus* was put to the test of flames. From this

Theodoor Galle (1571–1633), *St. Dominic's Student Days*, 1611. Burin, pl. c.: 15 × 9.2 cm. Joannes Nys (?–1622), *Vita et Miracvla S. P. Dominici Prædicatorii Ordinis Primi Institvtoris, Antverpiæ, Apud Theodoru[m] Gallæum*, 1611. Amsterdam, Rijksmuseum, RP-P-OB-6768. Photo credit: Rijksmuseum (Amsterdam)

ordeal, it flew out intact and hit a chimney beam. Since the nineteenth century, the relics of the beam and the stone from the fireplace in the incident have been kept in the parish church of Fanjeaux. This is not far from the "House of Saint Dominic," which a recent tradition considers to have been the lodging of the founder of the order. The single bay window of the room converted into a chapel was replaced in 1955 with a stained-glass window commissioned by the Dominican Alex-Ceslas Rzewuski (1893–1983), then occupant of the vicariate. The series was designed by Jean Hugo (1894–1984), great-grandson of the celebrated Victor Hugo. The stained-glass window, divided

Jean Hugo (1894–1984), *The Ordeal (or Miracle of Fire) reported to the King by the Consuls of Fanjeaux*, 1954–1955. Stained glass window, 43.3 × 30.5 cm. Fanjeaux, Maison Saint-Dominique. Photo credit: Henri Gourdin, biographer of Jean Hugo

into two sections, was completed by Paul Bony (1911–1982), who also worked in Vence with Henri Matisse. Among the six depictions chosen by Jean Hugo to summarize Dominic's stay in Lauragais is the scene of the miracle of the fire: proof of the incident's importance in the local cult. On the left and facing the praying canon, three heretics watch incredulously as the manuscript escapes the fire. The work is characterized by its lively colors. In the center, yellow patches form an *ichthus*, echoing the tones of the founder's tunic and the parchment, and their shape recalls the dance of the flames that revealed the divine judgment in this test of the faith.

Unidentified Artist (Italy), *St. Dominic Supporting the Church*, ca. 1450. Xylograph, copy on illuminated paper, 27.3 × 10.8 cm. Washington, DC, Rosenwald Collection, National Gallery of Art, 1963.11.7. Photo credit: National Gallery of Art (Washington, DC)

The Dream of Innocent III

Xylography, the carving of a mold in wood, makes it possible to multiply the prints of a single drawing. The copies, whether they are on parchment or paper, can then be colored. The strokes are often simple and the outlines sharp, but the details can be refined, as in the twisted columns that support the scalloped arch framing this full-length portrait of St. Dominic. The image emphasizes the church's recognition of the holiness and charisma of the founder. In the right hand are set the Book of the Word and the crucified Christ, as well

Santi di Tito (1536–1603), *Apparition of Saints Peter and Paul to St. Dominic*, 1581–1584. Fresco a tempera, 400 × 380 cm. Florence, Santa Maria Novella, large cloister (west). Photo credit: Fr. Lawrence Lew, OP

as a branch of lilies, symbols in medieval thought not only of purity but also of Christ being preached. In his left hand, Dominic holds an image of the church that he and his order support through their preaching ministry. The upper register reinforces these iconographic symbols of the founder. On the right, the Italian artist of the fifteenth century recalls Pope Innocent III's vision of Dominic raising a church threatened with ruin. On the left, the artist places the vision of Reginald of Orleans, signifying that this new order, represented by its distinguishing habit, is a grace offered for the church; of this, Dominic is the most radiant gift.

The Vision of Saint Peter and Saint Paul in Rome

The creation of artistic works representing St. Dominic is not always due to the initiative of the order itself. Thus, the impulse for the decoration of the great cloister adjoining the Basilica of Santa Maria Novella was given in 1565 by Cosimo Medici I. Other prestigious Florentine families became patrons of this project, and the best artists of the city, including Santi di Tito (1536–1603), were engaged to complete the frescoes. On two sides of the cloister, a cycle of the life of St. Dominic is displayed, and this is interspersed with portraits of prominent Dominicans. The apparition of Saints Peter and Paul, confirming Dominic's founding of an order closely following an apostolic life, adorns a lunette on the west side and is paired with the preaching of Christ and the apostles. The painter takes care to place the handing on of the apostolic staff in St. Peter's Basilica in Rome where the event took place. Such a setting is a location in which the faithful have the right to expect strong and firm preaching, centered on Christ, whose golden *IHS* is the only decoration on the altar's retable. The vision is for the benefit of both Dominic and the faithful. It informs us of the apostolic nature of the mission of the members of the young order, who, as seen far in the background on the left of the fresco, will have to go out two by two carrying the Word, symbolized by the book handed to Dominic by St. Paul. The Order of Preachers is an order of new apostles fully aware of their vocation.

The Raising of Napoleon Orsini from the Dead in Rome

The depiction of the miracle of the resurrection of the young Napoleon Orsini was popular in fifteenth- and sixteenth-century Italy, as evidenced by the predella[9] of Fra Angelico's *Coronation of the Virgin*[10] (or Lorenzo Lotto's oil on wood[11]). Between the creation of these two works, Bartolomeo degli Erri (*c.* 1467–1474) also made a tempera on this theme. His work belongs to the predella of an altarpiece dedicated to St. Dominic, now dismantled and part of a series of polyptychs commissioned for the church of San Domenico in

9. A painting or sculpture on the front of a raised shelf above an altar, which typically forms the base for an altarpiece.

10. *c.* 1430–1432, tempera on wood, for the convent of San Domenico in Fiesole, Paris, Louvre, inv. 314.

11. *c.* 1513–1516, oil on wood, Bergamo, Accademia Carrara, inv. 58AC00070.

Bartolomeo degli Erri (active 1460–1479), *Saint Dominic Resuscitating Napoleone Orsini* (predella panel of the altarpiece of the Church of the Preachers in Modena), ca. 1467–1474. Tempera on canvas transferred to wood, 25.6 x 44.5 cm. The Bequest of Michael Dreicer, 1921. New York, Metropolitan Museum of Art, 22.60.59. Photo credit: Metropolitan Museum of Art (New York)

Modena. The structuring of the work is hardly comparable with the two famous works referenced; the field of the scene, enclosed by imposing architecture, differs from the depth of perspective conveyed by Fra Angelico, and the static postures of the characters contrast with the animation that gives rhythm to Lotto's painting. Interestingly, Bartolomeo degli Erri's composition superimposes two narrative moments. In the foreground, Napoleon Orsini is lying at the feet of his horse. Leaning over the body, St. Dominic revives the nephew of the Cardinal of Fossanova. In the background, he reunites the two men before the surprised witnesses of this miracle. A dog is lying peacefully in the middle of the space serving as the transition between the different groups.

Verotius (active in the eighteenth century), *The Miracle of the Meal* (stall back from the Priestly Convent in Trier, Germany), 1754. Oil on canvas, 126.5 × 104 cm. Toulouse, Maison Seilhan, MS-HT-09. Photo credit: Laetitia Guneau

The Miracle of the Loaves Brought by the Angels

Depictions of the miracle of the loaves abound. The oil on canvas painted in 1754 by Verotius for the Dominican convent in Trier, Germany, offers many distinctive characteristics. The composition of the scene is traditional and recalls portrayals of the Last Supper. The similarity is accentuated by the presence of a basin and a jug in front of the central table, evocative of the washing of feet in the Gospel of John. In the background, the picture of Christ on the cross is framed by a portrait of his Mother and the beloved disciple. But while the fourth Gospel does not record the institution of the Eucharist at the Last Supper, the painting announces that amidst the service of charity and carried out in the gift of the life of each brother, God will provide bread and wine without fail. The painting is one of the six panels that adorned the convent choir stalls. It is likely that it was placed as close as possible

Unidentified artist, *The Death of Saint Dominic*, late seventeenth century. Oil on canvas, 155 × 200 cm. Salamanca, Convent of San Esteban, inv. SAL. P. 02. Photo credit: Fr. Lawrence Lew, OP

to the altar and the Eucharistic table, across from the image of Dominic's death. Thus, it would link the Passover of Christ, that of Dominic, and the promise of bread offered always by God for the life of the brothers in their bodily needs as well as in their spiritual needs.

The Death of Saint Dominic

On August 6, 1221, Dominic's eyes closed against the light of day. At the words "Come to his aid, saints of God," the saintly founder's soul "traded this dwelling of mourning for the eternal consolation of a heavenly dwelling." After recommending his brothers to the heavenly Father, Dominic's eyes opened to the Light that is not extinguished.

The brothers' overwhelming compassion and sorrow turned into peace and confidence. The founder's last will and testament, commending charity, humility, and voluntary poverty to the brothers, united the circle of brothers who continued the work begun by Dominic. The candle of faith was lit, the water of blessing sprinkled. Nothing ended; it had only just begun for the Order of Preachers. The Spanish artist of the seventeenth century, whose name has been lost, knew how to play on the contrast between the static position of Dominic's already stiffened body and the realism of the faces of the friars, expressions so similar to the Dominicans of today. From the thirteenth to the twenty-first centuries, the diversity of persons, perceptible in the expression of the faces in the image, and the collegiality of the religious body impress a particular mark on the order. The debating of ideas can be lively and passionate, but it is animated by a quest for truth. The desire to share and communicate the truth urges its study and contemplation, and by it, fraternity becomes sweeter. The charism of St. Dominic is a heritage that bears fruit in *verbo et exemplo*, and the friars know they can count on their founder's intercession in heaven. They received the promise of it with his last breath.

The Vision of Blessed Guala of Bergamo

The decoration of the initial 'M' [*Mundum vocans ad agni nuptias*] in the first responsory of first matins on the night of the feast of St. Dominic testifies to the diverse facets of veneration paid to the founder. In the medieval manuscripts, the saint may be standing blessing a friar (Philadelphia Library, ms. Lewis E M 71:3), receiving a scroll from Christ and passing it on to the community (Philadelphia Library, ms. Lewis E M 74:4–7), or sheltering the nuns under his cappa (Philadelphia Library, ms. Lewis E M 26:32–33). Some illuminators, however, such as the one on the Poissy antiphonary (Melbourne, State Library Victoria, ms. *096.1/R66A), followed the example of this page of the Bolognese school (*c.* 1265) and evoked the vision of Brother Guala. The decoration of the lettering is clearly divided into two levels. In the lower one, the funeral of Dominic takes place. The holy body, solemnly displayed, is already attracting the poor and the sick who seek relief by touching it. The upper part, invisible to the audience but known to the four friars in the spandrels, depicts what

Unidentified illuminator, *Initial M*: *The Vision of Brother Guala at the Death of St. Dominic*, ca. 1265, Bologna. Illumination (tempera, gold) and ink on parchment, 52.5 × 37.3 cm. (page). Los Angeles, J. Paul Getty Museum, Ms. 62 (95.MS. 70), recto. Photo credit: J. Paul Getty Museum (Los Angeles)

only Friar Guala witnessed: the elevation to heaven of Dominic's soul, drawn by Christ and his Mother. The latter symbolizes this *post-mortem* ascent, which was thereafter told throughout the order, especially to the novices (Toulouse, Bibliothèque municipale, ms. 418, f. 94v), as an example of holiness through the living of the religious life here on earth.

The Translation of the Body of Saint Dominic

The French sculptor Jean-Baptiste Boudard was commissioned by the Dominicans of Bologna to decorate the front of the *Arca* (the

Jean-Baptiste Boudard (1710–1768); Giuseppe Boni (dates unknown), after Carlo Bianconi (1732–1802), *The Entombment of Saint Dominic*, 1768. Carrara marble. Bologna, Basilica of San Domenico, front of the *Arca*. Photo credit: Fr. Lawrence Lew, OP

tomb of St. Dominic in Bologna). The work was completed in Parma by his pupil Giuseppe Boni in 1768. Curiously, the bas-relief's details do not correspond to any account of Dominic's burial in 1221 or of the transfer of his relics in 1233. The body is heavy, like that of a dead man, but supple in its abandon. There is no stiffness in this shrouded figure, who, being laid in the tomb, is crowned with rays of light. In the place of a mother veiled in long draperies bows instead the cardinal, a representative of Mother Church that Dominic never stopped serving. Already the halberds stand guard, and a soldier marks out the space with his back turned, his fist on his hip, his gaze scarcely concerned by the burial of the saint. Other witnesses, chatting amongst themselves or stroking their beards, wonder: who is this whose fragrance of holiness is already emanating? We see a flood of hope at the time of the transfer of the remains for the woman with the child and the astonished expressions of the podestas (magistrates), who are now convinced that a canonization is imminent. Was this an inaccurate entombment or an idealized translation of a body that would be as limber as it was at the last breath? The sculptural outcome of the *Arca* surpasses any historical account, but it cannot misconstrue the graces obtained from the one whose body is enclosed there. Such graces are engraved in hearts, not marble.

Saint Dominic the Preacher

When the pope offered the religious orders the possibility of erecting a statue of their founder in St. Peter's Basilica in Rome, the Master of the Order, Antonin Cloche (Master General from 1686 to 1720), seized the opportunity. Sculpted by Pierre Legros II (1666–1719) from the drawings of Brother Baptiste Monnoyer, the white marble statue, despite opposition to the excessive prominence, was placed in the right-hand niche of the apse. This exceptional work was mentioned in many travel reports and guidebooks of Rome beginning in the eighteenth century as one of the masterpieces of the edifice. The style is strongly dynamic. The movement of the folds of the wide, sharply edged cape reinforces the attitude of the preacher, full of audacity and ardor. The saint is in the midst of disputation, his right index finger pointing to heaven and his left hand holding an open book against him. The gaze is directed toward the viewer, who cannot help but feel called by such vehemence of gesture into the work of preaching. The parted lips seem to deliver the message of faith. The very intertwining of the curls of the hair and the wrinkles on the forehead portray the energy that Dominic exerts. At his feet, the dog with the flaming torch has a conquering attitude, as resolute as his master's. So that no one is deceived about the identity of this apostle, the statue is placed on a pedestal with a large plaque indicating the name of the founder.

Saint Dominic at Prayer

Of all the ways of prayer of St. Dominic that have been depicted, the one that is seen most often is the act of flagellation. Beyond the spectacular side of such a depiction, the scene recalls the penitential dimension of the Order of Preachers and the existence of a lay form of Dominican life called the "Order of Penance of St. Dominic." In

Pierre Legros (1666–1719), sculptor, after Brother Baptiste Monnoyer (dates unknown), draftsman, *Ordo Prædicatorvm Fvndatori* (detail), 1706. White carrara marble, height: "fourteen Roman palms, which are nine feet seven inches and a half." Rome, St. Peter's Basilica. Photo credit: Fr. Lawrence Lew, OP

their chapels or private rooms, laypersons could thus link their movement directly to the founder through works such as this. In the painting, Dominic is kneeling before the private altar in his cell. The lace cloth, the bouquet of roses in colors evocative of the mysteries of the rosary, and the hourglass measuring time on the work table all suggest a place where one lives in intimacy with Christ. Filippo Tarchiani, who perfectly masters the Roman artistic codes of the early seventeenth century, depicts Dominic as a muscular figure with perfect proportions. He does not place the emphasis on the bloody exer-

Filippo Tarchiani (1576–1645), *St. Dominic in Penitence*, ca. 1607. Oil on canvas, 132.1 × 109.2 cm. Gift of Brian J. Brille, 2015. New York, Metropolitan Museum, 2015.761. Photo credit: Metropolitan Museum (New York)

cise, however. The flaying and tearing of the flesh is suspended, the face is raised and taut. The gaze is not so much imploring mercy as it is absorbed in the pains suffered by Christ for the salvation of men. Thus, those who could not adhere to the penance of St. Dominic find in him the model of a soul transfixed by Christ, conversing day and night with his crucified Lord.

Gathered by Christ: The Dominican Family

The vision of Dominic in which he beheld the Virgin sheltering the brethren of the Order of Preachers under her blue mantle conveys a declaration of confidence. The friars are, as in other religious families, under the patronage of Mary, who assures them of her protection from the radiance of heaven, where they are already counted

Sister Mary of the Compassion (1908–1977), OP, *The Saints of the Order of Preachers at the Foot of the Cross*, n.d. [ca. 1950]. Mixed media, 244 × 122 cm. Washington, DC, Dominican House of Studies, Refectory. Photo credit: Fr. Lawrence Lew, OP

among the blessed. Gradually, depictions of this event moved away from the primitive accounts such that nuns and lay Dominicans were introduced under the mantle. The order, with its many members, found other ways to show its collegiality and unanimity. Trees growing from the body of the founder offer the most beautiful fruits of holiness nourished by the same sap (see the *Radix Dominicus* painted in 1675 by J. Rolbels, kept in the monastery of Estavayer-le-Lac in Switzerland). Less numerous, but just as representative, are the Dominican saints kissing the wounds of Christ together (see the oil on canvas of Odoardo Fialetti, painted around 1610, in the sacristy of the convent of Saints John and Paul in Venice). From the medieval Madonna of the Cloak to the veneration of the wounds of Christ, artists such as Dominican Sister Mary of the Compassion (Constance Mary Rowe) gathered the saints of the order not for self-glorification but for a reorienting of souls to the Crucified and to his mother. Placed in the refectory of the House of Studies in Washington, DC, her painting reminds the brothers while at table that the blood poured out by Christ unites them more intimately in one body than the bread they share in community.

Jan Luyken (1649–1712), *Banners of the Inquisition in Spain and Goa*, 1692. Etching, 16.3 × 26.6 cm. Plate for Philipp van Limborch, *Historia Inquisitionis*, Amsterdam, by Henri Wetsten, 1692. Amsterdam, Rijksmuseum, RP-P-1896-A-19368–933. Photo credit: Rijksmuseum (Amsterdam)

Saint Dominic the Inquisitor

In 1692, Philipp Limborch reprinted in Amsterdam the text and illustrations of the work of the Frenchman Charles Dellon (1650–post-1709), published in Paris in 1688, after a stay in the East Indies, during which he was condemned by the tribunal of the faith. Although Charles Dellon denounces forcefully, his work is not outrageous but relates a personal experience and details the sources, sinister in many respects, of the inquisitorial operation. A document of the utmost importance, the text was constantly republished and the illustrations copied. The banner of the Inquisition of Goa holds the attention insofar as it establishes St. Dominic himself as promoter of inquisitorial justice. Emerging from a cloud, Dominic holds the sword of justice and an olive branch, which were also the symbols of the Spanish Inquisition. Philip Limborch explains the symbolism: "The olive branch in the right hand and the bared sword on the left show that in the sentences of the Inquisition mercy is the companion of justice.

Giorgio Vasari (1511–1574), *The Madonna of the Rosary* (detail), c. 1569. Oil on canvas, 330 × 230 cm. Florence, Church of Santa Maria Novella. Photo credit: Fr. Lawrence Lew, OP

All the efforts of mercy having been exhausted without effect, the inquisitors, albeit with regret, will then arm themselves with the sword that God gave them for the execution of his justice." The interpretation expresses more an ideal than a reality, which has tarnished the image of St. Dominic and of Dominicans for a long time, forging a tenacious "black legend" in which the dog with the torch is only there to light the pyres on fire.

Saint Dominic and the Rosary

With the devotion of the rosary, promoted by Alain de la Roche (situated here below the Child Jesus), the wide blue mantle of the Virgin

Mary no longer houses only the members of the Order of Preachers but all the faithful who implore the Queen of Heaven. Men and women, children and adults, rich and poor, all share in the mysteries of the life of Christ and his Mother, delicately recalled in grey medallions. Blessings and graces will not be lacking from God, the Father, the Son, and the Holy Spirit. Surprisingly, in contrast to many other works, the patrons and the artist, Giorgio Vasari, did not make Dominic the recipient of the gift of the rosary but the transmitter of a filial devotion to the Virgin Mary. The founder tenderly kisses the Marian hand by which she is giving him the habit of the order. It is this order that will seek to develop devotion to the rosary, a prayer both simple and rich. With his left hand, Dominic distributes this precious gift in the form of rosaries made of pearl. The ultimate goal of this practice unfolds across the whole width of the lower part of the painting: charity. Love bestows her gifts—the heart of Christ, held in the hand of the Dominican Pope Pius V, configuring the soul to Christ as shown by the stigmata of Catherine of Siena and the evocation of her martyred patron saint, Catherine of Alexandria (left). This generous love is symbolized by the allegory of Charity, a woman feeding many children, including all those numbered among the church.

CHAPTER 6

At the Table with Saint Dominic

Eleonora Tioli and Gianni Festa

The oldest image of Saint Dominic is the painted panel known as the *Tavola de la Mascarella* in the church of Santa Maria della Mascarella in Bologna, and it is a precious testimony to the history of the Order of Preachers. Many believe the work is the first image of St. Dominic ever painted, and it is at least the oldest one in Bologna that has come down to us. The saint, crowned with a halo, is depicted in front of a richly laid table, behind which forty-eight friars are seated, surrounding him on both sides.

In addition to its iconographic value, the Mascarella panel is rich in cultural significance. According to a Bolognese tradition dating back to the fifteenth century, the table was identified as the refectory table at which St. Dominic multiplied the bread in order to feed his brothers. This miracle of the multiplication of the loaves is known from Friar Rodolfo of Faenza's testimony during the canonization inquiry, which took place in Bologna in 1233:

> Whenever the house ran short of bread, wine or any item of food, the witness used to go to Dominic and say: "We have no bread—or wine." He would answer: "Go and pray, for the Lord will provide." So the witness would go to the church to pray, often followed by Brother Dominic. God heard them, for they always had enough to eat. Sometimes, at Dominic's command, the witness took the little bit of bread they still had and put it on the tables, and the Lord supplied the lack.[1]

In the version of this story that has been popularized in the legend of Constantine of Orvieto, two friars from the convent of

1. *Acta canonizationis*, Bologna, 31; Lehner, 120.

San Sisto in Rome were sent to beg for food and returned to the convent with "hardly any bread, just a tiny morsel." However, as St. Dominic prayed joyfully in the refectory before this meager pittance, surrounded by the forty or so friars present, "Two young men, with the same habit and appearance, entered the refectory, carrying the folds of the garment which hung around their necks filled with those loaves of bread which the baker who sent them knew well how to make."[2] This miracle is also referenced by Humbert of Romans and Sister Cecilia. The latter insists on the angelic nature of the visitors.[3] The Mascarella table could therefore have great spiritual value and be considered a second-class relic, since it was touched by the saint's body and held the miraculous bread brought by the angels.

Iconography and History of the Panel

For stylistic reasons, the Mascarella panel can be dated to the 1240s or 1250s. It is possible that the work was produced following the canonization of St. Dominic in 1234, as a form of homage to the saint, who died in Bologna in 1221. Due to a rather complicated history, the work has lost its original appearance; nevertheless, it can be reconstructed. Originally, it was just over six yards long, and the height of the panel has remained almost unchanged: approximately 1 foot, 5 inches. An inscription, now lost, bordered the lower end of the painting. Finally, while the painting originally depicted forty-eight friars surrounding St. Dominic, it now depicts just forty.

The image shows St. Dominic and his brothers seated before a table abundantly furnished with bread and crockery: plates, knives, jugs, and chalice-shaped cups. A series of richly decorated arches and columns frame the friars, grouped in pairs, with the exception of St. Dominic, who occupies the space normally shared by two friars. The image of the saint does not differ much from the other friars, only in his size, which is more prominent, his central position, and his halo.

In this ancient image, St. Dominic is represented as a character in a narrative scene rather than as the portrait of an iconic and iso-

2. Constantine of Orvieto, *Legenda*, 37; Bériou-Hodel, 899–900.

3. Sister Cecilia, *Miracula*, 3; Lehner, 168.

lated figure. The Mascarella table seems to celebrate the Order of Preachers as a group rather than just its holy founder. In this sense, Dominican iconography is clearly different from Franciscan iconography, which exalts St. Francis as an extraordinary man. St. Dominic, on the other hand, is often depicted among the other friars, as a *primus inter pares*: first among equals.

In 1332, the church of *La Mascarella* underwent alterations. The thirteenth-century painting was turned over and its memory was lost: a new image was painted on the back of the piece of wood, which until then had been devoid of any representation. The original image showed a typical scene of fraternal conviviality, while the fourteenth-century image depicts the miracle of the loaves in a way that conforms more closely to the hagiographic sources. St. Dominic is depicted seated at a table surrounded by twelve brothers while two angels bring bread. The iconography is reminiscent of the Last Supper in which the twelve apostles are seated at table with Christ. While the early Dominican community was more associated with the apostolic community, a century later, St. Dominic was seen to occupy the place reserved for Christ. The original representation did not impose this interpretation; it merely suggested the parallelism with the Last Supper by presenting forty-eight friars (a multiple of twelve) around the saint.

The new fourteenth-century painting responded to a need to update not only the iconography but also the style. The linear and flowing forms of the new image contrasted with the thirteenth-century's stately figure of Dominic in the midst of his brethren. The new version of the work, in contrast, responded to fourteenth-century Bolognese tastes and preference for Gothic art.

A Table Considered as a Sacred Object

The identification of the Mascarella table with that of the miracle of the loaves is attributed for the first time in the *Chronicle* of Girolamo Albertucci de' Borselli, prior of the convent of San Domenico in 1497. On November 14, 1497, the Dominican friars dared to steal the "relic" from the Mascarella and take it home. The Bolognese chronicler, Fileno della Tuata, who was contemporaneous with the events, reports the confrontation between the friars and the parishioners at Mascarella. The latter recovered the table, which they took back to their church in procession.

This unsuccessful attempt at theft paradoxically underscores the venerated status that the table had acquired. Later Bolognese sources also attest to the object's significant cultural value, giving rise to a strong local tradition. It is possible that the Dominican friars were motivated by the desire to exercise a monopoly on the cult of their founder: the Mascarella panel was the only Bolognese relic of Dominic that was not kept in their basilica where the body of the saint already lay.

The Basilica of St. Dominic and the church of *La Mascarella* were therefore the two places of prime importance to the local Dominican community. At the beginning of 1218, the primitive community of the Bolognese Preachers had in fact settled in Mascarella before moving in the spring of 1219 to the new convent in St. Nicholas of the Vineyards. The church of the Mascarella could therefore be seen as significant due to its link with the history of the order in Bologna, while the patriarchal convent of St. Dominic was the holy place *par excellence* because it housed the relics of Dominic's body.

The Bolognese sources are the only ones to place the miracle of the loaves in the church of the Mascarella, maintaining the belief that the table was the table of the miracle. In order to overcome the contradiction with other hagiographic accounts, some local sources proposed to distinguish between two miracles that occurred in Bologna: the first in the Mascarella, when angels brought bread, and the second in San Domenico, when they offered the friars bread and figs. In the choir of San Domenico's patriarchal basilica, the predella by Vincenzo Spisanelli bears witness to this position by means of an iconographic *unicum*: the painter depicted the miracle that is said to have taken place in San Domenico by painting four angels, one of whom carries a basket of figs.

Before the attempted theft by the Dominicans, the Mascarella panel was hung on a beam in the church at Mascarella, as witnessed by Leander Alberti in his *History of Bologna* (1541). It was later placed against the wall of a chapel dedicated to the Madonna, and St. Dominic was located on the right in the presbytery, protected by a grille. In 1823, the panel was moved to the second chapel on the right, dedicated to the Assumption of Mary. It was sawn into three equal parts that could be folded over each other. The intent was to divide the fourteenth-century painting of the miracle of the loaves, but this also affected the thirteenth-century scene painted on the opposite side, which at that time was hidden from view.

On December 19, 1881, the panel was temporarily transferred to the room occupied by the Confraternity of the Blessed Sacrament in at Mascarella. It was then that the hidden original thirteenth-century painting was rediscovered. In 1912, the panel was finally transferred to the chapel of San Domenico and affixed to the left of the high altar, and in 1923, the two pictorial surfaces of the panel were definitively separated: the fourteenth-century painting, divided into three parts, was transferred to a canvas, while the thirteenth-century painting remained on its original wooden support.

The Mascarella Table Today: A Possible Theological Meaning

Because of its dual status as a work of art and a sacred object, the history of the Mascarella panel is particularly complex. While the entire fourteenth-century painting is preserved in the church of La Mascarella in the third chapel on the left in the form of three canvases hung on the wall, the original thirteenth-century painting on wood has been separated into six pieces. Two of the three pieces from the 1923 division are on display with the three fourteenth-century canvases at the Mascarella. Looking at the thirteenth-century version as a whole, the central panel and the one on the right have been retained and are installed in the front of the church's altar. The canvases produced from the fourteenth-century version hang on the wall by a side altar in the same location. The remaining left part of the table has been divided into four parts. The first part, representing five friars, hangs in *La Mascarella* with the three canvases. The second, originally depicting eight friars but no longer including them, has been in the Convent of San Domenico in Bologna since 1931, in Master Moneta of Cremona's cell. The third, representing two brothers, has been kept since 1961 in the museum of the Basilica of Santa Sabina in Rome, while the last fragment, representing a single brother, has unfortunately been lost.

The thirteenth-century panel depicts St. Dominic with a halo, occupying the central position. Beside him, in a series of niches, preaching friars are seated in pairs before a table covered with bread. The anonymous artist has individualized the faces: the friars seem to come from different parts of Europe. Could the painter have crossed paths with the Dominicans on the occasion of a general chapter, when many would be gathered from across the continent? The chapter was celebrated every year until 1245 either in Bologna or in Paris. The meaning of the painting could then find its inspiration in the prologue of the *Legend* of Peter Ferrand, which was inspired by the text of the canonization bull of St. Dominic, *Fons Sapientiae* (1234, Rieti) The *Legend* states:

> *While in the past, on several occasions and in several ways, God* had invited the chosen ones to the heavenly banquet, in these *last days,* that is to say, *at the eleventh hour, he sent his servant to tell those invited to come, for from then on, everything was ready.* This servant, according to the interpretation of Saint Gregory, is an order of preachers who were to be sent in the last days, to warn the spirits of men of the coming of the Judge. The Scripture has indeed announced that there would be a new order of preachers, which it declared very clearly to be sent towards the end of time, saying: *He has sent his servant at supper time.* The hour of the supper is the end of the world, and we are the ones for whom *the end times have come. At the hour of supper,* that is, in the last days, a new order was sent out; new, I say, as well as old: new in institution, old in authority; new, or better, last in time, but first in office. These are the Preachers, the order which divine Providence has provided for in order to provide for the peril of these last times, so that at the coming judgement which will be carried out by the one to whom, in humiliation, judgement has been denied, the number of witnesses will increase.[4]

The Mascarella painting, therefore, offers perhaps the earliest image depicting how the Order of Preachers might have perceived its mission in the church at the time of St. Dominic's canonization.

4. Peter Ferrand, *Légende de saint Dominique*, 1; Bériou-Hodel, 797–98.

Part IV

REFERENCES AND SOURCES FOR THE HISTORY OF SAINT DOMINIC

Chronology of the Life of Saint Dominic

Prepared by Simon Tugwell, OP

In 2005, the English Dominican historian Simon Tugwell published "A Chronological Outline of the Life of St. Dominic" in which he synthesized the results of the work he had previously published annually in the journal *Archivum Fratrum Praedicatorum*, with the addition of an explanation of some developments in his studies. This outline was not intended to "interpret Dominic's personality" but rather to outline, in the form of an annotated chronology, some solidly established facts of the life of the founder of the Order of Preachers. We are pleased to present a simplified version of this chronology with the author's permission.[1]

1170–1174

According to the *Life of St. Dominic* by Dietrich of Apolda, a Dominican author who seems to have been well informed, Dominic's parents were married in 1170. Spanish tradition gives us their names as Felix and Jane. Dominic was born at Caleruega in Castile around 1174. We know of two brothers of Dominic, one named Mannes, who became a Dominican, and the other, also a priest, who dedicated himself to the service of the poor. Dominic also had two *nepotes* who were members of the order. The term *nepos* can refer to nephews in the literal sense, children of a hypothetical sister, or to children of cousins. According to Dominican chronicler Galvano Fiamma, a hermit *nepos* went to Rome in 1300 for the Jubilee.

ca. 1187

After preliminary studies with his uncle, Dominic studied at Palencia. He first studied the liberal arts for about seven years, then went on to study theology for another four.

1. Simon Tugwell, "Schéma chronologique de la vie de Saint Dominique," in *Domenico di Caleruega e la nascita dell'Ordine dei Frati Predicatori*, Acts of the 41st International Historic Conference, Todi, October 10–12, 2004 (Centro italiano di Studi sull'alto medioevo, 2005), 1–24.

1196–1198

Dominic sold his books to help the victims of a local famine. This action brought him to the attention of Bishop Martin of Osma (or perhaps the prior of the chapter, Diego). In 1197 or 1198, the prelate persuaded him to become a regular canon of Osma.

1201

Dominic is documented as being subprior in Osma.

1203–1204

Between October 4, 1203, and February 26, 1204, Diego, now Bishop of Osma, went to Denmark to negotiate a marriage on behalf of the son of the King of Castile. Dominic accompanied him. While passing through Toulouse, the two men became aware of the extent of the problem of heresy in that region. Their host was a heretic, and Dominic converted him. On the way back to Spain, Diego made a detour to Cîteaux to seek a group of monks for the oversight of a monastery of sisters that he had founded in his diocese.

1205

At some point after May 19, Diego was sent back to Denmark to bring the prince's fiancée to Spain. Dominic accompanied him once more, but in the meantime, the bride had died. Rather than return to Spain, Diego, moved by what he had been told about the pagan Cumans, went with Dominic to Pope Innocent III. He asked the pontiff for permission to renounce the episcopate so that he might devote himself to converting these heretics. The pope did not allow Diego to do so and asked him to return to his diocese.

1206

In January, or at least before mid-March, Diego happened to meet the papal legates in Montpellier and convinced them of the need to go on foot "without gold or silver" to counter the influence of the heretics. Diego probably knew from experience that one could overcome the obstacle of the widespread anticlericalism of that time by only being free of any semblance of worldliness. One had to present oneself as *vir evangelicus*, a man of the Gospel. The counsel of poverty seems to have been directed more to combat the anticlericalism that accompanied heresies than against the heresies themselves.

Diego sent his baggage and his companions back to Osma except for one companion, who was undoubtedly Dominic. Then with two of the legates, he set out to preach against the heretics and to hold disputes with them.

On his return to Osma before April 29, Dominic renounced the office of subprior. He returned to the Midi with Diego and some companions, probably in July, accompanying Bishop Fulk of Toulouse to preach against heresy.

At the Cistercian General Chapter, which began on September 14, a preaching campaign was organized to counter the heretics in the Midi following the strategy suggested by Diego.

Before November, Diego went a second time to Pope Innocent III to propose a long-term mission in the South of France. It would be characterized by a more radical poverty than the one he had convinced the legates to adopt. Supporting this mission, the pope wrote to the legate Raoul of Fontfroide giving him authorization to recruit preachers from among the religious in the region to preach against heresy. Diego himself must have received a new mandate from the pope. Indeed, back in the Midi, he established a *predicatio* (preaching mission) centered in Prouille, which by August 1207 had acquired institutional stability, allowing it to receive *donati* (people) and donations. With its limited objectives, the Cistercian mission was certainly not capable of this. As Diego's vicar, Dominic had become the effective head of the mission.

The seal used by Dominic, which bore the inscription "*sigillum Christi et praedicationis*," may be that of Diego's *predicatio* or, more probably, that of the *praedicatio* revived in 1211 under the aegis of Fulk.

Fulk donated the church at Prouille to Diego before March 25, 1207, at Dominic's request so that women "converted by the preachers against heresy" (by Dominic and his companions) could live there as religious.

1207

Between February 3 and March 16, Diego's presence is documented in Castile, likely because Dominic remained in Languedoc as vicar to his bishop.

In March and April, Diego and Dominic took part in a major doctrinal dispute in Montreal. The small group of preachers was then joined by the Cistercians under the authority of Abbot Arnaud Amalric, who held a meeting with the bishops of the region.

Between May 3 and June 2, Diego was in Spain while the first Cistercian mission was taking place in the south of France.

Between August and September, a regional meeting of clergymen that Diego attended was held in the city of Pamiers. It sought ways of continuing the mission after the departure of the Cistercian preachers. It seems that there was another dispute with the Waldensians, but we are not sure that Dominic took part.

Before September 25, Diego returned to Spain. At the Cistercians' General Chapter, Guy des Vaux-de-Cernay was entrusted with their second apostolic mission, which took place from October 1207 to January 1208.

Diego died on December 30, 1207.

1208–1210

In January 1208, informed of his bishop's death, Dominic returned to Osma, where it seems he remained until 1211. In the meantime, Bishop Fulk of Toulouse had granted the church of Prouille to the "converted ladies" who lived nearby.

According to the testimony of Brother John of Navarre, Dominic was elected bishop of Comminges. If this is true, we must place the event in 1209 or 1210, perhaps even 1206 or 1207, but we have no evidence of Dominic's presence in the region at that time.

1211

Before June 20, Dominic returned to the Midi with the consent of the Most Reverend Menendo, the new bishop of Osma. He was accompanied by other canons, some of whom would later become Dominicans. He thus resumed his role as *praedicator*.

At the end of the year, Fulk entrusted the direction of the nuns of Prouille to Dominic and provided him with the means to build a real monastery there.

1212

Dominic spent the Lenten period from February 7 to March 25 accompanied by a *socius* working to convert a group of women with a heretical bent. He won their conversion through an asceticism that surpassed even that of the heretics.

In December, when he was elected Bishop of Béziers, Dominic declared that he would "flee by night with his staff before accepting a bishopric or any other dignity."

1213–1214

From January 1213 to May 1214, Dominic resided in Carcassonne as vicar to Bishop Guy. His *socius* was Stephen of Metz, who later became a Dominican. Dominic probably remained there until the marriage of Amaury de Montfort (son of Simon), which he celebrated in June.

Between December 1211 and May 26, 1213, Prouille was regularly referred to as a monastery or abbey in the records, but these designations disappeared on February 1, 1214, which suggests that group was being gathered for the *praedicatio* and that Prouille was part of it.

1214

The citizens of Toulouse submitted to the church and were reconciled on April 25. Dominic was then appointed head of the *predicatio* by the legate, Peter of Benevento, or by Fulk in the legate's name.

Before May 25, Fulk gave the benefice of Fanjeaux to Dominic as a way of financing him and his companions, but it is not known whether Dominic resided there.

In the latter half of the year, Dominic moved to Toulouse. As "minister of preaching," he gave a certain Raimond Guilhermy of Auterive temporary permission to house a converted heretic, Guilhem Hugues.

On August 18, Simon de Montfort conquered Casseneuil and gave it to Dominic "and to all those who would assist him in the office which inaugurated salvation" (*in officio inchoatae salutis*). The *praedicatio* was thus to be an institution capable of receiving goods.

Between the middle of 1214 and the middle of 1215, Dominic was elected bishop of Couserans, but he did not accept the appointment on the pretext that he had to look after "the very young establishing of preachers."

1215

At the beginning of January, the brothers Peter and Thomas Seila "offered" or gave themselves to Dominic; it seems that they were the first disciples to bind themselves to him by a vow. That is not all: Peter also gave him his houses in Toulouse, and it was there that Dominic took up residence. When on April 25 the Seila brothers divided their inheritance, Dominic received Peter's share for himself, for his successors, and for those who resided in the house established by him.

At that time, Dominic, together with six companions "wearing the same habit," attended the theology courses given by a professor in Toulouse. Around the month of May, Fulk granted this group the status of diocesan preachers in perpetuity, "who have religiously proposed to walk in evangelical poverty and to preach the word of evangelical truth." For this purpose, he granted them a part of the tithes of the diocese. Diego's dream of having a group of preachers dedicated to total poverty was thus realized, but their field of action was limited to the diocese of Toulouse. A bishop had no authority to transform a pontifical mission into a diocesan institution without the provisional consent of the legate; such a step required papal confirmation. It was also necessary to look for ways to ensure the expansion of the *praedicatio* beyond the diocese of Toulouse. For this purpose, Dominic accompanied Fulk to Rome, when the latter was obliged to go there for the Lateran Council.

In addition to his other demonstrations of support, Fulk had previously donated a hospice in Toulouse *ad portam Arnaldi Bernardi* to Dominic for "converted women," which indicated he probably intended to found a monastery in Toulouse, as in Prouille.

On August 28, Brother John of Navarre, or of Spain, "received the habit from the hand of Brother Dominic, who planted this Order and was its first Master; and on that day he made profession in the hands of this brother in the church of Saint-Romain in Toulouse."

On October 8, Innocent III put the community and property of Prouille under his protection, but instead of immediately confirming the *praedicatio* of Toulouse, he advised Dominic to return to his companions and with them choose an already approved rule, not granting his confirmation until later. It is likely that the pope thought that with the unquestioned status of "orthodox" religious preachers from Toulouse, these men would be safe from the inconvenience that lay groups such as the Poor Catholics had encountered. Moreover, these religious could more easily establish themselves in the rest of their old mission territory to combat heresy and thus contribute, within the whole church, to the renewal of preaching, according to the instruction of the ecumenical council that had just been celebrated. Dominic, aware that his brethren were too few to respond to this broader vision of their role, was comforted—according to Gerard de Frachet—by a vision he had in a dream in which he saw the brethren going out to preach in pairs throughout the world.

1216

On his return to Toulouse, Dominic reported the pope's directions to the friars. The rule chosen was that of Saint Augustine, with some additions taken from the customs of Prémontré. The friars renounced *possessiones*, or landed property (as opposed to the practice of the Cistercians, who would have developed it), but they retained revenues from rents (until 1221, they continued to receive the tithes that Fulk had assigned to them in 1215) and land, which were sources of income. In July, the diocese gave the church of Saint-Romain to the friars.

The transformation of the group of preachers into a religious community was henceforth complete, and there was nothing to prevent Dominic from returning to the pope to ask for the confirmation he had been promised. In the meantime, Innocent III had died, and the new pope, Honorius III, was apparently unaware of the Toulouse *praedicatio* and of Innocent's hopes for it.

On 22 December, therefore, Dominic received only the "confirmation" of the religious community of Saint-Romain from the new pontiff.

1217

Between January 19 and February 7, numerous bulls were issued by the Roman Curia at Dominic's request. One of them requested that teachers and students from the University of Paris go to Toulouse to support the efforts of the local church; another granted him and his brothers the title of *praedicatores in partibus Tholosanis.*

Dominic confided to William of Montferrat, who he had met at the home of Cardinal Ugolino, his desire to go and "convert the pagans who lived in Prussia and other northern regions." But William first had to study theology in Paris for two years.

Dominic had obtained only the recognition of the mission of the friars in the Diocese of Toulouse from the pope. Now back in the Midi, and aware of the rebellion attempts that were being prepared in Toulouse against Simon de Montfort, Dominic understood the perils that threatened the community of Saint-Romain. It was in August that he decided to disperse the brothers as the situation had become critical. Instead of bringing Parisian teachers to Toulouse, he sent some brothers to Paris to study and establish a convent; others went to Spain.

Matthew was elected "abbot" of the friars and sent to Paris because it was expected that the order would develop following the model of a central abbey with dependent priories. At the same time, Brother Sueiro Gomez was probably appointed superior of the friars going to Spain. The technical terms "province" and "provincial prior" did not yet exist, but their reality took two different forms: Matthew would be in charge of a territory as superior of a convent, while Sueiro would be in charge of a territory where there was not yet a convent. Once the latter was founded, he would not become the convent's prior but would instead continue to be *prior fratrum praedicatorum in Hispania.*[2]

2. Prior of the Friars Preachers in Spain.

The preaching status of Dominic's friars had no validity outside the Diocese of Toulouse. Everywhere else, they were juridically only canons regular. The friars in Paris therefore behaved as canons, and in accordance with the statutes governing the conduct of canons, they no longer went on foot or without money. The ambiguity of the poverty of the southern preachers was felt here: was their poverty a strategy for the mission against the heretics, or was it an essential dimension of the life of an evangelical preacher?

In Paris, the friars attracted the attention of Jordan of Saxony, who in 1218 or 1219 began writing a *Libellus*, which he continued at intervals until 1221. His information about Dominic's youth and the origins of the order seems to have come mainly from John of Navarre, who was well informed about what Dominic had told the brothers in Toulouse.

By mid-December, Dominic set out to explain the development of the preachers to Pope Honorius III.

1218

There is nothing to suggest that Dominic wanted to found a convent in Rome. The only location he decided on in the Italian peninsula was that of Bologna, where he had sent friars as early as January. If he went to Rome again, it was only to attend to his business with the Papal Curia. He was waiting for news from the brothers in Paris and Spain, and perhaps also from those he had left in Toulouse. In the meantime, he was carrying out an apostolate among the nuns of Rome.

During his stay in Rome, Dominic met Reginald, dean of Saint-Aignan in Orléans. Reginald was accompanying his bishop on a pilgrimage to the Holy Land, the group spending their Lent in Rome. Reginald dreamed of a life dedicated to preaching and poverty; Cardinal Ugolino confided to him that his desire would be fulfilled in Dominic's order, and Reginald decided to enter. Falling ill, Reginald was healed by the Virgin, who also indicated to him the order to which he should commit himself. Then having made his profession in Dominic's hands, and after completing his pilgrimage to the Holy Land, Reginald was sent by Dominic to Bologna as his vicar.

On February 11, Dominic received the first bull of recommendation for his brothers addressed to the prelates of the whole church. Here we find the expression *fratres ordinis praedicatorum* used for the first time. Honorius III not only showed the support of his curia for the new order, which was extended to several countries, but also gave it its name.

At the beginning of May, Dominic left for Spain with Peter Seila, who had recently joined him in Rome with some of the friars. He spent several days in Bologna and probably left some of his companions in Narbonne with a view to founding a convent there. From there, he went to Catalonia. When the death of Simon de Montfort was announced on June 25, he sent Peter Seila to Paris to establish a foundation at Limoges. In Madrid, he gave the habit to the first nuns of a monastery there to be established on the model of Prouille. Before Christmas, he was in Segovia, where he founded the first Dominican convent in Spain.

1219

It is not known precisely when Dominic left Spain. He probably stayed there for a few months and arrived in Toulouse shortly before Prince Louis of France laid siege to it on June 17, 1219. After spending perhaps a few days in Prouille and Toulouse, he arrived in Paris in early July. It was probably at this time that he restored the independence of the southern brothers and appointed Bertrand of Garrigue as their superior. The latter thus became the fourth *de facto* provincial before the name was adopted. In Paris, he urged the friars to return to the way of life they had practiced in Toulouse and invited them to give up their income. It seems clear that the friars were not convinced. Another of Dominic's proposals met with such opposition from the friars that he gave it up: that of entrusting full authority to the lay brothers for the administration of temporal affairs.

During his visit to Paris, Dominic received William of Montferrat (with whom he discussed some new missionary projects) into the order. Although he had spoken of the Prussians two years earlier, it seems that Dominic was now thinking more of the Saracens and Cumans.

By mid-August, Dominic arrived in Bologna, where he found a flourishing convent thanks to the high-quality recruits Reginald had attracted to the order. The brothers of the still-fledgling community shared Dominic and Reginald's ideas of austerity and poverty. Dominic understood that in Bologna, more easily than in Paris, he would be able to realize the ideal of conventual mendicancy that was to characterize the new Order of Preachers. This way of life involved a renunciation not only of property but also of rents and income of any kind. It was perhaps in the hope that Reginald would be able to impart the same spirit in Paris as in Bologna that Dominic decided to send him there.

The order had developed in northern Italy more rapidly than in France or Spain. New locations followed in Florence, Bergamo (perhaps even before Dominic's arrival), Milan, and Verona. The model of a central abbey surrounded by a network of priories was not suitable for Italian cities that were fiercely attached to their independence. The title of abbot was also less common there than in France, and these structures had to be abandoned.

Reginald's preaching in Bologna had attracted not only men but also some women to the order. Soon after his arrival, Dominic received the profession of Diana d'Andalò, who undertook to build "a house of women which would be, and would be named, a house of the Order."

Toward the end of October, Dominic joined the papal court that was staying in Viterbo. He wanted copies of the bull of recommendation for the new locations in progress. He also wanted to tell the pope about the missionary hopes he had entrusted to William of Montferrat in 1217. However, before undertaking a mission to unbelievers, he first had to complete the organization of the order to be presented at the general chapter planned for 1220.

Dominic's missionary ambition was soon thwarted, however. Honorius III entrusted him with a project inherited from Innocent III, which consisted in gathering the nuns of Rome in a newly restored monastery built next to the basilica of San Sisto, which was nearing completion. While waiting for the arrival of the nuns, some religious from Bologna were installed in San Sisto. In this way, the first Dominican convent in Rome was founded.

In the meantime, news had arrived from Paris. Reginald had managed to convince the friars to renounce their income and to embrace the poverty so desired by Dominic. This decision was confirmed by a bull of December 12, certainly written at Dominic's request. On December 8, Honorius III had already issued a bull of recommendation that stressed the importance of preaching and radical poverty and mentioned for the first time the existence of a "prior" of the order. There was sufficient documentation to support the expansion of the order, but it is likely that the main purpose of this new text was to provide some sort of official definition of the order in preparation for the general chapter. In addition, the pope gave Dominic full *disponendi, ordinandi, corrigendi* authority[3] for the entire order.

Around December, Dominic received the profession of a priest from Friesach and allowed him to return to Carinthia to found a convent.

1220

Toward the end of February, Dominic returned to Bologna. At the beginning of May, he had to go again to Viterbo at the request of the pope to take charge of some religious who had been gathered, it seems, by Cardinal Ugolino for a mission against the heretics in northern Italy. It is not known what happened, but the existence of a great "preaching against the heresies in Lombardy" led by Dominic, as suggested by some historians, is very doubtful.

On May 20, the first general chapter began in Bologna. Dominic submitted to its authority and asked to be deposed. The capitulars refused his request and urged him to continue as Master of the Order. The customs of the order were revised: the first distinction (the "monastic" part) was corrected, while the second (which was to regulate the order as an *Ordo Praedicatorum*) was redrafted. The titles of the superiors were fixed: *magister* (*ordinis*), *priores provinciarum vel regnorum*, *priores* (*conuentuum*).[4] The term *abbas* disappeared. In addition to the traditional conditions for the foundation of a new community, the presence of a *doctor* (teacher) as well as a superior was added; each convent had to include a school of theology. Furthermore, the chapter decided that "our friars shall have no possessions or income in the future." It was decided to found a convent in Palencia, without doubt in connection with the foundation of the university. Two Scandinavian friars left for Sweden with a cleric from Sigtuna, but the hope of founding a convent there did not materialize.

3. Translation: authority of disposing, ordering, and correcting.

4. Translation: Master of the Order, priors of provinces or territories, priors of convents.

On the occasion of this general chapter, or the one of 1221, Dominic sent a letter to the nuns of Madrid, who he entrusted to his brother Mannes.

After the chapter, Dominic seems to have resided most of the time in Bologna, with the exception of a visit to Milan in June and a trip of unknown duration between September and November.

1221

The construction of the monastery of San Sisto in Rome was almost complete, and Dominic went there in January. The pope had appointed three cardinals to oversee the opening of the monastery; Dominic collaborated with them in the drafting of the constitutions. On February 28, 1221, the nuns, including Sister Cecilia, were able to enter the new building, receive the Dominican habit, and practice their profession in Dominic's hands. The friars who had been occupying the premises left San Sisto for the church of Santa Sabina, which the pope had given them.

On March 25, the pope appealed to the European metropolitans to provide him with at least two religious who would be able to preach to unbelievers. On March 29, Dominic received a bull of personal recommendation from the Holy Father. It is probable that he intended to participate in the pope's missionary project, perhaps even lead it. In a copy of the bull of recommendation addressed to the king of Denmark and dated May 6, 1221, the pope introduced a new element into the text: the Dominicans were not only presented as preachers of the Gospel but also as "evangelizers of the pagans." After the General Chapter of 1221, a Danish friar was sent to his country with the papal letter and letters from Dominic to the king and the archbishop of Lund. It can be deduced from this that Dominic's missionary goal had been clarified: he now wanted to evangelize the pagans in Estonia, where the Danes had just settled.

Dominic remained in Rome until mid-May to care for the formation of the sisters of San Sisto. He abandoned the project of transferring the entire community of Prouille to Rome but had eight nuns from the Lauragais region come, including Blanche, who became prioress. They probably made the journey with Fulk, whose presence is documented in Rome in April 1221. Dominic took advantage of the visit of this prelate to renounce the tithes that the friars received from the Diocese of Toulouse; Fulk, for his part, gave Dominic and his successors the church of Fanjeaux. It may be assumed that it was hoped to establish a house of the order in the town.

The General Chapter of Bologna began on June 2. It was decided to divide the order into several provinces. The word province acquired its technical meaning of an administrative district of the order. Brothers were sent to England, Hungary, Denmark, Poland, and perhaps even Greece.

In July, Dominic, traveling with Friar Paul of Venice, reached the Marche of Treviso. Toward the end of the month, he returned to Bologna very tired and fell seriously ill. He died on August 6, 1221. Miracles seem to have occurred at his tomb and gave rise to a cult, but the friars, "fearing that they would be reproached for their greed," prevented the devotion of the faithful.

Jordan of Saxony arrived in Bologna shortly after Dominic's death and resumed writing his *Libellus*, which he soon had to abandon, unfinished.

1233

The preaching of the "great Alleluia" by John of Vicenza and other preachers led to a revival of Dominic's cult. Instead of suppressing it, the friars collected accounts of miracles, which were included in the dossier sent to the pope for canonization. Jordan revised the text of the *Libellus*.

On May 24, during the solemn translation of Dominic's body, a wonderful fragrance emanated from the old tomb when it was opened. Several people have left testimonies of this experience. The scent of this perfume was still noticeable eight days later, when Dominic's relics were exposed for the veneration of the friars who had not been able to attend the translation. The official investigation into Dominic's sanctity and miracles was conducted during the summer.

1234

On July 3, St. Dominic was canonized in Rieti by Gregory IX (the former Cardinal Ugolino) in the Cathedral of Santa Maria Assunta.

Sources and Bibliography

Sources of the History of Saint Dominic and Bibliographical Abbreviations

The authors have chosen to return the reader to the editions of the Latin sources published by the Historical Institute of the Order of Preachers (IHOP) in the collection of the *Monumenta Ordinis Prædicatorum Historica* (MOPH) but also in the journal *Archivum Fratrum Prædicatorum* (AFP). This editorial choice, in a book for the general public, is intended to facilitate access to the sources themselves. Notes have been abbreviated to indicate only essential elements of the source (author, title), followed by the chapter number in the referenced edition. A second reference, abbreviated as Bériou-Hodel, usually follows this one. It refers to the translations edited by these two historians in the book *Saint Dominique de l'ordre des frères prêcheurs: Témoignages écrits fin* XIIe–XIVe *siècle* [*Saint Dominic of the Order of Friar Preachers: Testimonies written at the end of the 12th–14th century*], textes traduits, annotés et présentés par Nicole Bériou et Bernard Hodel avec la collaboration de Gisèle Besson [texts translated, annotated, and presented by Nicole Bériou and Bernard Hodel with the collaboration of Gisèle Besson] (Paris, Éd. du Cerf, 2019). The texts in their original version are available in a PDF file on the website of les Éditions du Cerf: https://www.editionsducerf.fr/librairie/livre/18834/saint-dominique-de-l-ordre-des-freres-precheurs-temoignages-ecrits.

AFP	*Archivum Fratrum Prædicatorum*
AGOP	*Archivum Generale Ordinis Prædicatorum* (Rome, Santa Sabina)
ASOP	*Analecta Sacri Ordinis Prædicatorum*
Bériou-Hodel	*Saint Dominique de l'ordre des frères prêcheurs: Témoignages écrits fin* XIIe–XIVe *siècle* [*Saint Dominic of the Order of Friar Preachers: Testimonies written at the end of the 12th–14th century*], textes traduits, annotés et présentés par Nicole Bériou et Bernard Hodel avec la collaboration de Gisèle Besson [texts translated (into French), annotated, and pre-

sented by Nicole Bériou and Bernard Hodel with the collaboration of Gisèle Besson] (Paris, Éd. du Cerf, 2019).

MOPH *Monumenta Ordinis Prædicatorum Historica*

A Spanish edition of the sources for the history of St. Dominic was recently published by Vito-Tomás Gómez Garcia, *Santo Domingo de Guzmán: Escritos de sus contemporáneos* [*Saint Dominic de Guzman: Writings of his contemporaries*], prólogo [foreword by] José A. Martinez Puche (Edibesa, 2011). Furthermore, the Società Internazionale per lo Studio del Medio Evo Latino (SISMEL) recently edited a bilingual (Latin-Italian) edition of Dominican sources: *Domenico di Caleruega alle origini dell'Ordine dei Predicatori: Le fonti del secolo XIII* [*Dominic of Caleruega at the origins of the Order of Preachers: The sources of the thirteenth century*], a cura di Gianni Festa, Agostino Paravicini Bagliani, Francesco Santi, SISMEL (Firenze, Edizioni del Galluzzo, 2021). We cannot thank the authors enough for making the preparatory work for this edition available to us free of charge.

For the diplomatic sources of the history of St. Dominic and the documents attesting to his presence among the Albigensians:

- *Monumenta diplomatica Sancti Dominici.* Edited by Vladimír J. Koudelka, OP, *auxiliante* Raymundo J. Loenertz, OP. MOPH 25. Institutum Historicum Fratrum Prædicatorum, 1966. [abbreviation: *Monumenta diplomatica*]
- Pierre des Vaux-de-Cernay, O. Cist. *Histoire albigeoise* [*Albigensian history*]. Nouvelle traduction par Pascal Guébin et Henri Maisonneuve [new translation by Pascal Guébin and Henri Maisonneuve]. J. Vrin, 1951. [abbreviation: Pierre des Vaux-de-Cernay, *Histoire albigeoise*]
- Guillaume de Puylaurens. *Chronique: Chronica magistri Guillelmi de Podio Laurentii* [*Chronicle: The Chronicle of Master William of Puylaurens*]. Texte édité, traduit et annoté par Jean Duvernoy [text edited, translated, and annotated by Jean Duvernoy]. Éd. du CNRS, 1976. [abbreviation: William of Puylaurens, *Chronica*]

Enriched with personal memories, the *Libellus* [booklet] of Jordan of Saxony offer along with the acts of the canonization process a precious personal witness to record the life of St. Dominic and understand the expansion of the nascent order:

- *Monumenta historica Sancti Patris Nostri Dominici*, fasc. II, MOPH 16. Institutum Historicum Fratrum Prædicatorum, 1935. The text of *Libellus de principiis Ordinis Prædicatorum* of Jordan of Saxony is edited by Heribert Christian Scheeben, pp. 1–88. [abbreviation: Jordan of Saxony, *Libellus*]
- *Monumenta historica Sancti Patris Nostri Dominici*, fasc. II, MOPH 16. Institutum Historicum Fratrum Prædicatorum, 1935. The text of the Bologna depositions is edited by Angelus Walz, pp. 123–67. [abbreviation: *Acta canonizationis*, Bologna]
- *Monumenta historica Sancti Patris Nostri Dominici*, fasc. II, MOPH 16. Institutum Historicum Fratrum Prædicatorum, 1935. The text of the Toulouse depositions is edited by Angelus Walz, pp. 176–87. [abbreviation: *Acta canonizationis*, Toulouse]

After the canonization of St. Dominic, the lives and legends of Dominic—but also the memories of a nun who had known him when she was a young sister—nourish the devotion to and the memory of the father of the Preachers:

- *Petri Ferrandi legenda sancti Dominici.* Edited by Simon Tugwell, OP, MOPH 32. Angelicum University Press, 2015. [abbreviation: Peter Ferrand, *Legenda sancti Dominici*]
- *Monumenta historica Sancti Patris Nostri Dominici*, fasc. II, MOPH 16. Institutum Historicum Fratrum Prædicatorum, 1935. The text of the *Legenda* of Constantine of Orvieto and the *Libellus of* Jordan of Saxony are edited by Heribert Christian Scheeben, pp. 286–352. [abbreviation: Constantine of Orvieto, *Legenda*]
- *Humberti de Romanis legendæ Sancti Dominici*, ed. Simon Tugwell, OP, MOPH 30. Institutum Historicum Ordinis Fratrum Prædicatorum, 2008. [abbreviation: Humbert of Romans, *Legenda maior*]

- Thierry d'Apolda, OP. *Livre sur la vie et la mort de saint Dominique* [*Book on the life and death of Saint Dominic*]. Traduit et annoté par Amédée Curé [translated and annotated by Amédée Curé]. Œuvre de Saint-Paul, 1887. [abbreviation: Dietrich of Apolda, *Vita sancti Dominici*]

- Vito-Tomás Gómez Garcia, OP. *Santo Domingo de Guzmán: Escritos de sus contemporáneos* [*Saint Dominic de Guzman: Writings of his contemporaries*]. Prólogo [prologue by] José A. Martinez Puche. Edibesa, 2011, 581–624 (translation into Castilian, after the translation of Carro and the *Annalium*). [abbreviation: Rodrigo de Cerrato, *Vita*]

- Fratris Gerardi de Fracheto, OP. *Vitæ Fratrum Ordinis Prædicatorum necnon Cronica ordinis ab anno MCCIII usque ad MCCLIV* [*The Life of the Brethren of the Order of Preachers and the Chronicle of the Order from 1203 to 1254*]. Edited by Benedictus Maria Reichert, MOPH 1. Typis E. Charpentier & J. Schoonjans, 1896. [abbreviation: Gerard de Frachet, *Vitæ fratrum*]

- *Miracula S. Dominici a sorore Cecilia recitata et a sorore Angelica in scriptis redacta* [*The miracles of Saint Dominic recited by Sister Cecilia and recorded in writing by Sister Angelica*]. In Simon Tugwell, OP, "*Scripta quædam minora de S. Dominico* [*Some minor writings on Saint Dominic*]." AFP 83 (2013): 64–115. [abbreviation: Sister Cecilia, *Miracula S. Dominici*]

- *De quattuor in quibus Deus prædicatorum ordinem insignivit* [*Of the four in which God distinguished the order of preachers*]. Edited by Thomas Kaeppeli, OP, MOPH 22. Institutum Historicum Ordinis Fratrum Prædicatorum, 1949. [abbreviation: Stephen of Salagnac-Bernard Gui, *De quatuor in quibus*]

The first legislation of the order was the subject of work that has not yet been replaced:

- *De oudste Constituties van de Dominicanen: Voorgeschiedenis, tekst, bronnen, ontstaan en ontwikkeling (1215–1237)* [*The Oldest Constitutions of the Dominicans: History, text, sources, origin, and development (1215–1237)*]. Edited by Antonin H. Thomas, Bibliothèque de la Revue d'histoire ecclésiastique, 42. Leuven, 1965. See also *A Cathedral of Constitutional Law: Essays on the Earliest Constitutions of the Order of Preachers with an English Translation of Fr Antoninus H. Thomas's 1965 Study*, ed. Anton Milh and Mark Butaye, Bibliothèque de la Revue d'Histoire Ecclésiastique 112 (Turnhout, 2023).

See as well:

- Dominicus Planzer. "De Codice Ruthenensi miscellaneo in Tabulario Ordinis Prædicatorum asservato" ["The Miscellaneous Code of Ruthenian in the Archives of the Order of Preachers"]. AFP 5 (1935): 5–123.
- *Acta Capitulorum Generaliu Ordinis Prædicatorum. I. 1220–1303.* Edited by Benedictus Maria Reichert, OP, MOPH 3. Institutum Historicum Fratrum Prædicatorum, 1898.

For the letter of canonization of Saint Dominic, see:

- *Humberti de Romanis Legendæ sancti Dominici, necnon Materia prædicabilis pro festis sancti Dominici et testimonia minora de eodem, adiectis miraculis Rotomagensibus sancti Dominici et Gregorii IX bulla canonizationis eiusdem [Humbert's Roman History of St. Dominic, as well as the preaching material for the feasts of St. Dominic and minor testimonies concerning the same, additional miracles at Rotomagens, the Bull of the same canonization of St. Dominic and Gregory IX]*. Edited by Simon Tugwell, OP, MOPH 30, 56–57. Institutum Historicum Ordinis Fratrum Prædicatorum, 2008.
- Saint Dominic's letter to the nuns in Madrid was edited by Simon Tugwell, OP. "St. Dominic's Letter to the Nuns in Madrid." AFP 56 (1986): 5–13.

The works of Humbert of Romans have been published under the title *Opera de vita regulari.* Edited by Joachim Joseph Berthier. 2 vols. Marietti, 1956.

Bibliography

Apart from listing some references to the figure and work of St. Dominic, we limit ourselves to indicating some of the studies to which we have referred in writing this book. The reader will not find here a complete bibliography but rather some suggestions on the basis of which he can engage in a more in-depth study. He will also enjoy reading the *Archivum Fratrum Prædicatorum*, *Mémoire dominicaine*, *Dominican History* newsletter, and the rich collection of *Cahiers de Fanjeaux*.

Saint Dominic and the Beginnings of the Order of Preachers

The classic academic biography devoted to St. Dominic is that of Marie-Humbert Vicaire, OP, *Histoire de saint Dominique* [*History of St. Dominic*], 2nd ed. (Éd. du Cerf, 1982). See as well Guy Bedouelle, OP, *Dominique ou la grâce de la parole* [*Dominic: The grace of the word*] (Fayard-Mame, 1982) and Simon Tugwell, OP, *The Way of the Preacher* (Darton, Longman, and Todd Ltd., 1979). We will add to these readings the details and corrections made by Simon Tugwell in his articles published by the journal *Archivum Fratrum Prædicatorum* [abbreviation: AFP]: Simon Tugwell, "Notes on the life of St. Dominic," AFP 65 (1995): 5–169; AFP 66 (1996): 5–200; AFP 67 (1997): 27–59; AFP 68 (1998): 5–116; AFP 3 (2003): 5–141. We will also refer to his "Schéma chronologique de la vie de Saint Dominique" ["Chronological diagram of the life of St. Dominic"], in *Domenico di Caleruega e la nascita dell'Ordine dei Frati Predicatori* [*Dominic of Caleruega and the birth of the Order of Preachers*], Proceedings of the XLI International Historical Conference, Todi, October 10–12, 2004 (Italian Center for Studies on the Early Middle Ages Foundation), 1–24. Finally, concerning the development of the hagiographic image of St. Dominic, his cult, and the self-representation of the order: Luigi Canetti, *L'invenzione della memoria: Il culto e l'immagine di Domenico nella storia dei primi frati Predicatori* [*The invention of memory: The cult and image of Dominic in the history of the first Preachers*], Biblioteca di Medioevo Latino 19 [Library of the Latin Middle Ages 19] (Centro italiano di Studi sull'alto medioevo, 1996).

An important stage in the historiography dedicated to Saint Dominic was represented by the colloquium: *Domenico di Caleruega e la nascita dell'Ordine dei Frati Predicatori* [*Dominic of Calaruega and the birth of the Order of Preachers*], Atti del XLI Convegno storico internazionale, Todi, ottobre 10–12, 2004 (Centro italiano di Studi sull'alto medioevo, 2005) [Proceedings of the XLI International Historical Conference, Todi, October 10–12, 2004 (Italian Center for Early Middle Ages Foundation, 2005)].

On Dominic's family origins: Anthony John Lappin, "On the Family and Early Years of Dominic of Caleruega," AFP 67 (1997): 5–26. From the same author: "From Osma to Bologna, from Canons to Friars, from Preaching to the Preachers: The Dominican Path Towards Mendicancy," in *The Origin, Development, and Refinement of Medieval Religious Mendicancies*, ed. Donald Prudlo, Brill's Companions to the Christian Tradition 24 (Brill, 2011), 31–58.

On the Inquisition, besides the collection *des Cahiers de Fanjeaux* [*Fanjeaux Notebooks*]: Jean-Louis Biget, *Hérésie et inquisition dans le Midi de la France* [Heresy and inquisition in the *South of France*] (Picard, 2007) and *Dizionario storico dell'Inquisizione* [*Historical Dictionary of the Inquisition*], ed. Adriano Prosperi, with the collaboration of Vincenzo Lavenia and John Tedeschi (Edizioni della Normale [Editions of the Normale], 2010).

On the first stage of the preaching of Diego and Dominic: Simon Tugwell, OP, "L'évêque Diègue et la lettre du pape au légat Raoul" ["Bishop Diego and the Pope's letter to legate Raoul"], *Mémoire dominicaine* 21 [*Dominican memoirs*] (2007): 119–33, and Anne Reltgen-Tallon, "*Innocent III et saint Dominique* [Innocent III and St. Dominic], *Innocent III et le Midi* [Innocent III and the south of France]," ed. Michèle Fournié, Daniel Le Blévec, and Julien Théry-Astruc, *Cahiers de Fanjeaux* [*Fanjeaux Notebooks*] 50 (2015): 337–53.

For the foundation of Prouille: Simon Tugwell, OP, "For Whom Was Prouille Founded?" AFP 74 (2004): 5–125. Concerning the nuns in the origins of the order: Marco Rainini, OP, "La fondazione e i primi anni del monastero di San Sisto: Ugolino di Ostia e Domenico di Caleruega" ["The foundation and the first years of the monastery of San Sisto: Ugolino of Ostia and Dominic of Caleruega"], in *Il velo, la penna e la parola: Le domenicane: storia, istituzioni e scritture* [*The veil, the pen and the word: The Dominicans: History, institutions and scriptures*], Atti del Convegno internazionale di studi [Proceedings of the International Conference of Studies], Bologna, October 11–13, 2007, ed. Gianni Festa, OP, and Gabriella Zarri, Biblioteca di Memorie Domenicane 1 [Library of Dominican Memoirs 1] (Nerbini, 2009), 49–70.

On the canonization of St. Dominic and its circumstances, see the studies of Marco Rainini, OP, "*Giovanni da Vicenza, Bologna e l'Ordine dei Predicatorini*" ["*Giovanni da Vicenza, Bologna and the Order of Preachers*"], in *L'origine dell'Ordine dei Predicatori e l'Università di Bologna* [*The origin of the Order of Preachers and the University of Bologna*], Atti del Convegno di Studio [Proceedings of the Study Conference], Bologna, February, 18–20, 2005, ed. G. Bertuzzi, *Divus Thomas* 109 (2006): 146–75; "I Predicatori dei tempi ultimi: La rielaborazione di un tema esatologico nel costituirsi dell'identità propetica dell'Ordine domenicano" ["The Preachers of the Last Times: The reworking of an eschatological theme in the establishment of the prophetic identity of the Dominican Order"], *Cristianesimo nella Storia* 23 (2002): 307–43.

Dominican History

Among the works that contributed to renewing Dominican historiography: Daniel-Antoine Mortier, *Histoire des Maîtres généraux de l'Ordre des Frères Prêcheurs (1170–1904)* [*History of the Masters General of the Order of Friars Preachers (1170–1904)*], 8 vols. (Picard et fils, 1903–1920) and William A. Hinnebusch, OP, *The Dominicans: A Short History* (Alba House, 1975). See also, more recently: *L'Ordine dei Predicatori: I Domenicani: Storia, figure, istituzioni* [*The Order of Preachers: The Dominicans: History, Figures, Institutions*] *(1216–2016)*, ed. Gianni Festa, OP, and Marco Rainini, OP (Laterza, 2016) and Massimo Carlo Giannini, *I Domenicani* [*The Dominicans*] (Il Mulino, 2016).

On the mission of the Order of Preachers in France: *Les Dominicains en France (XIIIe–XXe siècle)* [*The Dominicans in France (12th–20th century)*], ed. Nicole Bériou, André Vauchez, and Michel Zink, Actes de Colloque [Conference proceedings], Paris, December 10–12, 2015, Académie des Inscriptions et Belles-Lettres (Éd. du Cerf, 2017).

A complete catalog of Dominican saints was published by a Spanish Dominican historian on the occasion of the eighth centenary of the birth of the order: José A. Martínez Puche, OP, *El año dominicano: 800 años de santitad en la Orden de Predicadores: Santos, Beatos, Venerables y Servios de Dios* [*The Dominican year: 800 years of sanctity in the Order of Preachers: Saints, Blesseds, Venerables and Servants of God*] (Edibesa, 2016). On the policy of holiness in the Order of Preachers, starting with the canonization of Saint Dominic: *Fra trionfi e sconfitte: Aa politica della santità nell'Ordine dei Predicatori* [*Between triumphs and defeats: The politics of holiness in the Order of Preachers*], ed. Gianni Festa, OP, and Viliam S. Doci, OP (Istituto Storico Domenicano, 2021).

For the organization of studies in the order: Célestin Douais, *Essai sur l'organisation des études dans l'ordre des frères prêcheurs au treizième et quatorzième siècle* [*Essay on the organization of studies in the Order of Friar Preachers in the thirteenth and fourteenth centuries*] (Picard-Privat, 1884) as well as Michele M. Mulcahey, *"First the bow is bent to study": Dominican Education Before 1350*, Studies and Texts 132 (Pontifical Institute of Mediaeval Studies, 1998).

For the history of the Dominican liturgy, we refer to William R. Bonniwell, OP, *A History of the Dominican Liturgy: 1215–1945* (J. F. Wagner, 1945) as well as the rich volume *Aux origines de la liturgie dominicaine: le manuscrit Santa Sabina XIV L1* [*At the origins of the Dominican liturgy: the manuscript Santa Sabina XIV L1*], under the direction of Leonard Boyle, OP, and Pierre-Marie Gy, OP, Collection de l'École française de Rome, 327 [Collection of the French School of Rome, 327] (École Française de Rome, 2004).

On the history of the laity attached to the order: Gilles Gérard Meersseman, OP, *Dossier de l'Ordre de la Pénitence au XIIIe siècle* [*Dossier of the Order of Penance in the 12th century*] (Éd. Universitaires de Fribourg, 1982) and Catherine Masson, *Des laïcs chez les Prêcheurs: De l'ordre de la Pénitence aux fraternités laïques, une histoire du Tiers-Ordre dominicain* [*From the laity to the Preachers: From the Order of Penance to lay fraternities, a history of the Dominican Third Order*] (Éd. du Cerf, 2016). On the cooperator brothers: Augustine Thompson, OP, *Dominican Brothers: Conversi, Lay and Cooperator Friars* (New Priory Press, 2017).

For the history of iconography: *Études d'iconographie dominicaine: Europe occidentale (XVe–XXe siècle)* [*Dominican iconography studies: Western Europe (15th–20th centuries)*], ed. Augustin Laffay, OP, and Gabrielle de Lassus Saint-Geniès, Dissertationes historicæ 35 (Institutum Historicum Ordinis Prædicatorum—Angelicum University Press, 2017).

Index

The name of Saint Dominic appears on every page in this book dedicated to him; he has not been included in this index.

The abbreviations Bériou-Hodel and Lehner, which appear in the footnotes, refer to publishers and translators of medieval authors. The indexing refers to the authors cited and not to these translators.